TOO BRAVE
TO LIVE,
TOO YOUNG
TO DIE

TOO BRAVE TO LIVE, TOO YOUNG TO DIE

TEENAGE HEROES FROM WORLD WAR I

NIGEL CAWTHORNE

metro

Published by Metro Publishing,
an imprint of John Blake Publishing Ltd,
3 Bramber Court, 2 Bramber Road,
London W14 9PB, England

www.johnblakebooks.com

www.facebook.com/johnblakebooks 🅵
twitter.com/jblakebooks 🅴

This edition published in 2015

ISBN: 978 1 78418 811 5

British Library Cataloguing-in-Publication Data:

A catalogue record for this book is available from the British Library.

Design by www.envydesign.co.uk

Printed in Great Britain by CPI Group (UK) Ltd

1 3 5 7 9 10 8 6 4 2

Papers used by John Blake Publishing are natural, recyclable products made from
wood grown in sustainable forests. The manufacturing processes conform to the
environmental regulations of the country of origin.

ROLL OF HONOUR

1. Driver Job Drain VC, 18, Royal Field Artillery, Le Cateau, France, 26 August 1914
2. Driver Frederick Luke VC, 18, Royal Field Artillery, Le Cateau, France, 26 August 1914
3. Gobar Sing Negi VC, 19, 39th Garhwal Rifles, Neuve Chapelle, France, 10 March 1915*
4. Private Edward Dwyer VC, 19, East Surrey Regiment, Hill 60, Zwarteleen, Belgium, 20 April 1915
5. Midshipman Wilfred Malleson VC, 18, HMS *River Clyde*, Gallipoli, Turkey, 25 April 1915
6. Second Lieutenant George Moor VC, 18, Hampshire Regiment, Krithia, Gallipoli, Turkey, 5 June 1915*
7. Second Lieutenant Sidney Woodroffe VC, 19, Prince Consort's Own (Rifle Brigade), Hooge, Belgium, 30 July 1915*
8. Private John Hamilton VC, 19, 3rd Battalion, Australian Imperial Force, 'Lone Pine', Gallipoli, Turkey, 9 August 1915

9. Private George Peachment VC, 18, King's Royal Rifle Corps, Loos, France, 25 September 1915*

10. Temporary Lieutenant Richard Jones VC, 19, Loyal North Lancashire Regiment, 'Broadmarsh Crater', Vimy, France, 21 May 1916*

11. First Class Boy John 'Jack' Cornwell VC, 16, HMS *Chester*, Jutland, Denmark, 31 May 1916*

12. Private William (born John) Jackson VC, 18, 17th Battalion, Australian Imperial Force, Armentières, France, 25 June 1916

13. Private John Cunningham VC, 19, East Yorkshire Regiment, Ancre, Hebuterne Sector, France, 13 November 1916

14. Second Lieutenant Thomas Maufe VC, 19, Royal Garrison Artillery, Feuchy, France, 4 June 1917

15. Second Lieutenant Dennis Hewitt VC, 19, Hampshire Regiment, Ypres, Belgium, 31 July 1917*

16. Private Harry Brown VC, 19, 10th Battalion, Canadian Expeditionary Force, Hill 70, Loos, France, 16 August 1917*

17. Corporal Ernest Egerton VC, 19, Sherwood Foresters, Bulgar Wood, Ypres, Belgium, 20 September 1917

18. Private Thomas Holmes VC, 19, 2nd Battalion, Canadian Expeditionary Force, Passchendaele, Belgium, 26 October 1917

19. Lance Corporal Robert McBeath VC, 19, Seaforth Highlanders, Ribecourt, near Cambrai, France, 20 November 1917

20. Second Lieutenant Alan 'Babe' McLeod VC, 18, No. 2 Squadron, Royal Flying Corps, Arras, France, 27 March 1918

21. Rifleman Karanbahadur Rana VC, 19, 3rd Queen Alexandra's Own Gurkha Rifles, El Kefir, Egypt, 10 April 1918

22. Private Jack Thomas Counter VC, 19, King's Regiment (Liverpool), Boisleux St Marc, France, 16 April 1918

23. Able Seaman Albert McKenzie VC, 19, HMS *Vindictive*, Zeebrugge, Belgium, 22–23 April 1918
24. Sergeant John Meikle VC, 19, Seaforth Highlanders, Marfaux, France, 20 July 1918*
25. Lance Sergeant Edward Smith VC, 19, Lancashire Fusiliers, Serre, France, 21–23 August 1918
26. Private Thomas Ricketts VC, 17, Royal Newfoundland Regiment, Ledegem, Belgium, 14 October 1918
27. Acting Corporal Roland Elcock VC, 19, Royal Scots (Lothian Regiment), Capelle St Catherine, France, 15 October 1918
28. Private Norman Harvey VC, 19, Royal Inniskilling Fusiliers, Ingoyghem, Belgium, 25 October 1918

* Awarded posthumously

INTRODUCTION

The river of poppies outside the Tower of London was a vivid reminder of those who had sacrificed their lives in the British armed forces during the First World War. Most of those who lost their lives were very young – by and large it is young men who go, or are sent, to fight. All of them were very brave, simply to have gone into the hell of combat. Some of them were braver still because they were so young that their lives had barely begun.

Private Sidney Lewis was only twelve years and five months when he enlisted in the East Surrey Regiment in August 1915. At thirteen, he fought for six weeks in the First Battle of the Somme as a machine-gunner, only to be sent home and discharged in August 1916 when his mother sent his birth certificate to the War Office. Undaunted, he returned to service before the end of the war and worked in bomb disposal in World War II.

Thousands of boys, like Lewis, lied about their age to sign up – and not just at the beginning of the war when it was still thought to be a big adventure. Brave youngsters were still enlisting when it was plain that the fighting was purely mechanised slaughter and no one could figure out what they were dying for.

Some of these young men won medals for gallantry for deeds so daring that they scarcely seem credible. All the teenage heroes in this book won the highest decoration for valour – the Victoria Cross.

Instituted at the end of the Crimean War in 1956, the Victoria Cross was awarded for conspicuous courage in the face of the enemy. During World War I, it was conferred 628 times on 627 recipients. Captain Noel Chavasse won it twice, one of only three people to do so.

He was a doctor in the Royal Army Medical Corps and won his first VC for his actions on 9 August 1916 during the First Battle of the Somme. The citation appeared in *The London Gazette* on 24 October 1916 and read:

Captain Noel Godfrey Chavasse, M.C., M.B., Royal Army Medical Corps.

For most conspicuous bravery and devotion to duty.

During an attack he tended the wounded in the open all day, under heavy fire, frequently in view of the enemy. During the ensuing night he searched for wounded on the ground in front of the enemy's lines for four hours.

Next day he took one stretcher-bearer to the advanced trenches, and under heavy shell fire carried an urgent case for 500 yards into safety, being wounded in the side by a shell splinter during the journey. The same night he took up a party of twenty volunteers, rescued three wounded men from a shell hole twenty-five yards from the enemy's trench, buried the bodies of two Officers, and collected many identity discs, although fired on by bombs and machine guns.

Altogether he saved the lives of some twenty badly wounded men, besides the ordinary cases which passed through his hands. His courage and self-sacrifice were beyond praise.

His second VC was won at the Battle of Passchendaele, also known as the Third Battle of Ypres, for his actions between 31 July and 2 August 1917. The citation published in *The London Gazette* of 14 September 1917 read:

War Office, September, 1917.

His Majesty the KING has been graciously pleased to approve of the award of a Bar to the Victoria Cross to Capt. Noel Godfrey Chavasse, V.C., M.C., late K.A.M.C., attd. L'pool R.

For most conspicuous bravery and devotion to duty when in action.

Though severely wounded early in the action while carrying a wounded soldier to the Dressing Station, Capt. Chavasse refused to leave his post, and for two days not only continued to perform his duties, but in addition went out repeatedly under heavy fire to search for and attend to the wounded who were lying out.

During these searches, although practically without food during this period, worn with fatigue and faint with his wound, he assisted to carry in a number of badly wounded men, over heavy and difficult ground.

By his extraordinary energy and inspiring example he was instrumental in rescuing many wounded who would have otherwise undoubtedly succumbed under the bad weather conditions.

This devoted and gallant officer subsequently died of his wounds.

Captain Chavasse was buried in the war cemetery at the small village of Brandhoek in Belgium. He was just thirty-two. However, the men remembered in this book were much younger. They all won the Victoria Cross before the age of twenty. The youngest was sixteen-year-old First Class Boy John 'Jack' Cornwell of HMS *Chester*, who did not survive his first action.

He was not the youngest ever to have won the VC. That honour is shared by Andrew Fitzgibbon and Thomas Flinn, who were both just fifteen years and three months old when they showed great bravery respectively in the Third China War in 1860 and the Indian Mutiny – also known as the Sepoy Mutiny or the Indian Rebellion – in 1857. The exact day on which Flinn was born is not known, only the month, so it cannot be determined whether he was a few days older or younger than Fitzgibbon.

Their citations were brief. Fitzgibbon's appeared in *The London Gazette* of 13 August 1861 and read:

Hospital Apprentice Arthur Fitzgibbon
For having behaved with great coolness and courage at the capture of the North Taku Fort, on the 21st of August, 1860. On the morning of that day he accompanied a wing of the 67th Regiment, when it took up a position within 500 yards of the Fort. Having quitted cover, he proceeded, under a very heavy fire, to attend to a Dhoolie-bearer, whose wound he had been directed to bind up; and, while the Regiment

was advancing under the Enemy's fire, he ran across the open to attend to another wounded man, in doing which he was himself severely wounded.

Fitzgibbon was with the Indian Medical Establishment and it is thought that he had the VC with him when he was buried in 1883, having died at the age of thirty-eight.

Drummer Thomas Flinn was with the 64th Regiment. Gazetted on 12 April 1859, his citation read:

Drummer Thomas Flinn
Date of Act of Bravery,
28th November, 1857
For conspicuous gallantry, in the charge on the Enemy's guns on the 28th November, 1857, when, being himself wounded, he engaged in a hand to hand encounter two of the Rebel Artillerymen.

He, too, survived the action and lived to the relatively ripe old age of fifty.

None of the VC winners in this book are quite that young. They were teenagers. Some died during the action they were decorated for. Others died later in the slaughter of World War I or, weakened by their injuries, in a pandemic of Spanish flu that followed it. Some died seeing action again in World War II, still comparatively young then. A few even died of old age in the comfort of their own bed.

Even so, in the action that won them their VCs, they risked almost certain death, exhibiting a bravery that, hopefully, none of us will ever be called upon to match. We will never know whether we would be able to find the valour that they so effortlessly plucked from within themselves. For these boys – who proved themselves to be men – were too brave to live, too young to die.

Nigel Cawthorne
Bloomsbury
November 2015
www.nigel-cawthorne.com

DRIVER JOB DRAIN, 18, AND DRIVER FREDERICK LUKE, 18

ROYAL FIELD ARTILLERY

Le Cateau France, 26 August 1914

Barking in Essex is extremely proud of its young VC winner. His house at 42 Greatfields Road, Barking, carries a blue plaque and, in November 2009, the borough erected a bronze statue of Driver Job Drain in his army uniform outside the Broadway Theatre in the town centre. A commemorative paving stone – one of those to commemorate all VC winners from World War I – was laid in front of the statue on 27 August 2014. The ceremony was attended by Lance-Sergeant Johnson Beharry VC, who won his Victoria Cross in Iraq in 2004, aged twenty-four.

It was awarded for 'two individual acts of great heroism by which he saved the lives of his comrades. Both were in direct face of the enemy, under intense fire, at great personal risk to himself (one leading to him sustaining very serious injuries)...' The full citation is much too long to include here, but can be read at www.thegazette. co.uk/London/issue/57587/supplement/3369.

Born on 15 October 1895, Job Henry Charles Drain attended

Barking Church of England School before he enlisted in the regular army in Stratford on 27 August 1912 to escape unemployment. He was just seventeen.

When Britain declared war on Germany on 4 August 1914, he was in Ireland with the 37th Howitzer (H) Battery of the Royal Field Artillery. Two weeks later, on 17 August, his battery sailed from Dublin, arriving at Le Havre two days later. On the 21st, they headed for the front.

Britain had gone to war not because she was allied to France but to defend the neutrality of Belgium, guaranteed by the Treaty of London of 1839. By the time Drain's battery arrived, the British Expeditionary Force had moved up to Mons in south-west Belgium. There they were to defend the left flank of the French 5th Army and took up positions along the Mons-Condé canal. That day, a British bicycle reconnaissance team met a German unit at the village of Obourg, where Private John Parr of the 4th Battalion of the Middlesex regiment became the first British soldier to be killed in the war.

Having lied about his age, Parr had joined the Army in 1912 when he was only fourteen. He was just seventeen when he died. The circumstances of his death remain a mystery. In later years, a Belgium woman who was eight years old at the time said that she had seen him holding off a German patrol, allowing other Allied force soldiers to escape. But he may have been killed by friendly fire.

The military records still listed him as serving with his battalion on 27 January 1915, though his commanding officer listed him as missing after the Battle of Mons on 23 August. His mother only discovered he was dead when she received a letter from Berlin, from one of his chums who was a prisoner of war, saying he had been

2

shot. He was buried in St Symphorien military cemetery, east of Mons. His headstone gives his age as twenty.

The BEF under Marshal Sir John French held the line at Mons against a superior force in the first major actions that earned them the nickname 'The Old Contemptibles' after the Kaiser was thought to have given an order on 19 August 1914 for German forces to 'exterminate... the treacherous English and walk over General French's contemptible little army'. This may have been propaganda.

On 23 August, the French retreated, exposing the British right flank and forcing them to pull back too. Soon after they arrived, Drain and 37th (H) battery found themselves caught up in the retreat from Mons.

At 02.00 hours on 26 August, there was a meeting of the senior commanders at Bertry, in France, thirty miles south of Mons. The army was in disarray. Major General Edmund Allenby reported that cavalry were scattered and no longer an effective fighting force and Major General Hubert Hamilton, commanding the 3rd Division, said he could not get his men out of harm's way until 09.00 hours. The 5th Division were also in no position to beat a hasty retreat. So Brigadier General Sir Horace Smith-Dorrien decided that they would have to halt the German advance with a short stopping blow at Le Cateau, just four miles away. That would give the rest of the army time to get away in good order.

Unfortunately, Smith-Dorrien was depending on the support of I Corps under General Sir Douglas Haig. He did not know until 05.30 hours that Haig was already in full retreat, but it was too late to change his plans.

On the field were fifty thousand men of the 3rd, 4th and 5th Divisions of II Corps. Opposing them were five divisions of German cavalry. But the Battle of Le Cateau was to be principally an artillery battle. The British had 225 guns, while the Germans had six hundred.

The 37th (H) Battery were with the 5th Division when they withdrew from Mons. At Bavay, eighteen miles north-east of Le Cateau, the battery stopped to provide a rearguard. The division arrived at Le Cateau and set up its headquarters in the village of Reumont, three miles to the south-west. Meanwhile the infantry deployed on the gently sloping fields between Reumont and Le Cateau to the west of the River Selle.

The artillery from XV Brigade was moved up as close as possible to the infantry to give them maximum support. But this left them exposed. The 37th (H) Battery were with three other batteries, with twenty-four guns in all, between the 2nd Suffolks, who made up the front line to the north-east, and their supporting infantry. The battery itself straddled the road that ran from Le Cateau to Reumont. They camouflaged themselves as best they could and dug into the soft soil of the recently harvested fields. To their right flank was a small stream and two machine guns manned by B Company of the 2nd King's Own Yorkshire Light Infantry. On top of a small rise the XVth Artillery Brigade had an observation post.

When the Germans arrived, they occupied the high ground to the west of Le Cateau. Approaching down the valley of the River Selle, they took Le Cateau at 06.00 hours. At the same time, German guns at the forest to the north-east of Le Cateau began pounding the positions of the 5th Division. In response, the 37th (H) Battery and the other guns of the XVth Brigade fired at their muzzle flashes, with some success. The Howitzers quickly silenced two German guns, but it was difficult for them to operate so close to the infantry.

Drain wrote in the diary of 37th (H) Battery: 'There was little cover or hiding place and when the battle began there were

4

18-pounder batteries on either side, with a siege battery to the rear of them and hundreds of infantry men were going up to meet up with the enemy. Terrible shells came over in sixes and were bursting all over the place and over the tops of our guns and wagon lines with plenty of bullets flying about. Man after man was becoming wounded and horses were being killed and batteries smashed to pieces. I just don't think there was a man on the field who did not say his prayers for a general retirement to be ordered.'

Shells intended to hit the battery fell short and the 2nd Suffolks suffered heavy losses. Then, just before 07.00 hours, Major E.H. Jones commanding the 37th (H) Battery was wounded.

At 10.00 hours, the German infantry began to attack the 2nd Suffolks and 2nd Manchesters to their flank in small groups. The XVth Brigade turned their fire on them, inflicting heavy casualties. Soon they were running short of ammunition. At around 13.30 hours, the order came to retrieve the guns and leave the battlefield, but the artillery continued firing until they were almost out of shells.

The 37th (H) Battery were still firing at 13.45 hours when other artillery units were leaving the field. It was clear that the British were going to have to withdraw and the 37th (H) Battery began taking their guns out.

On the other side of the Reumont road, 52, 123 and 124 batteries found themselves so close to the front line that they decided to abandon their guns, first taking out their breech blocks and smashing their sights. Fourteen of the twenty-four guns of XV Brigade were pulled out, but the teams from the 37th (H) and 80th were the last to leave as they were trying to rescue the last four Howitzers and five field guns, rather than abandon them.

Douglas Reynolds, a thirty-one-year-old captain with the battery, was searching for spare gun-carriage teams to haul another two howitzers away. He did not find them, so he disabled the guns and withdrew towards Reumont with his men. There he found two gun-carriage teams, who volunteered to go back for another attempt to rescue the guns. One of them comprised Lieutenant E.G. Earle, who was already wounded, and Lieutenant W.D. Morgan, along with Drivers Ben Cobey, Job Drain and Frederick Luke.

Born on 29 September 1895, Frederick Luke was from Lockerley in Hampshire, where his father was a mill worker. He was one of a family of five boys and eight girls, two of whom had died in infancy. After school, he worked briefly on a local farm before enlisting at Winchester in January 1913. At seventeen, he was still underage when Britain declared war on Germany on 4 August the following year.

Luke was another driver with 37th (H) Battery. The job of these soldiers was to handle the teams of horses that pulled the gun carriages. The equines were harnessed in pairs, with one driver per pair.

Under the command of Captain Reynolds, they headed up the road at a slow trot. Then, when they approached the guns, they broke into a gallop. As the gun carriages bounced across the rough ground, the crew leaned forward in an attempt to steady themselves. The advancing German infantry were taken by surprise by the sight of the gun carriage racing towards them. They were now on three sides of the battery, finishing off those of the 2nd Suffolks, who were still putting up resistance.

XV Brigade were still firing at the advancing Germans as the gun-carriage team approached the wall of shrapnel ahead of them. The artillery commander ordered a brief ceasefire. This allowed the Germans, who were just a hundred yards away, free rein.

While Luke and Lieutenant Morgan were bringing out one gun,

Cobey was shot dead. His whip flew up in the air, but Captain Reynolds, who was riding alongside, managed to catch it and urge the horses on. Drain, who had been running alongside, jumped on to the horse and spurred it on. Captain Reynolds and Driver Drain then sped to safety past the astonished Germans, stunned by the audacity of the manoeuvre.

The wounded Lieutenant Earle did not fare so well. His team hooked up the second Howitzer, but only made it fifty yards before two horses were shot and killed. Earle and Sergeant Bower were unhooking them, when two of his other men were shot dead. They abandoned the gun and, with Sergeant Bower's help, Earle, who had been wounded again in the eye and forehead, made it back to Reumont. Only four of the eighteen officers in the brigade were left unscathed and Major Jones of 37th (H) battery had been wounded and also captured.

Captain Reynolds and Drivers Drain and Luke were all awarded the VC. Reynolds's citation appeared in *The London Gazette* on 16 November. It read:

> At Le Cateau, on 26th August, he took up two teams and limbered up two guns under heavy Artillery and Infantry fire, and though the enemy was within 100 yards he got one gun away safely. At Pisseloup, on 9th September, he reconnoitred at close range, discovered a battery which was holding up the advance and silenced it. He was severely wounded on 15th September, 1914.

The two drivers' awards were gazetted on 25 November. Their joint citation read:

> At Le Cateau on 26th August, as volunteers, helping to save guns under fire from hostile infantry who were 100 yards away.

Five VCs were awarded at the Battle of Le Cateau. Some thought that Driver Cobey should have been awarded the VC posthumously and he appears in a heroic pose in depictions of the action.

Lieutenant Earle was recommended for the VC, but the War Office turned down the award on the grounds that he was under the orders of a superior officer, rather than acting on his own initiative. He got the Distinguished Service Order instead. Sergeant Bower was given the Distinguished Conduct Medal. This was also awarded to Trumpeter S.F.G. Waldron, who was wounded bringing up horses under heavy fire. Later, the 37th Howitzer Battery was given the honorary title of 'Le Cateau'.

For these brave young men the war was far from over. They continued the retreat deep into France for the next ten days. In the summer heat, the horses sometimes collapsed with exhaustion. Those that became lame were shot at the roadside. Men were also overcome with the heat and fell by the wayside. The Germans were just twenty miles from Paris when they were finally halted along the River Marne. Then the French and the British Expeditionary Force began to push them back.

On 9 September, the fourth day of the Battle of the Marne, Captain Reynolds ordered the 37th (H) Battery to take out a German battery that was holding up the advance, reconnoitring it at close quarters. This incident was also mentioned in his VC citation.

During the ensuing Battle of Aisne, the battery crossed the river on a pontoon bridge and the men were billeted at a farm near Soissons. On the 14th, the second day of the battle, Drain recorded that the guns fired all day.

Reynolds was wounded in the chest by a piece of shrapnel. Promoted to major, he was given a new Howitzer battery to command.

Drain and Luke only heard that they had been awarded the Victoria Cross when they were fighting together in the trenches near Bethune and a field officer told them that the King, who was in France, wanted to see them. Given no time to clean up, Drain and Luke were decorated in the field by George V at Locon on 1 December 1914. He warned them not to lose their medals in the mud. Instead, he told them that they should give them to their commanding officer, who would see that they were sent home.

Reynolds received his VC at Buckingham Palace on 13 January 1915. Meanwhile, the 37th (H) Battery was sent north to Flanders, where its soldiers fought with distinction in the First and Second Battles of Ypres in November 1914 and April–May 1915.

Just before Christmas 1915, Reynolds was gassed after being mentioned in despatches another two times. He died of septicaemia in hospital in Le Touquet on 23 February, aged thirty-three, shortly after his son was born back in England.

When Drain returned to Barking, there was a ceremony where he was presented with a purse of gold, a watch and an illuminated copy of the formal address (a calligraphed document on special paper, presented either as a scroll or a panel, with official wording). He went through the rest of the war without being wounded. In 1920, he was one of the VC winners who formed the guard of honour at the internment of the Unknown Warrior in Westminster Abbey. He went into the reserves in 1919 and was discharged with the rank of sergeant in 1924. Drain's father also served in the First World War.

Drain himself married Patricia Murray in 1919 and they had two children. But he found the transition back to civilian life difficult.

He found a job as a Whitehall messenger. Later, he became a Billingsgate fish porter and then was a bus driver. Until his death on 26 July 1975, he continued living in Barking. He was buried in Ripplesdale Cemetery.

For the rest of his life he remained close friends with Frederick Luke, who also served in the Army for the remainder of the First World War. But he was wounded and spent time in hospital in Todmorden, where he met his future wife, Jenny Husband. They had three sons and a daughter.

Discharged from hospital, Luke was transferred to D180 Battery of the 16th Division. He left the reserve in 1929 with the rank of sergeant and became a janitor at Glasgow High School for Boys. During the Second World War, he joined the RAF and served as a ground gunner. Back in civvy street again, he became a store man in an engineering firm.

In 1962, he returned to Le Cateau with Brigadier Earle, where he was given the freedom of the town. He returned the following year to mark the fiftieth anniversary of the battle with the successor to the 37th (H) Battery, 93 (Le Cateau) Battery. In 1981, he visited the battery in Paderborn, Germany, where he was given a champagne lunch in the officers' mess, sitting under a painting of the three holders of the VC rescuing the gun at Le Cateau. The commanding officer of the 4th Division, Major General Richard Vickers, said that he hoped they would never go to war again.

'Well, if you do,' said Luke, 'and you need any help, just give me a call.'

For several years before he died, Luke was the oldest living recipient of the Victoria Cross and he held the record for being the longest holder of the medal, clocking up over sixty-nine years.

He died on 12 March 1983 at the age of eighty-seven. He was

cremated in Linn Crematorium, Glasgow, and his ashes were scattered in the crematorium gardens there.

Along with Drain and Reynolds, his name appears on the VC memorial in the Royal Artillery Chapel in Woolwich, south-east London. Both Drain's and Luke's VCs are on display in the Lord Ashcroft Gallery at the Imperial War Museum, London.

GOBAR SING NEGI, 19

39TH GARHWAL RIFLES

Neuve Chapelle, France, 10 March 1915

We have a problem with Rifleman Gobar Sing Negi VC. Due to poor record keeping in Uttarakhand, northern India, his date of birth is variously given as 21 April 1895 – which would have made him nineteen when he won his VC – or 21 April 1893 – which would have made him twenty-one. And his name is given variously as Gobar Sing Negi, Gabar Singh Negi and Gabbar Singh Negi.

Sources generally agree that he was born at Manjood village near Chamba, Tehri in the Garhwal district of Uttarakhand and joined the Garhwal Rifles in October 1913. He was with the 2nd Battalion of the 39th Garhwal Rifles.

When World War I broke out, both the 1st and 2nd Battalions were sent to France. On 13 October 1914 they arrived at Marseilles as part of the Garhwal Brigade. They mustered at Orleans and entered the front-line trenches at Richeburg on the night of 29–30 October. The trenches were already under heavy shellfire. On the night of 4 November, about eighty Germans advanced on the trenches occupied by the 1st Battalion. A party of sixteen riflemen charged and put them to flight.

By the night of 9–10 November, a German trench had extended to within fifty yards of the 2nd Battalion, who decided that they had better attack it. Some fifty riflemen crawled to the German parapet without being seen. Once the signal was given, they jumped down into the trench and captured six prisoners. The rest fled.

A few days later they decided to carry out another night raid, but on a larger scale. Fifty men from the 2nd Battalion were detailed, along with 250 from the 2nd/3rd Queen Alexandra's Own Gurkha Rifles on their right. A party of sappers and miners and two more platoons of riflemen were to follow in order to occupy the German trench once it had been captured.

However, since the last raid, the Germans had been improving their trenches and had also installed a searchlight. The raid was also preceded by a short artillery bombardment, so the Germans knew that an attack was coming. The advance was met with heavy fire. Though many of the men reached the German trench, they found it impossible to capture it. There were heavy casualties. Two British officers and one Garhwali officer were killed.

After three weeks in the trenches both the 1st and 2nd Battalions were relieved. Then on 23 November, the 1st Battalion was sent to reinforce the Ferozepur Brigade in the Pas-de-Calais. The Sikhs there had lost a part of their trenches to the Germans and, despite repeated counter-attacks, had failed to retake it.

When the 1st Battalion, Garhwal Rifles arrived, it was decided to attack the German flank. The raid was to be led by a party of seven bombers borrowed from the 57th Rifles. Several traverses – right-angled bends in the trench to prevent enfilading fire (a volley of gunfire directed along a line from end to end) – were taken at the point of a bayonet, after the bombers had done their work. Between thirty and forty prisoners were taken. When the bombs ran out, the riflemen charged, killing or taking prisoner any Germans who stood their ground. They captured the rest of the trench and, by dawn, the original line had been restored.

During the action Naik Darwan Sing Negi, thought to be thirty-three, was wounded twice in the head and once in the arm, yet he refused to give in. He continued to head the party, pushing round each successive traverse in the face of heavy fire. He was awarded the VC. The citation, which appeared on the front page of the supplement to *The London Gazette* published on 7 December 1914, read:

His Majesty the KING-EMPEROR has been graciously pleased to approve of the grant of the Victoria Cross to the under-mentioned soldier of the Indian Army for conspicuous bravery while serving with the Indian Army Corps, British Expeditionary Force:

1909, Naik Darwan Sing Negi, 1st Battalion, 39th Garhwal Rifles.

For great gallantry on the night of the 23rd–24th November, near Festubert, France, when the regiment was engaged in retaking and clearing the enemy out of our trenches, and, although wounded in two places in the head, and also in the arm, being one of the first to push round each successive traverse, in the face of severe fire from bombs and rifles at the closest range.

Directly under Naik Darwan Sing Negi's citation came that of Sepoy Khudadad Khan, who had won the VC at the First Battle of Ypres. It read:

> 4050, Sepoy Khudadad, 129th Duke of Counaught's Own Baluchis.
>
> On 31st October, 1914, at Hollebeke, Belgium, the British Officer in charge of the detachment having been wounded, and the other gun put out of action by a shell, Sepoy Khudadad, though himself wounded, remained working his gun until all the other five men of the gun detachment had been killed.

Both also appeared in the *Gazette of India* on 15 January 1915. Though they were both awarded the medal on the same day Sepoy Khudadad Khan's came from an earlier action, so he is considered the first Indian winner of the VC.

In the action at Festubert, one British officer, one Garhwali officer and eighteen men were killed, and one British and two Garhwali officers and thirty-three men were wounded. The battalion captured two machine guns, one trench mortar and 105 prisoners. They held the captured trench until the night of 25–26 November when they were relieved by the 2nd Battalion, who occupied it for three days and suffered heavy casualties, exhuming and re-burying the German dead under intense fire. This dangerous and unpleasant work was undertaken for sanitary reasons.

After one day out of the line, the 2nd Battalion returned to the trenches near Richebourg, alongside the 1st. Although the shelling was now less intense, both battalions still suffered casualties daily. At the end of December, they were relieved and marched some twenty miles behind the lines, where they could rest.

They returned to the front line in the last week of January 1915. The weather was bad and the trenches were flooded. Consequently, there was little fighting until the Battle of Neuve Chapelle began on 10 March. This was to be the first large-scale organised attack undertaken by the British Army during the war.

By then more divisions had arrived in France and the British Expeditionary Force was split into two armies. The action at Neuve Chapelle would be undertaken by General Sir Douglas Haig's First Army.

French Commander-in-Chief, General Joseph Joffre, considered it vital that the Allied forces should take advantage of their growing strength on the Western Front, both to relieve German pressure on Russia and, if possible, break through in France. British commander Sir John French agreed and pressed the BEF to adopt an offensive posture after the months of defence in waterlogged trenches. Joffre planned to reduce the great bulge into France punched by the German advance in 1914, by attacking at the flanks in Artois and the Champagne. The plan was to take the railway running across the plain of Douai, forcing the Germans to evacuate a large part of the ground they held. The British were asked to attack at Neuve Chapelle.

The attack was undertaken by the IV Corps under General Sir Henry Rawlinson on the left and the Indian Corps under General Sir James Willcocks. The battle opened with a thirty-five-minute bombardment of the front line, then thirty minutes of shelling on the village and reserve positions. The bombardment, for weight of shell fired per yard of enemy front, was the heaviest that would be fired until 1917.

'At 7.30 am the artillery bombardment commenced, and never since history has there been such a one,' said Captain W.G. Bagot-

Chester MC, 2/3rd Gurkha Rifles, Garhwal Brigade, Meerut Division. 'You couldn't hear yourself speak for the noise. It was a continual rattle and roar. We lay very low in our trenches, as several of our guns were firing short.'

The 1st Battalion was on the right of the brigade. They strayed too far south and found the German wire there practically untouched. Under intense fire the Garhwalis showed great bravery and determination, taking heavy casualties. Eventually they broke through and took around two hundred yards of trench. However, they had become separated from the battalion to their left by around the same distance. This meant they had Germans on three sides of them. All their British officers had been killed in the advance and the battalion was under the command of Subadar (Lieutenant) Deb Sing Mahar until he, too, was killed. Sudadar Kedar Sing Rawat then took over and the 1st held off the Germans until British troops closed the gap.

The 2nd Battalion had a comparatively easy time of it. In their sector, the artillery bombardment had done its job. They captured over two hundred prisoners and three machine guns.

It was during the advance that Rifleman Gobar Sing Negi distinguished himself. He was one of a bayonet party attacking the flank. Once in the enemy trench, he was the first to go round each traverse in the face of fierce German resistance, killing several of the enemy. When the NCO in his party was killed, he took over command and drove the Germans back until they surrendered.

Gazetted on 28 April 1915, the citation to his VC read:

His Majesty the KING has been graciously pleased to approve of the grant of the Victoria Cross to the undermentioned man for his conspicuous acts of bravery and devotion to duty while serving with the Expeditionary Force:

No. 1685 Rifleman Gobar Sing Negi, 2nd Battalion, 39th Garhwal Rifles.

For most conspicuous bravery on 10th March, 1915, at Neuve Chapelle. During our attack on the German position he was one of a bayonet party with bombs who entered their main trench, and was the first man to go round each traverse, driving back the enemy until they were eventually forced to surrender. He was killed during this engagement.

By nightfall the remains of the village had been taken and the Germans had been pushed back a further four hundred yards to the River Layes. But, during the night, the Germans reinforced their second line in front of the Bois du Biez beyond and all further attempts to push them back further proved futile.

Before the German counter-attack at dawn on 12 March, the 2nd Battalion was ordered back when it was found the trenches had become overcrowded. But the 1st Battalion stayed in the captured trench. After suffering heavy bombardment, they played their part in repulsing the enemy. Their machine-gun detachment defeated every effort of the Germans to recapture the trenches, killing hundreds. The following day the 1st Battalion was relieved.

For the part they had played in the battle, both battalions were mentioned by the Corps Commander as having especially distinguished themselves. A message to this effect from the commander-in-chief of the British Army in the field was published in *India Army Orders*. The two battalions were at the head of the units cited.

During the action 1st Battalion lost seven British officers, three

Garhwali officers and 120 other ranks killed, and five British officers, four Garhwali officers and 190 other ranks wounded. Due to their losses, the two battalions were amalgamated as The Garhwal Rifles.

Gobar Sing Negi's name is recorded on the Neuve Chapelle Memorial. However, back in Chamba, he is remembered as Gabar Singh Negi, where an annual Gabar Singh Negi Fair is held in his memory every 20 or 21 April, depending on the Hindu calendar. In 1971, the Garhwal Regiment adopted the fair and a memorial was constructed. With the inclusion of the Army in the ceremonies, the Gabar Singh Negi Fair began attracting villagers from far and near to pay homage to the brave young soldier. It is the only fair of its kind in the state.

The fair is also a recruitment rally for the Garhwal Rifles, which still exists as an infantry regiment in the Indian Army.

'The saga of Negi's bravery continues to inspire the youth from this part of the world to join the Army,' says local writer Kunwar Prasoon.

PRIVATE EDWARD DWYER, 19

EAST SURREY REGIMENT

Hill 60, Zwarteleen, Belgium, 20 April 1915

Private Edward Dwyer was at the Second Battle of Ypres with B Company of the 1st East Surreys. Born in 1895 in Fulham, he was baptised Edwin at St Thomas of Canterbury's Roman Catholic Church in Rylston Road and was educated at St Thomas's Parish School, living with his parents in Lintaine Grove nearby.

After leaving full-time education, he worked as a greengrocer's assistant. At the age of sixteen, he ran away from home shortly after the reading of the banns for the marriage of his father, private builder James Dwyer, and his mother Mary Ann. It is thought that he could not bear the shame of his newly discovered illegitimacy.

Although he was short for his years – 5 foot 3½ inches – he lied about his age and enlisted in the Army at Kingston-upon-Thames as Edward Dwyer. He was with the 1st Battalion of the East Surreys when they were posted to Ireland and was in hospital with a venereal disease when war broke out. He embarked for France with the

British Expeditionary Force on 13 August 1914, just nine days after war had been declared.

The 1st Surreys were with the BEF when they advanced on Mons.

'That march to Mons was a nightmare,' Dwyer said. 'Unless you've been through it, you can't imagine what an agonising time it was. We used to do from twenty to twenty-five miles a day. We filled haversacks with biscuits and ate them as we marched along.'

It was at Mons he first saw action.

'The first big scrape we had was at Mons at twelve o'clock Sunday noon,' he said. 'The Germans don't take any account of Sundays. You people over here don't realise what we went through in those days.'

He then experienced the humiliation of the retreat from Mons. Then, from the River Marne, the 1st Surreys moved up to relieve the French, covering as much as forty miles in one day.

'We had a four-hour sit-down and then we went straight into action in open formation,' said Dwyer. 'That was when we pushed them back fifteen miles in three weeks. I remember September 30 too. It was the day we drew the first pay since we'd been out there – five francs. It had to last as long as we could make it. No more pay until November. Five francs more on the fifth of November and bread was a franc a loaf.'

Afterwards, they moved up to Ypres. It was all this marching that Dwyer recalled particularly:

'There was only one thing that could cheer us up on the march,' he said. 'That was singing. We used to sing something made up by the chaps. "Tipperary" was in full swing then and they would always go on to something they had invented themselves. It used to buck us up and we would march all the better for it. Sometimes we would sing some of G.H. Elliott's songs. You know, the "Chocolate Coloured Coon". But we would always go into something we'd invented.'

The refrain was often the stoical: 'We're here because we're here because we're here…'

During the First Battle of Ypres, the German 30th Division captured Hill 60, near Zwarteleen to the south-east. The French had dug a tunnel under the hill and, when the British took over that section of the front, miners from Wales and Northumberland continued their work as it was the only part of the front in that area that was not waterlogged.

The British attacked on 17 April 1914, taking Hill 60 easily. The *Illustrated War News* of 28 April 1915 explained how they did it in a piece entitled: 'How the capture of Hill 60 was made possible – the explosion of a land-mine under an enemy trench'.

It read:

In places, land-mines are playing in the trench-warfare a part of immense local importance, and sometimes with wide-reaching results. Their immediate effect is that of a volcanic eruption, suddenly belching up in the midst of the trenches with a devastating burst of flame and dense smoke, the explosion excavating a gaping crater and killing or crippling all on the spot. Our photograph, taken from a trench in front at the moment of mine-explosion, vividly shows what onlookers would see. The blowing-up always immediately precedes a bayonet assault by the layers of the mine, before the survivors or their comrades in the adjoining trenches have time to pull themselves together. In that way our capture of the otherwise impregnable Hill 60, south-east of Ypres, was rendered possible.

The whole operation cost just seven British casualties. However, it created a salient that would be difficult to hold and the Germans began heavy shelling of the whole area in preparation for a counter-attack.

The following morning, the 1st East Surreys marched out of their billets in Ypres and took the road to the south-east that led to Hill 60. They were to support the Royal West Kents and the Kings' Own Scottish Borderers, who had taken the hill the previous day.

An account of the action was written by Captain James Price Lloyd of the Welsh Regiment, who served with Military Intelligence and wrote reports on the actions of VC winners. After the war, the government gave orders that it could not be risked to make these archives public, as they were thought to be too sensitive. Remarkably, some of the documents have survived in the personal records of Captain Lloyd. In a document headed 'Tales of the VC', stamped 5 March 1918, he wrote:

On Sunday morning, the expected German counter-attack developed. Again and again masses of infantry breasted the lower slopes, but they never gained the ridge. All the enemy's endeavours to recover their lost ground ended in failure. The British losses, too, had been heavy. Fresh troops were needed at once to relieve the weary battalions in the firing line.

Early on the morning of the 19th, the 1st East Surreys took their place in the front line, and for nearly two days, in spite of every effort to dislodge them, they clung gallantly to the tangle of craters which crowned the hill. Field gun and Howitzer, trench mortar and machine gun rained death upon them always. These could kill, but they could not conquer.

On 19 April, Dwyer found himself in a trench to the north-east of the hill, almost opposite a German strongpoint that stood at the end of a sap, or trench, that ran out from the German front line towards the British trenches. The following day, B Company were supposed to move up to the advanced trenches to relieve A Company. This was prevented by a German push that began on the afternoon of the 19th. While A Company were involved in heavy fighting, German troops were seen advancing down the sap under the protection of sniper fire from the stronghold and the trenches held by B Company were soon under threat.

Leading a platoon with A Company was twenty-three-year-old Lieutenant George Roupell, a graduate of Sandhurst who had been commissioned in the East Surrey Regiment in March 1912. According to Lieutenant Lloyd:

> Lt. George Rowland Patrick Roupell set a shining example of courage and endurance to his men. Although he had less than three years' service, he had been in command of a company since the 15th of September the previous year, and had shown that he was well worthy of such a responsible post. He had already on several occasions proved himself a brave as well as a capable officer. When his battalion was in action near Messines his brigadier recommended him for 'devising and carrying out a very brilliant reconnaissance, in which he displayed courage and coolness of a very high order'. These same qualities he showed in defence of Hill 60.
>
> The 19th was a day of comparative peace, but there was stormy weather ahead. Next day the full fury of bombardment beat down on Hill 60 once more, and when the shells had done their work, the German infantry came forward to bomb

the defenders out of their ruins. The company had lost heavily and Lt. Roupell himself had been wounded in several places, but the Surreys would not give an inch. Inspired by the personal example of their leader, the survivors manned what was left of their parapets, and drove the Germans back into their trenches.

Early on 21 April, Dwyer risked life and limb, leaving the trench under heavy bombardment to bandage wounded comrades. Eventually, he found himself alone in that section of the trench, apart from the dead and wounded. The Germans were only fifteen or twenty yards away and were throwing grenades into the trench. Dwyer, though, was ready to make a stand. He climbed up onto the parapet and began lobbing grenades back.

In that position, the enemy could fire directly on him. But the Germans, at first shocked by his audacity, soon found themselves the target of his fusillade. Single-handed, he kept the Germans at bay until reinforcements arrived. In recognition of his feat, he was promoted to lance-corporal on 24 April.

Captain Lloyd wrote:

For his gallantry during this attack and the bombardment that preceded it, Pte. Edward Dwyer, of the same battalion, was also awarded the Victoria Cross. When the shell-fire was at its height he left to bandage the wounds of several of his comrades who had been hit and were lying in the open. When the attack came, regardless of his own danger, Dwyer climbed up the parapet, where he was fully exposed, and hurled bomb after bomb at the advancing Germans. A party of Germans, who had crawled up an old communications trench to within a few yards of the parapet, showered bombs upon him, but, by some miracle, he escaped out of that Hill unhurt.

Three days later, Dwyer was hit in the head by a piece of shrapnel. He learnt that he had been awarded a VC the following month when he was recovering in a French hospital. The award had been gazetted on 21 May 1915 and the citation read:

For most conspicuous bravery and devotion to duty at 'Hill 60' on the 20th April, 1915. When his trench was heavily attacked by German grenade throwers he climbed on to the parapet, and, although subjected to a hail of bombs at close quarters, succeeded in dispersing the enemy by the effective use of his hand grenades. Private Dwyer displayed great gallantry earlier on this day in leaving his trench, under heavy shell fire, to bandage his wounded comrades.

Three other VCs were won on Hill 60 that day, another ten days later. One of them was awarded to Lieutenant Roupell. Captain Lloyd's account continued:

There was a lull after the failure of this attack, and Lt. Roupell took advantage of it to hand over his command and pay a hurried visit to the dressing station. The Medical Officer would have kept him there, but Lt. Roupell refused to stay. He had other work to do. At any moment the enemy might attack again, and most of his officers were gone. He would not leave his men.

So he went back to the front line. He had not long returned when the German guns began to speak again. The garrison of the hill was now desperately thin. Lt. Roupell at once went down to Headquarters, through the storm of shell-fire which swept the slopes, and returned once more at the head of the reinforcements which were so urgently needed. Badly wounded as he was, he remained with his company on Hill 60; until, on the morning of the 21st, the battalion was relieved.

Lieutenant Roupell's VC was gazetted on 22 June 1915. The citation read:

For most conspicuous gallantry and devotion to duty on 20 April 1915, when he was commanding a company of his battalion in a front trench on 'Hill 60', which was subjected to a most severe bombardment throughout the day. Though wounded in several places, he remained at his post and led his company in repelling a strong German assault. During a lull in the bombardment he had his wounds hurriedly dressed, and then insisted in returning to his trench, which was again being subjected to severe bombardment. Towards evening, his company being dangerously weakened, he went back to his battalion headquarters, represented the situation to his Commanding Officer, and brought up reinforcements, passing backwards and forwards over ground swept by heavy fire. With these reinforcements he held his position throughout the night, and until his battalion was relieved next morning.

This young Officer was one of the few survivors of his company, and showed a magnificent example of courage, devotion and tenacity, which undoubtedly inspired his men to hold out till the end.

Lance-Corporal Dwyer received the medal from George V at Buckingham Palace on 28 June, taking with him Father Browne from St Thomas at Canterbury, Fulham, who he had known since he was seven. Roupell got his decoration at the Palace on 12 July. Both he and Dwyer were also awarded the Russian Cross of St George Fourth Class. Roupell also won the Croix de Guerre and was mentioned in despatches – and was retrospectively appointed temporary captain. By 1918, he was a temporary major on the general staff.

Back in England, Lance-Corporal Dwyer told his story in a piece entitled 'How I Won the VC – my single-handed fight with the Huns at Hill 60', which appeared in the *Daily Chronicle War Budget* on 8 July 1915:

They gave me the VC because I was in a dead funk at the idea of being taken prisoner by the Germans.

It happened at 'Hill 60' on 20th April 1915. My trench was heavily attacked by German grenade-throwers. I climbed onto the parapet, and, although subjected to a hail of bombs at close quarters, I succeeded in dispersing the enemy by the use of hand grenades.

I am the youngest VC in the British Army, being what is known as 'eighteen and a bit'.

There was a time when I was a greengrocer's assistant in Fulham, in the far-off days when I lived with my father and mother.

But I got tired of the greengrocery and said to myself, 'The Army's the thing for a Man.' I was a very little chap, and not more than sixteen at the time when I ran away from home to join the British Army.

I think the recruiting sergeant must have been just a bit short-sighted on purpose, because he enlisted me without any trouble in the 1st Battalion of the East Surrey Regiment.

The other day, they gave me a few days' leave, which I was lucky enough to get extended, but I go back to the front in a few days' time. When I came home the King sent for me to go to Buckingham Palace. His Majesty shook hands with me, and I told him what I had done. He was ever so nice to me, and smiled when he shook hands after pinning the VC on my breast. He's a King worth fighting for, King George.

What I mean when I say that they gave me the VC because I was in a dead funk at the idea of being taken prisoner by the Germans is that the Huns never take one man alone alive. Anything less than a batch they won't be troubled with. So you can understand why I was afraid. If I have to die, I thought, I will die fighting.

Fear's a funny thing. It gets at you in all kinds of funny ways. When we've been skirmishing in open order under heavy fire all the while I've felt myself go dumb, my tongue a bit of cotton. Then the blood has rushed into my face, head and ears hot as fire, and the tip of my tongue swollen into a blob of blood. It's not nice, I can tell you, but the feeling passes. I've never expected to get out of any fight I've ever been in. And so I always just try to do my bit, and leave it at that.

Well, they were shelling our trench pretty badly, and after a time all our chaps were either killed or wounded. Some of the papers have said that the other chaps retired. They didn't retire – the wounded may have crawled.

At last I was the only unwounded man left in the trench. There were three steps leading up to the parapet of the trench, and I sat crouched on the middle step. Shells and hand bombs were bursting all over and around, but nothing touched me at all. We had a lot of hand grenades in our trench, and I added to my stock by gathering up all I could find. I suppose I had about three hundred in all.

Then I went back to crouch on the middle step of the trench. The fear of being taken prisoner was very strong upon me. A straight shot, a round hole in the forehead, is all right. A soldier can't complain at that. But to be taken prisoner by those Huns – ugh!

But funking drives a man to do mad things – I found myself on the trench parapet hurling hand grenades. I won't say it wasn't fine fun, but there was the dread at the back of my mind that the devils might miss me, and take me alive before the trench was relieved. So I gave it to them good and hot. I did a few of them in. If they had only known that I was the last man left they would have rushed me, and by now I should have been – a dead prisoner…

I was pretty well done when help did come; but I jumped down into the trench, mad with joy and without a scratch. The relieving party chipped me a lot and called me 'The King of the Hand Grenades'.

I got wounded by a flying piece of shrapnel about a week later and went into hospital, and while I was there the news came that they had given me the VC.

Since I returned home I have been doing a bit of recruiting. One day I got about thirty chaps to join. I tell them just straight that because we've not enough men there are soldiers still in the firing line who have earned a dozen holidays but can't be spared because there's nobody to take their places.

Some of the slackers who won't join grouse about the fighting conditions they'd have to put up with. I say if the officers can put up with the grub and the grind, and men with money can serve as privates, who've always lived soft before, nobody has any right to be too particular. The Army's what a man makes of it.

According to the newspaper: 'Corporal Dwyer kept his home leave secret for three days – then word got out and the ladies of Fulham showed their appreciation!'

Dwyer did not go back to the front in a 'few days' time' as he predicted. He spent six months helping the national recruiting drive, talking not only of his own service, but that of his father who enlisted in the Army Service Corps at the age of fifty, his elder brother James who served in the Royal Navy Division in Salonika and his younger brother Andrew, who was then in hospital after serving in the Dardanelles.

He told the *Observer* on 18 July 1915: 'There are hundreds of lads in the Army who are only seventeen years of age, but they said they were eighteen, and if they can do it, so can you.'

Dwyer also made a couple of recordings about the retreat from Mons and day-to-day life in the trenches. Just nineteen, his voice through the crackles is old beyond his years. He begins: 'They tell me that you would like to hear something of what our boys are doing at the front. And although I am only a youngster as soldiers go, I've seen about as much fighting as any man and there's still a bit of fight left in me yet if I get the chance to go out again…'

He did get that chance. But first, on 20 December, he married Maude Barrett-Freeman, a twenty-one-year-old nurse he called Billie, who had tended him when he was injured. She was a farmer's daughter from Balham. The wedding was at St Thomas at Canterbury's Catholic Church in Fulham, with Father Browne officiating. Dwyer told his mother of his marriage the following day.

Before he returned to France, he seems to have had a premonition that he would not be coming home again. He left his VC for safe-keeping with Father Browne, saying: 'The general rule is that a VC gets knocked out the second time.'

Promoted to acting corporal on 27 December, he returned to the front in January 1916, while his wife returned to nursing under her maiden name. He was made a full corporal on 27 July. He was killed leading his men in an attack at Guillemont on the Somme at noon on 3 September.

Two weeks later, a memorial mass was held at St Thomas's. A bronze plaque honouring him was unveiled in a ceremony in Fulham Central Library on 28 December 1918. The inscription reads:

IN GRATEFUL MEMORY

CORPORAL EDWARD DWYER V.C.

A FULHAM LAD EAST SURREY REGIMENT

KILLED IN ACTION 3RD SEPT. 1916 AGED 20

HE GAINED THE VICTORIA CROSS FOR
CONSPICUOUS BRAVERY AND DEVOTION

TO DUTY AT HILL 60 FRANCE APRIL

1915 IN DISPERSING GERMANS BY HAND
GRENADES AND BANDAGING UNDER

SHELL-FIRE WOUNDED COMRADES

He is buried at Flatiron Copse Military Cemetery in France.

In 1962, when Father – then Canon – Browne died, Dwyer's VC was found among his possessions. This was reported to the War Office and the medal was presented to the Regimental Museum of the East Surrey Regiment in Kingston.

In November 1996, the Public Record Office – now the National Archives – in Kew, south-west London, put on an exhibition that included Dwyer's army papers and the newspaper coverage of his deeds at the time. Fulham Library also put on a commemoration attended by children from St Thomas's School.

Roupell remained in the Army after the war. He was taken prisoner during the Allied intervention into the Russian Civil War in 1919. Later, he spent two years at the Royal Military College of Canada in Kingston, Ontario, and a year with British troops in China in 1934.

By the outbreak of World War II, he was a colonel and, as an acting brigadier, he was given command of the 36th Infantry Brigade, which took him back to France with the British Expeditionary Force. When his brigade headquarters in Doullens was attacked, he is reported to have said: 'Never mind the Germans, I'm going to finish my cup of tea.'

The brigade headquarters were then overrun and Roupell hid out at a farm near Rouen for nearly two years, working as a farm labourer. Eventually the French resistance escorted him to Spain and he returned to the UK via Gibraltar. He then became commanding officer of the 114th Infantry Brigade. Retiring from active service as a brigadier in 1946, he went on to become the last colonel of the East Surrey Regiment before it amalgamated with The Queen's Royal Regiment to form the Queen's Royal Surrey Regiment.

MIDSHIPMAN WILFRED MALLESON, 18
HMS *RIVER CLYDE*
Gallipoli, Turkey, 25 April 1915

Turkey and its Ottoman Empire that dominated much of the Middle East joined the First World War on the side of the Central Powers – Germany and Austria – on 1 November 1914. This was because Russia had declared war on the Ottomans, immediately bringing in its Western Allies, Britain and France. The British were particularly gung-ho as the Ottomans threatened the Suez Canal, Britain's lifeline to India.

To aid its Russian ally, Britain agreed to attack Turkey through the Dardanelles, the narrow strait that connects the Aegean Sea to the Sea of Marmara. From there, a British fleet could bombard Constantinople – now called Istanbul – which was then the capital of the Ottoman Empire.

Initially this was planned as solely a naval action so men would not have to be diverted from the Western Front. It would also use obsolete warships, too old for fleet action against the Germans in the North Sea. The attack was to begin by bombarding the Gallipoli

Peninsula to the west of the straits, but this proved ineffective against the modern fortifications there. So Winston Churchill, then First Lord of the Admiralty, proposed a combined amphibious operation. The British were to land at five beaches on the tip of the peninsula, known as Cape Helles, on 25 April 1915. The ANZACs – men of the Australian and New Zealand Corps – would land further to the north, while the French would land at Kum Kale on the Asian side of the straits to draw away Turkish reinforcements.

At eighteen years, five months, William St Aubyn Malleson was the youngest of the ten VC winners at Gallipoli that day. Born on 17 September 1896 at Kirkee in India, he was the eldest son of Major General Wilfred Malleson, a distinguished officer in the Indian Army.

He was sent to prep school at Edgeborough, near Guildford. After attending Marlborough College, he went to the Royal Naval College, Dartmouth, and joined the battleship HMS *Cornwallis* as a midshipman three days before the outbreak of war.

The *Cornwallis* took part in the ineffective bombardment of the Turkish defences in early 1915 and was then assigned to support the landings on Cape Helles on 25 April. As landing craft had yet to be invented, most of the soldiers and stores would be taken ashore by pinnaces rowed by sailors.

The British also had a converted collier, the *River Clyde*, which would carry 2,000 troops. The ship would be beached and the troops would rush ashore over lighters from doorways cut in her side. Just before the landings the news came that Rupert Brooke, the war poet who had joined the expedition as an infantry officer, had died of septicaemia on a hospital ship off the Greek island of Skyros. It was not an auspicious beginning.

At 05.00 on 25 April, the British began their barrage on Cape

Helles. At 06.00, the *River Clyde* set off, but had to slow down so the pinnaces could keep up. Then at 06.22, she beached. The Turks, who had remained hidden in their trenches up to this point, opened fire. Men were killed where they sat in their barges.

'One fellow's brains were shot into my mouth as I shouted for them to jump for it,' recalled Sergeant J. McColgan, who was shot in the leg. 'I dived into the sea. Then came the job to swim with my pack and one leg useless. I managed to pull out the knife and cut the straps and swim ashore. All the time bullets were ripping around me.'

Of his thirty-two men, only six survived.

The plan called for a steam hopper, or barge, to form a bridge from the ship to the shore. However, the Dardanelles current swept the hopper away so Captain Edward Unwin, commander of the *River Clyde*, and Able Seaman William Charles Williams dived overboard and, under heavy fire from the Turkish defenders, manhandled two lighters into position, lashing them together to form the bridge. When Williams was mortally wounded, Unwin went to his aid and the lighter he was holding was swept away. Unwin then collapsed from cold and exhaustion.

Others attempted to lash the lighters together and failed from sheer exhaustion. Then Midshipman Malleson took his turn. Under heavy rifle fire and the rake of a Maxim gun, he swam out and succeeded in lashing two lighters together. But the rope then broke and he had to make two more attempts.

Eventually, when the lighters were in place, men rushed from the doors in the side of the *River Clyde* – to be cut down. Only twenty-one of the first two-hundred men reached the shore. Munster Fusilier Tim Buckley was with them.

'I was talking to the chap on my left when I saw a lump of lead enter his temple,' he said. 'I turned to the chap on my right, his name was Fitzgerald from Cork, but soon he was over the border. The one piece of shrapnel had done the job for the two of them.'

Major David French of the Dublins also made it ashore.

'I was in the last boat of my "tow" and did not realize they had started at my boat until one of the men close to me fell back dead – shot,' French wrote soon after. 'I realized immediately that having practically wiped out those in the three boats ahead they were now concentrating their fire on us. I jumped out at once into the sea (up to the chest) yelling at the men to make a rush for it and to follow me. But the poor devils – packed like sardines in a tin and carrying this damnable weight on their backs – could scarcely clamber over the sides of the boat and only two reached the shore un-hit...'

French himself was lucky to escape.

'I had to run about 100–150 yards in the water and being the first away from the cutter escaped the fire a bit to start with,' he said. 'But as soon as a few followed me the water around seemed to be alive – the bullets striking the sea all round us. Heaven alone knows how I got thro'... When I was about fifty yards from the water's edge I felt one bullet go thro' the pack on my back and then thought I had got through safely when they put one through my left arm. I could find only thirty or forty men intact and we commenced to dig ourselves into the low cliff. Why the Turks with their vast preparations did not level this bank of earth down I cannot imagine. Had they done so, none of us would have escaped.'

The few who made it ashore took cover under that bank at the back of the beach. Even there they were in danger of artillery fire from the Asian shore but, fortunately, the shells proved defective. Nevertheless, the ensuing slaughter was appalling.

'The beaches were covered with bodies of the dead, and the slopes with limbs, heads and bodies,' said a Turkish soldier fighting there. 'The small dried-up streams were flowing with blood.'

Malleson was in the third wave on V Beach, but the Turkish resistance was so great that the British became embroiled in the furious fight to gain the tiniest toe-hold. Nevertheless Malleson spent six days unloading men and material, and guiding units ashore. He was the only one of the six winners of the VC on V Beach not to be injured. Physically exhausted, he was evacuated to Bighi Hospital on Malta, suffering from rheumatic fever.

The citation that appeared in the *Supplement to The London Gazette*, 16 August 1915 read:

Admiralty, 16th August, 1915.

The KING has been graciously pleased to approve of the grant of the Victoria Cross to the undermentioned Officers and men for the conspicuous acts, of bravery mentioned in the foregoing despatch: —

Commander Edward Unwin, R.N.

Midshipman Wilfred St. Aubyn Malleson, R.N.

Midshipman George Leslie Drewry, R.N.R.

Able Seaman William Chas. Williams, O.N. 186774 (R.F.R. B.3766) (since killed).

Seaman R.N.R. George McKenzie Samson, O.N. 2408A

Midshipman Malleson was promoted to acting sub-lieutenant on 15 May 1916. That autumn he joined his younger brother Rupert on HMS *Lord Nelson*, where his rank was confirmed on 30 December. He received his VC at Buckingham Palace on 2 January 1918, the last of the six VC winners from V Beach to receive his award.

Promoted to full lieutenant on 30 March, he was serving on the depot ship *Lucia*, under the command of Martin Dunbar-Nasmith VC, when the war ended. In peacetime, he served in submarines, gaining his first command in 1923. He returned to surface ships for two years before taking command of another submarine in 1927.

That year, he married Cecile Mary Collison in St Mary's, Marylebone. The couple moved to Plymouth, where Cecile gave birth to a daughter.

In his mid-thirties he was posted to the cruiser HMS *Berwick* on China Station. One of his contemporaries there said: 'He was known as "Mad Malleson". That is not meant to be pejorative "mad", but a chap who is a bit unpredictable. He was fiercely forgetful, abnormally so.'

By the outbreak of the Second World War, he was back in Devonport, serving as a commander. In 1941, he went on the retired list, only to be recalled and sent to Malta as the assistant captain of the dockyard there. He stayed there for the rest of the war, enduring the ferocious air attacks. His family joined him there in 1945, when he was promoted to captain of the dockyard and later King's harbour master, continuing in service on Malta until he retired in 1948.

Attempting to start a second career, he ran a hotel in Galloway, then, with his wife, a caravan park in Cornwall, settling finally in Truro, where they lived in a bungalow he had built. Wearing a monocle, he became the village eccentric. Though chairman of the local sea cadets, few knew of his naval exploits. He hid a painting depicting his endeavours at Cape Helles and refused all invitations to join the Victoria Cross and George Cross Associations.

His brother Hugh, also a retired naval commander, explained his modesty, saying: 'He reckoned that he and his companions trying to replace the landing barges at V Beach were available for any odd jobs, and this was an emergency. Of course, he was frightened, as were the others, but like truly modest men, he seemed to prefer keeping his reflections on the action to himself.

'The hours spent in the water, trying to get the lighters back into position, under heavy fire was one thing, but the visible execution of hundreds of our soldiers before slipping into the water might well have un-nerved others. On this subject, therefore, Wilfred's reluctance to talk or join in celebrations about VCs was initiated by his illness at Bighi Hospital and prolonged by the curious.'

Captain Malleson died on 21 July 1975, aged seventy-eight. He was the last of the V-Beach VCs to die. His ashes were scattered at sea off Falmouth. His medals were presented to Edgeborough School, but were later acquired by Lord Ashcroft and are on display at the Imperial War Museum.

SECOND LIEUTENANT
GEORGE MOOR, 18
HAMPSHIRE REGIMENT
Krithia, Gallipoli, Turkey, 5 June 1915

George Raymond Dallas Moor was Australian by birth, but was not at Gallipoli with the ANZACs. Instead he was a lieutenant in the Hampshire Regiment and was at V Beach, where he won his VC.

The family had a tradition of colonial service. His father, William Henry Moor, had worked in the Ceylon Civil Service before becoming auditor-general of the Transvaal, and his uncle, Sir Ralph Moor, had been high commissioner for Southern Nigeria.

George was born on 22 October 1896 in the home of his aunt, Ella Helen Moor, née Pender, in St Kilda, Victoria, Australia. With his father occupied in Pretoria, Moor was sent home to England to be educated. He attended prep school on the Isle of Wight, before applying to Cheltenham College in 1909, giving his intended career as the Egyptian Civil Service. At school he was a promising sportsman.

Though Moor clearly intended to follow in the family tradition, it seems that he wanted to put some distance between himself and his father. In 1914, his mother filed for a judicial separation on the grounds of adultery. With good reason. Her husband, she stated, had 'never interested himself in the boy' and she had paid for his education out of her allowance.

Still only seventeen, Moor enlisted at Barnstaple on 18 September 1914. He joined the 21st (Service) Battalion (4th Public Schools) of the Royal Fusiliers, which had been formed by the Public Schools and University Men's Force a week earlier. The medical officer noted he had a fresh complexion and 'very good physical development'. He was five-foot eleven inches tall and weighed 10½ stone.

Moor spent just forty days as a private before being commissioned into 3rd Battalion of the Hampshire Regiment, his father's old unit. After six months' training in England and Egypt, he went to the Dardanelles as a second lieutenant with the 2nd Battalion of the Hampshires, landing on V Beach on 25 April 1915 and surviving the bloodbath there. Three days later, he was wounded during the advance from the beachhead towards the village of Krithia, which had been practically undefended when they had landed. In the face of stiff Ottoman resistance, the British were forced back to their starting point.

Another attempt to take the village and neighbouring hill of Achi Baba on 6 May also failed. By then only 250 of the original thousand men of the 2nd Battalion were left and were badly in need of rest and recuperation. Nevertheless the units of the 29th Division continued to push forward, aiming to establish a front line less than two hundred yards from the Turkish defences, ready for another attempt to take the village, which was scheduled for 4 June.

Before then, the 2nd Hampshires were reinforced and Lieutenant Colonel Weir de Lancy Williams took over as the unit's fifth commanding officer since the landing. He had also distinguished himself on V Beach on 25 April. The 2nd Hampshires' strength was brought up to 382, with thirty-nine officers and men rejoining the unit from hospital. One of them was Moor.

The Third Battle of Krithia began at 11.20 on 4 June. To begin with, everything seemed to go well. When the first bombardment was over, the British then made a feint advance, drawing the Turks back into their trenches, only to be decimated by a second bombardment.

At noon, the advance began. Then things started to go wrong. The Indian Brigade on the left was quickly halted, with the exception of the Gurkha Rifles. A Sikh battalion was almost wiped out as it advanced along the floor of Gully Ravine. Following a stirring speech by Lieutenant-Colonel Williams, in which he expressed the hope that the regiment would win its first VC since the attack on the Taku Fort during the Opium Wars of 1862, the 2nd Hampshires advanced along Fir Tree Spur beside them, quickly capturing two lines of trenches.

While the assault units of the 29th Division managed to secure their objectives, the 42nd Division in the centre broke through. But on the right, the French advance failed. A reserve battalion from the Royal Navy Division went in and its soldiers were annihilated. Nevertheless, the Hampshires continued their advance, with Moor's 88th Brigade taking the lead.

But with the failure on the right, the 42nd Division's position was untenable and they were forced back. At 18.00 hours, the 88th Brigade was ordered to pull back. By then the 2nd Hampshires' casualties were around 50 per cent. The losses among the officers were particularly severe. After meeting what he called 'a tall, wild-looking dark-haired boy of eighteen' in one of the captured trenches,

Lieutenant-Colonel Williams remarked: 'Moor, myself and one other officer were the only officers left untouched.'

Williams said to Moor: 'Well done, boy! Hold what you have got.'

Soon after, Williams was wounded and Moor was left as the only officer in the sector.

While the Turks were held back by machine-gun fire, they were reinforced that night and then attacked in strength. Lieutenant Colonel A.G. Paterson with the King's Own Scottish Borderers who, with the 1st Essex, occupied the H12 salient to the left of the 2nd Hampshires and the 2nd Royal Fusiliers recalled:

There was a slight mist. At dawn heavy fire broke out and a message came through that H12 was lost. Almost at the same moment looking away to the right one saw what appeared to be the whole of our trench garrisons streaming back in hundreds to the old front line under heavy MG fire.

It was a most extraordinary sight and I shall never forget the sound made by the troops coming back – a sort of long drawn-out moan. An officer of the HQ with us (I am not sure whether it was the Essex or Borders) ran out towards Nine Tree Copse to rally these troops. They must have rallied quickly as we got in touch with the Essex later that morning. The Turks took no advantage of this momentary panic.

The Turks had burst through the line of the 1st Essex, who fell back on the trench occupied by the 88th Brigade. The Hampshires' regimental history says:

A disorganized mass of men was being pressed back against the Royal Fusiliers' left, where crowded and narrow trenches impeded any reorganization of the defence. The situation was becoming critical, officer-less men were retreating in confusion when Second Lieutenant G.R.D. Moor dashed across the open from the Hampshires' lines with a few men and stemmed the retirement by vigorous and forcible measures, actually shooting one or two panic-stricken fugitives. He did not stop here: having rallied and reorganized the men in a hollow, he led them back to the lost trench and cleared the Turks out, setting a magnificent example of bravery and resourcefulness.

According to the 29th Division's commander General Henry de Lisle, Moor 'had to shoot the leading four men and the remainder came to their senses.' De Lisle commended this as a 'remarkable performance' and said that Moor was 'one of the bravest men I have ever met.'

Australian war correspondent Charles Bean, reporting on the retreat from Krithia, said: 'Before the order to retreat came, however, a British lieutenant was said to have shot four of his own men who had bolted. Dallas Moor, only eighteen, claimed he had killed them to stop a mob desertion. It was subsequently reported he was awarded the Victoria Cross for his disciplinary measures.'

Although Moor had indeed shot four of his own men, it was thought that if the rout had been allowed to continue, the casualties would have been much higher. His counter-attack was also successful, though the H12 salient remained in Turkish hands.

The regimental history records: 'That evening, Second Lieutenant Moor had to be taken to Brigade Headquarters, being completely exhausted.'

He had spent twenty-five hours under continuous fire, fourteen of them in command of the captured trench.

There he received the congratulations of his commanding officer. But it was the officers from the 2nd Royal Fusiliers alongside who observed his actions and recommended him for the VC.

While Moor was evacuated to hospital on Malta, his award was gazetted on 24 July. The citation read:

For most conspicuous bravery and resource on 5 June 1915, during operations south of Krithia, Dardanelles. When a detachment of a battalion on his left, which had lost all its officers, was rapidly retiring before a heavy Turkish attack, Second Lieutenant Moor, immediately grasping the danger to the remainder of the line, dashed back some two hundred yards, stemmed the retirement, led back the men, and recaptured the lost trench. This young officer, who only joined the Army in October, 1914, by his personal bravery and presence of mind saved a dangerous situation. During the action he was for eleven hours under continuous heavy fire in the trenches, and it was fourteen hours before he recovered from the state of collapse brought about as a result of his great efforts. He had previously greatly distinguished himself at the landing in Gallipoli.

By August, Moor was back in the trenches outside Krithia. On 6 August, another attack was made in what became known as the Battle of Krithia Vineyard. Though a small patch of ground known as 'The Vineyard' was taken, the action cost over four thousand men. The Hampshires suffered 240 killed and 210 wounded. But Moor had miraculously been left out of the battle and emerged as one of only four officers left in the battalion. Even so, Major John

Gillam, a British supply officer who visited the trenches ten days later, recorded in his *Gallipoli Diaries* that he had been taken to one of the forward positions by 'a cheery young man named Moor, who had recently won the VC'.

A month later, Moor was invalided home with dysentery, but on 18 October 1915 was well enough to attend an investiture at Buckingham Palace, where he received his VC. Afterwards he went to visit his mother in Braunton, Devon. According to the *North Devon Journal*: 'As Lieutenant Moor and his mother walked from the platform to the waiting motor car the large crowd gave three hearty cheers, with an additional cheer for Mrs Moor. Lieutenant Moor, in acknowledgement, rose from his seat in the car and saluted.'

But it was plain he was ill.

'Lieutenant Moor, who was looking pale and was evidently very weak, briefly replied that he was very glad to be home,' the paper said.

At an official reception, he was presented with an illuminated copy of the address given by the chairman of Braunton Parish Council, who wished him: 'God speed and further success in whatever duties you may be called upon to perform in future' – to loud applause. Moor himself was too weak to respond with anything more than a single sentence of thanks.

On 4 December 1915, his doctor noted: 'Lieutenant Dallas Moor has been under my care suffering from dysentery with jaundice. Jaundice now improving but as yet he has no solid motion and does not gain in weight and probably will not until fluid motions cease. There is considerable nervous exhaustion. He is quite tired out after walking one mile. Reflexes are exaggerated and fields of vision contracted. I should suggest further complete mental rest and abundance of fresh air.'

But on 8 February 1916, Moor returned to the 3rd Hampshires at Gosport. That autumn he was deemed fit for front-line service. On 3 October, he joined the 1st Hampshires on the Somme. Promoted to full lieutenant on 30 October, he was wounded in the arm on 23 December. He was invalided home again and told that it would be months before he was fit for duty again.

While recovering in hospital, he received a message from Brigadier Seely, who was commanding the Canadian Cavalry Brigade in France, asking him to come out as aide de camp. But while awaiting his discharge from recuperation, he was seconded on to the staff of Weir de Lancy Williams, his former commanding officer from Gallipoli, now a major general commanding the 30th Division on the Western Front. This man had been trying to head-hunt Moor since he took command of the division in April 1917.

He wrote later: 'My first thought was for young Moor. I wrote to his battalion commander asking for him, saying "the boy has been at it so long he must want a rest". His CO wrote back that he could not spare him. Early in 1918, I heard from him that he was wounded and in England, and though he could not get passed as fit, he could come to me as ADC. He joined me on 20 March 1918, during our retreat before the German main attack.'

Though he had not regained the full use of his arm, Moor was not one to hold back. Williams wrote: 'The officer has a positive contempt for danger and distinguishes himself on every occasion. In the open fighting of the last few weeks of the war he was invaluable, day after day reconnoitring well out in front of our most advanced troops.'

He put himself in the way of danger. On the advance towards the River Scheldt, he was accompanied by fellow VC winner Philip Neame, who wrote: 'We had dismounted and handed our horses to our orderlies while I looked with my field-glass, when I heard the ominous roar of a heavy shell coming through the air. By experience I knew that it was a 5.9-inch howitzer shell, and that it was coming very close. There was no cover at all, so we just stood there. The shell landed with a thud within three yards of our feet: by good fortune it was a dud. Another day Moor and I were walking down a lane with the CRA, Brigadier General F.F. Lambarde, CMG DSO, when a German field-gun battery bracketed us with two salvoes. Moor and I, as I thought sensible at the time, made it into the ditch, where there was good cover. Lambarde frightened us by walking straight down the middle of the road without batting an eyelid, and for shame we went too, while the shells kept on coming, but behind us.'

These acts of bravery won Moor a Military Cross, gazetted on 2 December 1918. The citation read:

Lieutenant George Raymond Dallas Moor, V.C., Hampshire Regiment. For conspicuous gallantry and skill. He carried out a daylight reconnaissance all along the divisional front in face of heavy machine-gun fire at close range, in many places well in front of our foremost posts

Six months later, he was awarded another Military Cross. The bar citation read:

On 20 October 1918, near to Pijpestraat, the vanguard commander was wounded and unable to carry on. Owing to heavy shelling and machine-gun fire, the vanguard came to a standstill. Lieutenant Moor, Acting General Staff Officer, who was reconnoitring the front, noticed this; he immediately took charge, and by his fearless example and skilful leading continued the advance until the objective was reached. He has a positive contempt for danger, and distinguishes himself on every occasion.

Moor did not live long enough to receive either of these awards. After dicing with death repeatedly throughout the war, in its last days he caught the Spanish flu that was soon to sweep the world. He died of pneumonia on 3 November 1918 at the Canadian clearing station at Mouvaux, France, and was buried at Y Farm Military Cemetery, Bois-Grenier.

His name appears on the roll of honour in the parish church in Braunton. The illuminated address he was presented with is kept in the local museum and his regiment presented the village with a field gun that has since rusted away. In 1961, his older brother Sylvester, who served in the Royal Navy during the First World War, presented his medals to the Royal Hampshire Regiment Museum & Memorial Garden in Winchester, where they are now on display. George Moor was the youngest officer to receive a VC during the First World War and his commanding officer, Major General Williams, described him as 'a fine character and as fearless a soldier as ever lived.'

SECOND LIEUTENANT
SIDNEY WOODROFFE, 19
PRINCE CONSORT'S OWN (RIFLE BRIGADE)
Hooge, Belgium, 30 July 1915

The First World War extracted a terrible price from some
families. Henry Long Woodroffe and his wife Clara Clayton
lost three of their four sons. The youngest, Sidney Clayton
Woodroffe, was born in Lewes, Sussex, on 17 December 1895. He
followed his two older brothers to Marlborough College, where he
became senior prefect and captain of the Officer Training Corps,
winning the Medal of Merit, which carried the bust of Lieutenant-
Colonel Curzon Wyllie, an old boy of the school who had served
in India and was assassinated by a Hindu student at the Imperial
Institute in South Kensington in 1909.

The Woodroffe brothers excelled at sport. Sidney represented the
school in football, hockey and cricket. He won a scholarship to read
classics at Pembroke College, Cambridge. At the outbreak of war
the brothers joined up in The Rifle Brigade. They were part of the
New Army, often referred to as 'Kitchener's Army' or, disparagingly,
'Kitchener's Mob', initially an all-volunteer army raised afresh

since the outbreak of war. Sidney joined as a second lieutenant two days before Christmas in 1914 and was sent to France on 25 May 1915. His eldest brother was already there. Attached to The Welsh Regiment, Kenneth was killed in action at Neuve Chapelle in France on 9 May 1915. Mentioned in despatches, he was just twenty-two.

On 12 July 1915, Sidney wrote a long letter to his friend Aidan 'Boko' Aidan, back in Althorne, Essex, who had been head boy at Marlborough when Sidney was there. It read:

My dear old Boko,

I wonder if you would mind if this letter does for Jack Barnes, Paul and Thomas H. if they come to read it, as I owe them all letters and it is simply impossible to write. In that case one apology for not writing will do for all of you!

I don't know if I have told you anything so far, but anyhow for the first six weeks we wandered over Northern France and Belgium and no one seemed to have any use for us at all. We flopped about in the appalling heat and flopped into trenches in different parts of Europe, each lot being worse than the last, and losing a few men here and a few there, among others Hooker and Lawson-Walton. Nothing particularly exciting happened and I didn't even get lice. Then at the beginning of last week we were put into the worst trenches in the British Line. This is an absolute fact – I'm not trying to be funny – as no Division ever takes them over for more than a month or it becomes a platoon and a long roll of honour. We were stuck in these trenches for nine days on end and I will try to give you some idea how beastly it was.

The place was the extreme tip of the furthest advanced part of our line, i.e. at the end of the well known 'salient'. This means that we were enfiladed by guns from both sides, and so were fired on from three directions at once. There was one 8-inch howitzer that used to shell us regularly every evening right away from jolly old 'Hill 60'. One man in our company was hit when he was 400 yards away from the burst. Another shell, a 15-inch one, burst in Ypres the other morning and the base of it, weighing over a hundredweight, knocked down a wall 900 yards back.

All the water in this God-forsaken country is undrinkable, and every drop of water we consumed in the trenches was brought up by hand in petrol tins over a mile at night. In one part we were in all the streams had been poisoned with arsenic by these bleeding Bosches. You can occasionally find a Jack Johnson hole [a large shell crater named for Jack Johnson, the heavyweight champion of the world] into which water has drained – probably via an impromptu cemetery and a few refuse pits – and this affords a doubtful wash. You never get your boots off the whole time you are in the trenches, and after about ten days a change of socks is decidedly desirable!

One thing that practically turns you inside out at first is the flies. Every kind of disgusting and bloated bluebottle and fly in various stages of torpor buzz about or sleep on beams, and flop down your neck when you bang your head on them for the hundred-and-one-th time.

This last lot of trenches we were in were ones that were captured from the Germans about a month ago. We were in reserve for that attack and sweated with fear all one night that we would be pushed into it. Practically every trench and road out here has a nickname, generally absurd but cheery names like Piccadilly Circus, Eastbourne Pier, etc.; in this last lot it was 'Hellfire Corner', 'Suicide Corner' and 'Dead Man's Alley' and such like, which of course cheers one to start with!

Well, first of all our company was put in a support trench quite isolated, about half a mile in rear, and Rae's [one of the masters from Marlborough] platoon was in another little trench about 50 yards behind us. We were warned that they shelled us all day every day, and my goodness it wasn't far wrong. It was so bad that fires could only be allowed between 2–3 am (jolly time for a meal) as the smoke doesn't show in that misty light – otherwise shells galore. It is beastly hardly ever having anything hot to eat and drink, especially when you are tired and fed up. The one amusing thing was that most of the shells that just missed us generally used to get Rae's trench! You get pretty selfish out here – as long as the shell misses you personally it is all right!

The first day we were there they gassed us with (prussic acid) gas shells. My God, it is bestial. With these foul shells which possibly explode a few yards away from you, the stuff is on you and inside you before you have time to make a selection from your stock of respirators and helmets. (Once you have been gassed you take jolly good care.) It makes your eyes (and nose) simply stream, you cough and retch and have a beastly sore throat and violent headache. While suffering like this a confounded great horse-fly bit me on the hand and reduced me to an absolute frenzy of rage.

The next day we were treated to a similar gassing, one of the shells knocking down the parapet about five yards away from me and covering me with earth. That night I had the most horrible time I have ever had, and ever hope to have. I was sent with a party of [a] hundred men to clear up a trench which had never been touched or occupied since we had captured it from the Germans a fortnight before; since nicknamed 'Dead Man's Alley'. I had a look in the daylight first, though couldn't start work until dark as it was under fire, and the place nearly made me sick, although you get used to a good deal out here. There was I landed in the dead of night on my own entirely, to make a hundred none to [sic] willing men work in this perfectly godless place. Besides all the countless equipment, rifles, overcoats etc. we collected, we buried twenty-three corpses (four English), two heads, a dismembered hand and a foot. As it was a pitch-dark night what I had to do was to wander about by myself, and on smelling something that nearly knocked you over backwards, cautiously shine my torch until I saw a ghastly blackened face grinning up at me – and then tell off a small party to dispose of it! Every one of us had to wear our respirators the whole of the 3½ hours we were there, and at the end of it I had had quite enough. To add to the discomfort, once when I shone my torch in the sky by mistake for the ground, we were promptly treated to two shrapnel shells.

The next day we were gas shelled again – and properly this time. They got the range exactly and put them right on the parapet. The first smashed to pieces our one and only anti-gas sprayer; the second blew to blazes the stretcher bearers' dugout and buried a stretcher; the third blew the head clean off the captain of my company, killed two corporals in my platoon and wounded a sergeant and another man in about five places, and so on. You can't imagine how bestial it was with the place as an absolute fog, and everybody coughing and choking in their helmets. I was wearing three myself, so couldn't see or hear! In desperation, finally, to get out of the blasted place I got hold of a sergeant and we sweated off with one of the men on a stretcher. It was a pretty absurd thing to do as it meant haring down a road which can be seen and is invariably shelled if anyone shows his nose down it. One shell removed practically the entire road not more than ten yards in front of us and nearly knocked us silly. The man we were carrying on the stretcher had been hit in the head and practically the whole inside of his head came out on the way down, which didn't make things pleasanter. I continued to cart stretchers until I thought the gas might have departed a bit!!!

That night the powers decided that ours really was rather a ridiculous trench, so we were shifted up to the firing line trenches to recover! All except the wretched Rae's platoon – he was left there alone all the time.

It is extraordinary how the gas hangs about, especially low down on the ground. Two mornings later I took a small party in the still smaller hours of the morning – about 3.30 am, as that is when the German Gunners go to bed for a few hours – to try and dig out a lot of equipment and property that had been buried where the shells burst. It took us 3½ hours, simply because we couldn't stay in the place more than a minute at a time wearing all the respirators in the world.

That night it fell to my lot to take a ration party – about eighty men – a mile back from the fire trenches to draw out the next day's rations for the battalion. It was all down a long communication trench and road, both of which were invariably shelled. Ten men were killed in the trench alone on similar jobs while we were there. What makes it so beastly is that you have so little control over a vast string of men in single file.

That night they bombarded us and knocked the trenches about a lot; early the next morning a party of German bombers came and bagged the trench occupied by one of our platoons. I was shaken up in a very déshabillé and sleepy condition and told to take my platoon and help get it back. I had not the haziest idea what was happening and had never seen that particular trench before. Feeling extraordinarily frightened and trying not to look it, I collected a party of bombers and stalked up (unfortunately discovering on the way that the only kind of bomb we were carrying was the only kind I had never seen in my life and not knowing how on earth to use them). Luckily, a platoon of another regiment on our left came to the rescue and had helped to clear the devils out before I arrived. We slew about eight of them in all. The Germans then got sick and bombarded us until four in the afternoon, banging our trenches to pieces, knocking out a lot of men, and preventing me from getting anything to eat until 5 pm.

That night I was in charge of a ration party again. On the way we were cheered up by passing a man who had recently had the whole of his face blown off. The next morning there was a big attack on our left, which I expect you read about, and we bombarded the Germans opposite us in order to keep their guns quiet. This sounds all right, but unfortunately the Germans thoroughly entered into the spirit of the thing and gave the unoffending us back about twice as much as they received. Also they will insist on having these shows at the unchristian hour of three or four in the morning. I stood there shivering with cold and simply deafened by the appallingly ridiculous noise, and every now and then showered with earth and muck – net result – trenches again bashed in and more men knocked out. It was made unnecessarily unpleasant again by our having been told that we might be wanted to attack as well.

The next night we stood to arms the whole blessed night as there was the probability of a German counter-attack. However, besides a few scares entailing furious blasts of rapid fire at nothing at all and besides the usual nightly ration of a thousand odd shells, trench-mortars, grenades, etc. – nothing. What you do discover though is that the sleep you were so much looking forward to never seems to come off.

After nine days of this we were relieved. I had to guide part of the relieving battalion up, which meant an extra five miles walk for me. The billets we came to were 14 miles back, so in all I started at 8.30 pm and walked some 19 miles all through the night before eventually arriving here at 7.30 am. Trenches do not get you into the best of training; very little sleep and eating vile tinned things at irregular intervals. To make matters worse I was stricken for the last nine miles with the worst stomach ache of modern times, and arrived completely doubled up at this most delightful of farms, where I slept twenty-two out of the first twenty-four hours.

Such is life here. Time drags in the trenches, nothing done to further the interests of our country as far as one can see, and the battalion lost five officers and a hundred men, and the brigade about 350 in all. This is war!! The German supply of shells seems quite unlimited. If our guns fire we cheer; even when they lay out men by dropping them in our own trenches (which has happened twice to us) we don't like to discourage them. As a matter of fact, really their gunners aren't a patch on ours and it will make all the difference in the world when we get the ammunition.

The most humorous thing that has happened to me so far was when an absolutely spent rifle bullet hit me plumb in the back of the head – and simply bounced off, merely giving me a bruise!

There is going to be the hell of a battle soon. I bet you anything you like. The Germans I believe have massed about a million men and guns opposite this part, so we are led to believe. With any luck we shall get a move on too. All the same there is nothing out here to make one believe the war will be over for the hell of a long time. Also it is simply becoming a war of shells and hand grenades.

How I would love to be able to get over to M.C. before you all leave. If I ever see it again it will be so horribly different after this term. It was perfectly priceless about Cheltenham. I hope Jack Barnes treats Rugby in the same way. How's the tennis – also Lower? I shall begin snorting with delight shortly at the thought of you enmeshed in endless certificate exams. You can comfort yourself in return at the thought of a weary and fly-blown S.C.W. with a 15-inch shell. If you haven't heard a 15-inch just go and listen to Duck's motor bus and it will give you some idea. Nothing will give you any idea of the noise it makes when it bursts though.

Are you going to Camp? It sounds awfully nice. I live just around the corner from Swanage, i.e. Bournemouth. Isn't it simply rotten about Busslo. This stinking war. I saw him just before we left Aldershot. I see Heal is dead, too. Pretty creditable my surviving two months I think.

Will you give W-W my love and tell him Reggie Layden

came over today. He has been at Rouen lately. He is looking much older, rather sadder and slightly grey-haired.

Look here, quite seriously, however hard up you are for copy – and with certificate exams I know what it is like – please (we were once comrades in trouble) don't put any part of any letter I write in the *Malburian*! Otherwise I will never write again. I do mean this. Give my love to:

(1) The Walls

(2) The Perks

This is the longest and worst letter I have ever written. I won't afflict you again.

Very Best Love

S.C.W.

Sidney and his elder brother Leslie were with the 8th Battalion of the Rifle Brigade, who were sent to the trenches at Hooge, twenty miles north of Neuve Chapelle in Belgium, at midnight on 30 July to relieve their sister battalion, the 7th Rifle Brigade. The handover was complete by 02.00 hours, though 7 RB's bombers – that is, men who throw bombs – remained in place.

The British front at Hooge was cut in two by a crater ninety feet wide and forty feet deep, making the position difficult to defend. A Company went in the line there, with Lieutenant Woodroffe's platoon on the left of the crater and Lieutenant Carey's on the right and the bombers' posts abutting the edge of the crater itself. There was little barbed wire there. The trenches were deep and narrow, as were the zigzagged communication trenches that ran back to Zouave Wood, some five hundred yards behind the front, making communication along them very difficult. Worse still, the German lines were close, at some points just fifteen yards away.

The 8th Rifle Bridge had been in position for just three hours when the Germans attacked. The 8th had been called to stand-to, so the trenches were packed when, at about 03.25 hours there was a huge explosion in the stables, 150 yards to the right. Then there was an intense bombardment of the front trenches which lasted about two or three minutes, before the unexpected happened. Suddenly the whole of the front was engulfed in a sheet of flame and billowing black smoke.

World War I was notorious for its wholesale adoption of new and more terrible forms of weaponry – the machine gun, aerial bombing, gas, the tank. The 8th were about to come face to face with another new danger – the flamethrower.

While fire had been used as a weapon of war since ancient times, in 1901 German scientist Richard Fiedler submitted various designs to the German Army for evaluation, which were of a weapon that projected streams of burning liquid. His *Flammenwerfer* was not adopted until 1911, when a specialist regiment was formed. The weapon was used briefly against the French at Verdun on 26 February 1915, but the British had yet to face it. They were untrained and unprepared. And Hooge, with the trenches being so close together, turned out to be the perfect spot for the Germans to test the effectiveness of their terrible new weapon.

Already dazed by the bombardment, the 8th looked on in horror as 'liquid fire' was sprayed from hoses along the German lines. These primitive flamethrowers only had a range of twenty yards. That did not matter. The burning oil easily dowsed the narrow British trenches, so fully packed it was impossible for their occupants to run away. Eyewitness Private A.P. Hatton described the scene in the classic magazine series of war reminiscences, *I Was There*. He wrote:

We first heard sounds as of a splashing to our front, then there was a peculiar smoky smell just like coal-tar; next a corporal of C Company cried out that he had been hit by a shell; yet when we went to look at him we found that a huge blister as from a burn was on his forehead, while the back of his cap was smouldering.

We had no time to notice anything else, for after that preliminary trial the Boches loosened their liquid fire upon us with a vengeance. It came in streams all over the earthworks, while shells containing star lights ignited the black fluid. Sandbags, blankets, top-coats, and anything of the sort [that] was handy smouldered and then flared. We were choked by the smoke and half scorched by the heat.

Our first instinct had been to fly to our dugouts under the parapets where the liquid could not touch us. I know that C——, 'Robbie' and I had just made ourselves as safe as possible in our earthy nook, when the captain's whistle blew and we heard the non-coms yelling: 'Stand to arms.' The Germans were upon us. That dastardly liquid fire attack had been a mere preliminary, by which they had hoped to wipe us all out.

The flamethrowers had been aimed at the men in the trenches on either side of the crater. Under the cover of the smoke and flames, German bombers had swarmed forward through the crater, then swung around behind the trenches on either side. Others made a frontal assault, arriving on the parapets of the British trenches that had been hit by the fire. The casualties there had been almost 100 per cent.

However, the men with Carey to the extreme right and Woodroffe to the extreme left had escaped the flamethrowers. The fighting became confused and the four remaining machine guns were knocked out, but Carey and Woodroffe hung on as the Germans tried to bomb them out.

At around 03.30 hours, the two forward companies signalled an SOS to Battalion Headquarters by field telephone. By then Woodroffe was under attack by German bombers making their way along the trench from the crater to his right, as well as those who had fanned around behind the trench.

Private Hatton said: 'We had ample time to note that the first line of attackers were all fine picked men, the 126th and 132nd Regiments, but that behind them came a queer, hobbling non-descript rabble of *Landsturm* reserves, men dressed anyhow, all middle-aged, some with beards, many with glasses, and a number so fat that they could hardly waddle over the broken ground. I suppose it was pitiful that such men, fathers of families, should be sent as food for our British bullets; but we had no time to think.'

B Company under Captain A.L.C. Cavendish had been held back in reserve in Zouave Wood. At 04.00, they counter-attacked. By then, the Germans had occupied most of what had been the British forward trench. It was now bristling with machine guns in fortified positions and the counter-attack failed.

Woodroffe and his men were now virtually surrounded, but they continued to defend their position until they ran out of bombs. Then they retreated in good order, fighting their way back to the Menin Road, just south of the ruined stables. Through a culvert further down the road, they managed to get back to British lines.

The Germans were now making their way down 'the communication trenches that had been named 'The Strand' and 'Old Bond Street'. But the British had blocked these halfway down and managed to hold off the Germans for the rest of the day.

During the ensuing counter-attack, Private Hatton said: 'We were just filled with the lust of killing, a lust that had been fully fed by that wicked liquid fire; and so – we let them have it.' But he lost contact with his friends, Lance-Corporal C—— and 'Robbie'. 'Later, on my way back, I stumbled on the rigid body of poor "Robbie", shot clean between the eyes.'

C Company had virtually ceased to exist, while A and B Companies had suffered heavy losses. At 09.00 hours a company from the King's Royal Rifles arrived as reinforcements from brigade reserve. At noon orders came that, following a forty-five-minute artillery bombardment beginning at 14.00 hours, they were to counter-attack again.

Despite their losses, 8 RB was to take the lead. D Company under Captain C. Sheepshanks, which had been held back in Zouave Wood, was to attack with its right on The Strand, bombing the Germans in the trench as they went. What was left of A and B Companies were to do the same down Old Bond Street. But this was an attack across open ground with the enemy well established with machine guns in trenches. The battalion's War Diary notes: 'The whole ground was absolutely swept by bullets'.

Most men were cut down before they got halfway towards their objective. The reinforcements who followed fared little better. Only Woodroffe reached the wire and began to cut it.

In his account of the action, Captain James Price Lloyd, attached to Military Intelligence, wrote:

The German attack at Hooge at the end of July was noteworthy for the appearance in the field for the first time of the Divisions of Kitchener's New Army. This was the 14th Division, consisting of the 41st, 42nd and 43rd Brigades, under the command of General Couper.

The ruins of the village of Hooge and the heap of brick and rubble that was once the château stand on the crest of a low ridge along the road which leads from Ypres to Menin. A little north of the road, in front of the village, the 3rd Division had exploded a mine earlier in the month and the crater was now in British hands. South of the road was a stretch of open ground, and beyond this open ground, separated by a few fields, were two woods, which have become famous. Zouave Wood and Sanctuary Wood.

The 14th Division took over the line from the neighbourhood of the Roulers railway, half-a-mile north of the crater, down to Sanctuary Wood. The trenches in front of the crater, which were destined to bear the brunt of the assault, were held by two companies of the 8th Rifle Brigade from the 41st Brigade.

It was a poor legacy that had been bequeathed to them. There [sic] trenches had been dug only a short time before under fire. They afforded very little protection against shell-fire, and proved hopelessly inadequate for the ordeal which was so soon to come.

Early in the morning of the 30th of July the German bombardment began. From north and east, and even from behind Hill 60 in the south-west, shells rained down upon the doomed trenches. The work of destruction was not entrusted to the artillery alone. The enemy had already driven saps to within a short distance of the British lines, and at 3 am, they launched a torrent of liquid fire. This new terror in warfare had been in readiness since the beginning of the war. The Germans had only been waiting for the place and time to use it. The liquid fire attack was accompanied by showers of *minenwerfer* [trench mortar] bombs.

Shortly afterwards, the German infantry swarmed into the attack. They were confident that theirs would be an easy victory but they sadly misjudged the fighting qualities of the men of the New Army. The two companies of the 8th Rifle Brigade had been nearly blotted out by the bombardment, but dazed survivors clung grimly to their shattered trenches, and it was only after a bitter struggle that sheer weight of numbers forced them back into the second line.

Much of the credit for this gallant stand was due to Sidney Woodroffe, a mere boy of nineteen, who was in command of two platoons in the extreme left of the line. His position was heavily attacked on the flank, but with the help of the few men he had left, he built a barricade and held off the enemy until all his stock of bombs was exhausted. It was only when he saw that he was almost surrounded that he consented to retire.

Under intense fire, he succeeded in bringing his men back safely across nearly 200 yards of open ground, into the lines of the 9th Rifle Brigade of the 42nd Brigade, and afterwards led them down a communication trench which was being heavily shelled, to the headquarters of his battalion in the Zouave Wood.

An hour later, the 8th Rifle Brigade made a heroic effort to recapture their lost trenches. The 9th Rifle Brigade, who had hurried up from Vlamertinghe, seven miles away, accompanied them into action.

For three-quarters of an hour British shells screamed over Zouave Wood to burst in the German positions beyond, and at 2.45 the two battalions moved forward to attack. But it was doomed to failure from the beginning. There was not the weight of guns on the British side which was to come later.

The great German shells bursting amidst the tree-trunks in the Zouave Wood tore great gaps in the ranks, and the few that won through to the open ground beyond fell under the savage blast of the German machine guns on the ridge. Against such odds no human valour could prevail, yet 2/lt Woodroffe, with a mere handful of men, did indeed reach the barbed wire in front of the enemy's trenches. He reached it but could go no further. He ordered his men to lie down, crawled forward himself, and tried to cut his way through. He knew his own life was less precious to him than the lives of his men. Death came quickly to him: a few minutes later, he was struck in the head by a bullet and instantly killed.

The counter-attack had failed; but it was a splendid failure. For it showed that the soldiers of the New Army could face death so unflinchingly as their comrades of old. They had been weighed in the balance, and not found wanting.

Second Lieutenant Woodroffe's father received a letter from Lieutenant R.C. Maclachlan informing him of his son's death. It spelt out exactly how courageous the nineteen-year-old boy had been.

'Your younger boy was simply one of the bravest of the brave and the work he did that day will stand out as a record hard to beat,' Maclachlan wrote. 'When the line was attacked and broken to his right he still held his trench, and only when the Germans were discovered to be in the rear of him did he leave it. He then withdrew his remaining men very skilfully away to a flank, and worked his way alone back to me to report.

'He finally brought his command back, and then took part in the counterattack. He was killed out in front, in the open, cutting wire to enable the attack to be continued. This is the bald statement of his part of that day's action. He risked his life for others right through the day and finally gave it for the sake of his men. He was a splendid type of young officer, always bold as a lion, confident and sure of himself, too. The loss he is to me personally is very great, as I have learnt to appreciate what a sterling fine lad he was. His men would have followed him anywhere.'

Woodroffe's VC was gazetted on 6 September 1915, just five weeks after he lost his life. The citation read:

The enemy having broken through the centre of our front trenches, consequent on the use of burning liquids, this Officer's position was heavily attacked with bombs from the flank and subsequently from the rear, but he managed to defend his post until all his bombs were exhausted, and then skilfully withdrew his remaining men. This very gallant Officer immediately led his party forward in a counter-attack under an intense rifle and machine-gun fire, and was killed while in the act of cutting the wire obstacles in the open.

Leslie Woodroffe had been severely wounded alongside his brother in the action at Hooge. However, he was able to return to his battalion in France on 1 June 1916. That day, he was wounded again and died in hospital three days later.

Their parents received Sidney's VC at an investiture by King George V at Buckingham Palace on 29 November 1916. His body was never recovered. His name appears on one of the panels at the Menin Gate, on a tablet outside 42 Trinity Square, Tulse Hill, south-east London and alongside those of his brothers on the memorial at All Saints' Church, Branksome Park, Bournemouth, Dorset.

His rugger cap and sword were on display in All Hallows Church, Bournemouth, but the sword was stolen during the Blitz.

However, his name does not appear on the war memorial in Lewes, where he was born. His family had moved from Lewes before the war memorial was erected in 1922. However, a petition was organised to have it added, along with the names of another nineteen of the town's lost sons, on a brass plaque.

PRIVATE JOHN HAMILTON, 19

3RD BATTALION, AUSTRALIAN
IMPERIAL FORCE

'Lone Pine', Gallipoli, Turkey, 9 August 1915

Above Anzac Cove, where the Australians and New Zealanders landed on Gallipoli in May 1915, there was a height known as 400 Plateau. The Turks quickly fortified it with a system of trenches and tangles of barbed wire. It saw heavy fighting and became known to them as *Kanli Sirt* – which means 'Bloody Ridge'. The Aussies had another name for it. An artillery observer looking for points to range his guns spotted a solitary pine tree. The song 'The Trail of the Lonesome Pine' – later made famous by Laurel & Hardy – was popular at the time, so the strongpoint was dubbed 'Lone Pine'. In the three-day action to take the position, which the Turkish commanders considered impregnable, seven VCs were won.

This seemingly foolhardy assault was undertaken on 6 May to draw Turkish defenders away from the fresh landings that were taking place at Suvla Bay to the north. At 17.30 hours, 1,800 men from the New South Wales Brigade rushed along the hundred yards separating the first lines of trenches. The Turks were, seemingly, taken by surprise. However, they were in well-defended positions in trenches covered with logs, which had not been spotted by aerial reconnaissance. The fighting was costly, but within half an hour the Australians seemed to have achieved the impossible. They had taken Lone Pine by a frontal assault but that was not the end of it.

As darkness fell at 19.00 hours, a battalion of Australian reinforcements were moving when the Ottomans began their counter-attack. The fighting was carried out at close range, using bayonets and improvised grenades and bombs. The Aussies had their 'jam pot' grenades, which were often as dangerous to the thrower as to the intended victim, while the Turks were well supplied with small spherical grenades the size of cricket balls that were lobbed back and forth between the trenches two or three times before they exploded.

'It was soon perceived that a couple of seconds elapsed between the landing of the cricket-ball bombs and the explosion,' said Sergeant C.O. Clark. 'So the policy of returning the bombs was adopted with the most satisfactory results, although the practice occasionally led to casualties in our own ranks.'

The master of this was twenty-nine-year-old Leonard Keysor. Born to a Jewish family in London's Maida Vale, Keysor had arrived in Australia, via Canada, in 1914 and enlisted on 18 August. At Lone Pine, Keysor scorned danger. As Turkish bombs landed in his trench he would leap forward and smother the explosion with a sandbag or a coat. If time allowed, he would throw a bomb back. To the amazement of his Aussie comrades, he caught several in flight and returned them smartly as if he was playing cricket. Although wounded twice, he kept this courageous retaliatory action up for fifty hours. His bravery saved his trench and removed the enemy from a temporarily commanding position.

Soon after the battle he was struck down by enteric and was convalescing in hospital in England when he read in *The London Gazette* of 15 October 1915:

> For most conspicuous bravery and devotion to duty at Lone Pine trenches in the Gallipoli Peninsula. On 7th August, 1915, he was in a trench which was being heavily bombed by the enemy. He picked up two live bombs and threw them back at the enemy at great risk to his own life, and continued throwing bombs, although himself wounded, thereby saving a portion of the trench which it was most important to hold. On 8th August at the same place, Private Keysor successfully bombed the enemy out of a position, from which a temporary mastery over his own trench had been obtained, and was again wounded. Although marked for hospital he declined to leave, and volunteered to throw bombs for another company which had lost its bomb throwers. He continued to bomb the enemy till the situation was relieved.

He received his VC from George V at an investiture at Buckingham Palace on 15 January 1916.

Returning to his unit who were now in France, he fought at the Battle of Pozières in March 1916. Commissioned in 1917, he rose to become a lieutenant. He was wounded again in March 1918 and gassed two months later. In October 1918, he returned to Australia to head a recruiting drive and was discharged on medical grounds that December. He went back to live in London and was rejected for service in World War II, again on medical grounds.

On 8 August 1915, the New South Wales Brigade had been relieved by the 7th (Victoria) Battalion. Commanding D Company was Lieutenant William John Symons. Born in Eaglehawk, Victoria, in 1889, he had worked as a commercial traveller and served in the militia for eight years before enlisting in the Australian Imperial Forces on 17 August. As colour sergeant, he embarked with the 7th Battalion for Egypt on 18 October, landing at Gallipoli on 25 April 1915. The following day he was commissioned.

'The fire was terribly hot,' he noted.

The 7th were about to dig in when orders came to press on at once.

'We went up straight in the face of a point-blank fire from Turkish machine-guns and artillery,' said Lieutenant Symons. 'Of 1,100 odd who landed, we mustered, after two days' continuous fighting, only 300, and a good number of these were wounded.'

On 18 May, the 7th were transported down to Cape Helles and took part in the advance on Krithia. Again they suffered heavy losses. From time to time they received reinforcements, so when they went into action at Lone Pine on 8 August they were 750 strong.

At about 05.00 the following morning, the Turks made a series of determined attacks on Jacob's Trench at Lone Pine, where six Australian officers were killed or severely wounded. Learning that the position had been overrun, Lieutenant-Colonel Harold 'Pompey' Elliott ordered Symons to retake the trench.

'I don't expect to see you again,' he said, 'but we must not lose that post.'

Symons led the charge that drove off the Turks, but the enemy continued attacking from the front and both flanks. He asked permission to abandon fifteen yards of the trench and hold back the Turks with a new barricade. Although the enemy set fire to the overhead woodwork, Symons extinguished the flames and kept the barricade in place. Finally the Turks stopped their attacks.

'At Lone Pine I got wounded, a bullet striking my rifle and shattering it, with the result that portions of the barrel were embedded in my left hand,' Symons recalled. 'My wound, however, was not sufficient to incapacitate me, and it was not until later that I contracted enteric, and was after a time, invalided to England.'

Of the 750, only 148 men and three officers survived. When they were relieved, Symons wrote home to his mother:

'Since last writing, I have had a rough time, as you will perhaps have seen by the papers. The New South Wales boys charged the enemy's trenches, and by dint of hard and strenuous fighting, captured them. Our battalion was sent in to assist them, and I went in with a company of 141 men, and the other companies had about a similar number. Anyway, Abdul decided to take his trench at all costs but in vain. They came once and dropped about 1,000 bombs into our trench, and, I am sorry to say, did a great deal of damage, but I think we did decidedly more with ours for we were better throwers. The first attack was about half-past 3 o'clock in the morning. They came to us in hundreds, and made a special point of my position. I only had about forty men with me in the firing line, the others being in reserve, or else casualtied. We had to set our teeth and drive them back, which the lads did with great credit. When I came to muster them afterwards, we only had about fifteen. I got some of my reserve in, and made up to strength again just in time for another attack, which was equally unsuccessful. I had to build up again, and this time our trench was filled in some places four or five deep with dead and wounded Turks, and our own brave lads. They were just coming for a third attack, when a couple of shells were distributed kindly among them by our artillery, and they must have thought that discretion was the better part of valour, as they cleared out, leaving us still masters of the position. I was left with about forty men out of my company, and I don't think one of the remaining men was unwounded. I can tell you, I was not sorry that they were not game enough for the last attack. Well you can just imagine the pluck and endurance of our men after about four hours' fighting to get into a hole like that and come out successfully. They are heroes, every one of them.'

On the voyage to England, in a hospital ship, Lieutenant Symons said he did not think he would ever reach the old country. When he left Egypt for Gallipoli he weighed twelve stone and was just eight stone when he landed in England. He spent two months in hospital and a month in a convalescent home.

Then on 4 December he went to Buckingham Palace to receive his Victoria Cross from George V.

'I am proud to decorate an Australian with this cross,' said the King, as he pinned it on Symons's tunic. 'You may be interested to know that the intrinsic worth of this bronze cross is only 5½d [2p]. I hope you will live long to wear it.'

The citation read:

For most conspicuous bravery on the night of 8th-9th August, 1915, at Lone Pine trenches, in the Gallipoli Peninsula. He was in command of the right section of the newly captured trenches held by his battalion, and repelled several counterattacks with great coolness. At about 5 am on 9th August a series of determined attacks were made by the enemy on an isolated sap, and six officers were in succession killed or severely wounded, a portion of the sap being lost. Lieutenant Symons then led a charge and retook the lost sap, shooting two Turks with his revolver. The sap was under hostile fire from three sides, and Lieutenant Symons withdrew some fifteen yards to a spot where some overhead cover could be obtained, and in the face of heavy fire built up a sand barricade. The enemy succeeded in setting fire to the fascines and woodwork of the head-cover, but Lieutenant Symons extinguished the fire and rebuilt the barricade. His coolness and determination finally compelled the enemy to discontinue their attacks.

Lieutenant Symons returned to Australia, where he was fêted. In 1917, he went to the Western Front as a captain. He was wounded on 27 February and gassed during the Battle of Messines on 7 June, but rejoined his unit in January 1918 and fought at Dernancourt, France, in March.

Eventually he settled in England and served as a lieutenant-colonel in the Home Guard during World War II.

Symons's place in Jacob's Trench was taken by Lieutenant Frederick Tubb. Born in Longwood, Victoria, in 1881, he joined the Victoria Mounted Rifles in 1900 and served in the Australian Light Horse before joining the 7th Battalion as a second lieutenant on 24 August 1914. He reached Gallipoli on 6 July and was gazetted captain on 8 August.

He had already been in the front line for two days, under heavy shelling, when he wrote: 'Shrapnel is coming like out of a watering can, splattering all around me as I wait for instructions.'

He was then ordered to hold a captured trench at Lone Pine at 'any cost'. Early on the 9th, the Turks began the attack, advancing along a sap that had been barricaded with sandbags. Tubb and eight men fired at them from the parapet. In the trench, two corporals smothered enemy grenades with greatcoats, or caught them and threw them back. Even though Tubb was blown from the parapet and the barricade repeatedly wrecked, each time it was rebuilt. He inspired his men with jokes and encouragement until a huge explosion blew up the barricade, killing or wounding most of the defenders.

Wounded in the arm and scalp, Tubb was left with Corporals Alexander Burton and William Dunstan. He led them into action, shooting three Turks with his revolver and providing covering fire while the barricade was rebuilt. A bomb burst killed Burton and temporarily blinded Dunstan. Reinforcements arrived and Tubb fought on until the Turks called off the attack.

The official historian Charles Bean recorded the event:

Tubb had at that position ten men, eight of whom were on the parapet, while two corporals, Webb and Wright, were told to remain on the floor of the trench in order to catch and throw back the enemy's bombs, or else to smother their explosion by throwing over them Turkish overcoats which were lying about the trenches. A few of the enemy, shouting 'Allah!', had in the first rush scrambled into the Australian trench, but had been shot or bayoneted. Tubb and his men now fired at them over the parapet, shooting all who came up Goldenstedt's Trench or who attempted to creep over the open. Tubb, using his revolver, exposed himself recklessly over the parapet, and his example caused his men to do the same. 'Good boy!' he shouted, slapping the back of one of them, who by kneeling on the parapet had shot a sheltering Turk. As the same man said later: 'With him up there you couldn't think of getting your head down.'

But one by one the men who were catching bombs were mutilated. Wright clutched one, which burst in his face and killed him. Webb, an orphan from Essendon, continued to catch them, but presently both his hands were blown away and, after walking out of the Pine, he died at Brown's Dip. At one moment several bombs burst simultaneously in Tubb's recess. Four men were killed or wounded; a fifth was blown down and his rifle shattered. Tubb, bleeding from bomb-wounds in arm and scalp, continued to fight, supported in the end only by a Ballarat recruit, Corporal Dunstan, and a personal friend of his own, Corporal Burton of Euroa. At this stage there occurred at the barricade a violent explosion, which threw back the defenders and tumbled down the sandbags. It was conjectured that the Turks had fired an explosive charge with the object of destroying the barrier. Tubb, however, drove them off, and Dunstan and Burton were helping to rebuild the barrier when a bomb fell between them, killing Burton and temporarily blinding his comrade. Tubb obtained further men from the next post, Tubb's Corner, but the enemy's attack weakened, the Turks continued to bomb and fire rifles into the air, but never again attempting to rush the barricade.

Tubb recorded his own version in his diary, writing on 10 August:

Here I am sitting down in a dugout near the beach ready to go to Lemnos or Mudros. (I am wounded, but not too bad.) It would take a book to describe what happened since yesterday morning. I have no notes of it but can supply most particulars.

At Stand To, 0400 yesterday the fun started. I was whipped around my Coy to the firing line. The enemy was attacking. Well they attacked us three times but we licked them. I was put in charge of the 7th firing line section. We had a ding-dong scrap which on and off lasted till four in the afternoon when we were relieved by the 5th Battalion and what was left of us came down to this bivouac. We went in 670 strong and we came out 320. All the officers except the CO and Capt Layh were hit, even the Quarter Master Hopkins. I was extremely lucky and feel gratified for being alive and able to write. My luck was in all the time. It is miraculous that I am alive. Three different times I was blown yards away from bombs. Our trenches were filled with dead, mostly ours. Burton of Euroa deserved the highest award for his gallant action for three times filling a breach in the parapet till they killed him. Dunstan and Oates, Ellis, Caddy, Webb, Silver, Keating also did magnificent work. Ellis was killed throwing back bombs before they exploded. We were glad to get out. I cannot write of details but many of our brave boys were blown to pieces. As fast as we put men in to fill the breaches they were out. I kept sending for reinforcements and bombs, all our bomb throwers were killed and so were those that volunteered to fill their places. To cut a long story short, we beat the enemy. Once he nearly got us. We yelled and yelled and the black devils turned and we knocked 'em over like rabbits. I was wounded three times, but got my injuries attended to and kept going. I am suffering a bit now from reaction. The doc has fixed my head and arm up. My left eye is painful but otherwise I am fit. I reckon I'll be A1 again in a week for my injuries are slight. By Jove it was some scrap and a lot more of our good old 7th are gone. The

Brigadier came to see me this morning, congratulating me, etc. My haversacks are shattered; the iron rations inside one of them are smashed to pieces. Anyway the CO is very pleased with me and so is the Brigadier so I feel happy as Larry.

In a letter of condolence to Corporal Wright's sister, Colonel Elliott wrote: 'I recommended all these boys for the VC. Tubb, Dunstan and Burton got VCs, Webb the Distinguished Service Medal [this was an error; Web received the Distinguished Conduct Medal]. No doubt, had your brother lived, he would have got the DCM if not the VC. There are so many brave deeds that it is almost impossible to receive recognition for them.'

On 15 October *The London Gazette* carried the citations. Tubb's read:

For most conspicuous bravery and devotion to duty at Lone Pine trenches, in the Gallipoli Peninsula, on 9th August, 1915. In the early morning the enemy made a determined counter-attack on the centre of the newly captured trench held by Lieutenant Tubb. They advanced up a sap and blew in a sandbag barricade, leaving only one foot of it standing, but Lieutenant Tubb led his men back, repulsed the enemy, and rebuilt the barricade. Supported by strong bombing parties, the enemy succeeded in twice again blowing in the barricade, but on each occasion Lieutenant Tubb, although wounded in the head and arm, held his ground with the greatest coolness and rebuilt it, and finally succeeded in maintaining his position under heavy bomb fire.

Burton and Dunstan received a joint citation, which read:

> For most conspicuous bravery at Lone Pine trenches in the
> Gallipoli Peninsula on the 9th August, 1915. In the early
> morning the enemy made a determined counter-attack on the
> centre of the newly captured trench held by Lieutenant Tubb,
> Corporals Burton and Dunstan and a few men. They advanced
> up a sap and blew in a sandbag barricade, leaving only one foot
> of it standing, but Lieutenant Tubb with the two corporals
> repulsed the enemy and rebuilt the barricade. Supported by
> strong bombing parties the enemy twice again succeeded in
> blowing in the barricade, but on each occasion they were
> repulsed and the barricade rebuilt, although Lieutenant Tubb
> was wounded in the head and arm and Corporal Burton was
> killed by a bomb while most gallantly building up the parapet
> under a hail of bombs.

Alexander Burton was born in Kyneton, Victoria, in 1893. He
worked as an ironmonger before enlisting in the 7th Battalion on
18 August 1914, leaving for Egypt in October. Suffering from a
throat infection, he watched the landings from a hospital ship. But a
week later he was in the trenches. He fought at 400 Plateau, Krithia,
Monash Valley and Steele's Post. After being wounded in action, he
was promoted to lance-corporal, then corporal. He was twenty-two
when he died.

William Dunstan was born in 1895 in Ballaret East, Victoria. He
worked as a draper's assistant and served in the compulsory training
scheme, gaining the cadet rank of captain. In July 1914, he was
commissioned as a lieutenant in the militia. He enlisted as private in
the Australian Imperial Force on 2 June 1915. A fortnight later, he

sailed for Egypt as an acting sergeant with the 6th Reinforcements of the 7th Battalion, though he was an acting corporal at Lone Pine. He had been in action just four days when he won his VC.

Temporarily blinded, he was invalided out. Back in Australia, he joined the Citizen Forces, rising to the rank of lieutenant. In civilian life, he worked for Rupert Murdoch's father, Sir Keith Murdoch.

Tubb was sent to England to convalesce, where he suffered appendicitis. Returning to Australia, he managed to persuade the AIF medical board that he was fit and rejoined his battalion in France in December and was promoted to major on 17 February 1917. His company played an important role in the Menin Road attack on 20 September in the Third Battle of Ypres. Before the battle he was troubled by a hernia, but refused to be evacuated. Leading his company towards its objective, he was hit by a sniper. On being stretchered out, he was mortally wounded by shellfire.

While Tubb, Burton and Dunstan were occupied at Jacob's Trench, the Turks were also attacking in the northern sector, advancing along Sasse's Sap, threatening the 3rd Battalion's command post there. The battalion's adjutant, Captain Owen Howell-Price, emptied his revolver into them. At 04.00 hours, he ordered his men to climb up on the parapet to fire on the Turks' flank and stop the enemy attacking across the open ground. Among them was Private John Hamilton.

Born in Orange, New South Wales, on 24 January 1896, he was just nineteen. He described himself as a butcher, and he had served in the militia before he enlisted in the Australian Imperial Force on 15 September 1914. Embarking for Egypt the following month, he took part in the Anzac landings on 25 April 1915. In May he came down with influenza and was evacuated, returning to duty on 2 June.

At Lone Pine, Hamilton had already distinguished himself as a sharpshooter. He had gone over the top on the first day. A dab hand with the jam-pot (the Australian hand grenade), like Keysor, he would catch incoming grenades and return them.

Along with Brigadier-General Nevill Smyth, who had won the VC fighting the Dervishes in the Sudan in 1898, Captain Howell-Price took a party to the entrance of Sasse's Sap. They arrived just in time: the Turks were just fifteen yards away, advancing in a column three deep. Howell-Price discharged his pistol into the leading rank, killing three and narrowly dodging a bullet himself.

The Turks were then thrown into confusion as Hamilton and the others fired on them from the parapet. One shot from Private Ward hit a Turkish soldier who was just about to throw a grenade, which then exploded among his own men. A second Turkish bomber was despatched with the same result. Meanwhile, Hamilton and others began hurling bombs back at the enemy.

'Two of my bombers Norton and Hamilton – the latter won his VC there – were up on the parapet throwing bombs as fast as they could light them,' wrote Lieutenant A.F. Burrett. 'One burst prematurely in Norton's hands, and blew both of them to fragments. We sent him back to the dressing station. Next morning a doctor said to me: "Good God! It's wonderful. That man Norton is the gamest thing that ever breathed. After I had finished fixing him up for the beach he said, "Good-bye Doc., old sport. Sorry I can't shake hands."'

Sole survivor of the six and protected only by a few sandbags, Hamilton held his position. For six hours he lay out in the open, keeping up constant sniper fire and telling those in the trench below him where to aim their bombs.

By 10.00 hours, the danger had receded and Hamilton slipped

back into the trench. Soon after the 3rd Battalion was relieved by the 1st Battalion.

There were many acts of gallantry that day. Captain Howell-Price was awarded the Military Cross. His batman, Private P.H. Ward, who had helped hold off the original assault with a rifle, received a Distinguished Conduct Medal. The courage of the bombers was universal and Hamilton was awarded his VC:

> For most conspicuous bravery on 9th August, 1915, in the Gallipoli Peninsula. During a heavy bomb attack by the enemy on the newly captured position at Lone Pine, Private Hamilton, with utter disregard to personal safety, exposed himself under heavy fire on the parapet, in order to secure a better fire position against the enemy's bomb throwers. His coolness and daring example had an immediate effect. The defence was encouraged and the enemy driven off with heavy loss.

Less than three hundred men were left of the 883 that had started the action. Nevertheless the 3rd Battalion was reorganised in Egypt, leaving for France in March 1916, where it went into the line at Armentières. On 3 May Hamilton was promoted to corporal and fought at Pozières in July, Mouquet Farm in August and Flers in November. He was promoted to sergeant in May 1917. That year his battalion served at Bullecourt, Menin Road and Broodseinde.

He left the Army in 1919 as a lieutenant. Back in Australia, he worked on the docks. In World War II, he served as a lieutenant with the 16th Garrison Battalion and several training battalions. In 1942 he went to New Guinea with the 3rd Pioneer Battalion, eventually reaching the rank of captain.

The last of the seven VC winners at Lone Pine was thirty-three-year-old Alfred Shout. Born in Wellington, New Zealand, in 1881, he served in the South African War as a sergeant and was wounded at least once. He moved to Australia with his wife and daughter. A well-known sharpshooter, he was commissioned in the militia. On 27 August 1914 he joined the Australian Imperial Force as a second lieutenant in the 1st Battalion. He was promoted to lieutenant in Egypt.

The 1st Battalion landed on Gallipoli on 25 April. Shout was in the thick of the fighting that lost the battalion 366 officers and men over the next five days. He was noted for a number of conspicuous acts of bravery and won the Military Cross. The citation read:

> On 27th April, 1915, during operations near Gaba Tepe, for showing conspicuous courage and ability in organizing and leading his men in a thick, bushy country, under very heavy fire. He frequently had to expose himself to locate the enemy, and led a bayonet charge at a critical moment.

A soldier who was with Shout on Walker's Ridge on 27 April wrote: 'Lieutenant Shout was a hero. Wounded himself several times, he kept picking up wounded men and carrying them out of the firing line. I saw him carry fully a dozen men away. Then another bullet struck him in the arm, and it fell useless by his side. Still he would not go to the rear. "I am here with you boys to the finish," was the only reply he would make. A little later Lieutenant Shout was wounded again, and fell down. It was cruel to see him. He struggled and struggled until he got to his feet, refusing all entreaties to go to the rear. Then he staggered and fell and tried to rise again. At last some men seized him and carried him away, still protesting.'

On 29 July Shout was promoted to captain. A week after that, he led his men to Lone Pine, where, on 9 August, they relieved the 3rd Battalion.

That morning Captain Shout led a charge down enemy-held trenches and, using bombs, killed eight Turks and routed the remainder. In the afternoon, he and Captain Sasse joined forces to clear a part of Sasse's sap of the enemy. While Sasse carried a rifle, Shout again relied on bombs. They were accompanied by men carrying sandbags to build barricades at each stage of the advance along the sap. Under heavy fire Shout and Sasse pushed the Turks back and then found a position for the last barricade. Along the way Shout was laughing and cheering the men on. For the final dash, he lit three bombs. The last burst in his hand, blowing it away and shattering one side of his face and body. Despite terrible injuries, he remained in good spirits while being evacuated to the rear. Two days later, he died on a hospital ship and was buried at sea.

His VC was gazetted on 15 October. The citation read:

For most conspicuous bravery at Lone Pine trenches, in the Gallipoli Peninsula. On the morning of the 9th August, 1915, with a very small party Captain Shout charged down trenches strongly occupied by the enemy, and personally threw four bombs among them, killing eight and routing the remainder. In the afternoon of the same day, from the position gained in the morning, he captured a further length of trench under similar conditions, and continued personally to bomb the enemy at close range under very heavy fire until he was severely wounded, losing his right hand and left eye. This most gallant officer has since succumbed to his injuries.

PRIVATE GEORGE PEACHMENT, 18

KING'S ROYAL RIFLE CORPS

Loos, France, 25 September 1915

George Stanley Peachment was eighteen years and four months old when he was killed during the Battle of Loos. This was the first mass engagement of Kitchener's New Army and the first time the British used poison gas. By then the war on the Western Front had reached a stalemate, with lines of trenches running from the North Sea to the Swiss Border. Towards the end of September 1915, the British sought to break the deadlock. Peachment was with the 2nd Battalion of the King's Royal Rifle Corps, which were to attack a 600-yard front to the north of the town of Loos, which was in enemy hands. Their objective was to overrun the German trenches, then move south-easterly across the Loos valley and meet up with the 15th Division to the rear of the town. It was to be the largest British offensive mounted on the Western Front during 1915.

Peachment, a barber's son, was born near Bury, Lancashire, on 5 May 1897. After attending technical school, he became an apprentice fitter at Ashworth & Parker, and later at a second Bury firm, J.H. Riley, making steam engines. Giving a false date of birth, he enlisted into the 5th Battalion, King's Royal Rifle Corps on 19 April 1915. He was just seventeen years and eleven months old, but you had to be nineteen to serve overseas. Having been turned away earlier when he tried to sign up, this time Peachment wore his father's bowler hat to make himself look older. His military career got off to a bad start when he went missing from 7.30 pm on 2 July 1915 until 8.10 am on 5 July, and he was fined seven days' pay. Posted to France on 27 July 1915, Peachment then transferred into the 2nd Battalion, King's Royal Rifle Corps.

His military record did not improve. On 19 September 1915, he was confined to barracks for three days for having a dirty bayonet on parade. Six days later, he found himself in the thick of the action on the first day of the Battle of Loos.

After a four-day artillery barrage to soften up the enemy, the chlorine gas was released at 05.50 hours on 25 September. But things did not go according to plan. There was little wind and the gas cloud, released from canisters in the British lines, remained hanging over the British trenches instead of drifting towards the Germans. So when the advance began at 06.34 hours, the soldiers had to march through their own gas. Men found themselves coughing and choking in no-man's-land. Their primitive gas helmets did not work well and two hundred of the battalion, along with two hundred of the 1st Battalion Loyal North Lancs beside them, were gassed badly enough to be put out of action.

Smoke shells had been fired from mortars, but there were problems with these and some went off prematurely. Almost immediately, two enemy machine guns, which had escaped damage during the artillery bombardment, opened up and took a terrible toll on the advancing British soldiers. A few Tommies managed to reach the enemy's barbed-wire defences, but were then cut down by heavy fire. The attack faltered and soldiers were forced to take cover in shell holes and natural hollows.

At 07.30, the few that had survived began straggling back to their trenches. The young George Peachment was not among them. Showing great bravery, instead he went to the aid of his commanding officer, Captain Guy Dubs, who had been seriously wounded. Again, Captain James Price Lloyd of The Welsh Regiment serving with Military Intelligence takes up the story in 'Tales of the VC':

At 6.30 am on the morning of the 25th of September 1915 the whistles blew all along the British line from the La Bassée Canel to Grenay, and the great battle of Loos had begun. South of the Vermelles–Hulluch road the first division attacked the German positions on the low ridge before Hulluch. The 1st Brigade were rewarded with instant success. They swept forward for a mile and three-quarters, and before noon were storming the last German strongholds in the outskirts of Hulluch itself.

To the 2nd Brigade on their right fortune was not so kind. On the very threshold of their enterprise they were faced with tragedy of uncut wires.

The 2nd King's Royal Rifle Corps of that Brigade suffered very heavily. The battalion crossed no-man's land under the protection of a thick cloud of smoke, but it was the very thickness of it that was their undoing. It was not until the enemy's entanglements had been reached that it was realized that much of the wire was still standing.

It was in this extremity that a rifleman of this battalion

performed an action which cost him his life, but won for him the highest honour that a soldier can receive.

Private George Peachment had been chosen to act as orderly to the officer commanding A Company. He was only a boy, but that day he showed that his was the heart of a brave man. To the last he never left his captain's side.

When he saw that the leading waves were held up, the captain of A Company went forward, as he thought, alone to see what could be done. He had almost reached the wire, when a bomb thrown from the German trench just beyond exploded in front of him, wounding him severely in the head.

To his surprise, he then found that he was not alone. His orderly had followed him, and he now knelt down beside the captain, and began to bandage his head. As he was doing so the smoke lifted, and the Germans, who were not more than twenty or thirty yards away, opened fire upon this defenceless pair.

The remainder of the company had by this time retired to their trenches to reorganize, but Peachment preferred to stay with his officer, although he must have realized that it meant almost certain death. There was a shell-hole, too, quite near, but he refused to avail himself of its cover, and, still kneeling there in the open in full view of the enemy, went on quietly with his work.

He had not knelt there long when he was struck in the chest by a bomb which burst just in front of him. The captain, who had also been hit again, managed to drag himself and his orderly partly into the shell-hole. He could do nothing for the dying boy except try to keep him still with the one arm he could still use. Mercifully the end came soon. A minute later,

Peachment was shot in the head and killed instantly. He was only seventeen years old [sic] when he died.

Captain Guy Dubs survived and got back to British lines. A month after the battle, he wrote to Peachment's mother Mary, saying:

I cannot tell you how sorry I am that your brave son was killed, but I hope it may be some little consolation to you to know how bravely he behaved and how he met his end. When we reached the wire we found it absolutely untouched by our artillery fire and an almost impassable obstacle as a result. However, we had to push on, and I gave the order to try to get through and over it. Your son followed me over the wire and advanced with me about 20 yards through it till we were only about 15 yards from the German trench.

None of the other men of the line was able to get as far and he was the only man with me. As a matter of fact I had not noticed your son was with me, but at this point a bomb hit me in the eye, blowing it and part of my face away. I fell to the ground, but on sitting up, found your son kneeling beside me. The German fire was at this time very intense, but your son was perfectly cool.

He asked me for my field dressing and started bandaging my head quite oblivious to the fire. His first thought was to help me, and though there was a shell hole nearby where he might have got cover, he never thought of doing so. Of course the Germans were bound to see us sitting up, and one of them threw a bomb which hit your son in the chest while at the same time I received a bullet also in the chest.

Your son was beyond feeling any pain, though still alive. I

tried to drag him into the shell hole and at the same time keep him from moving, but at that moment a bullet hit him in the head and killed him. After his first wound he was bound to die, in fact he was already, immediately after he received it, unconscious to any pain. I lay beside him there all day, and eventually we were both picked up in the late afternoon when the trench was taken by a flank attack.

I can't tell you how much I admired your son's bravery and pluck. He lost his life in trying to help me and no man could have been braver than he was. I have recommended him for the VC and have heard that the Commanding Officer has seen the recommendation.

If he gets it, it is sad to think he is not in this world to receive all the congratulations he would get, but perhaps it may be a comfort to you. Your son died the finest death that man can die, he showed the greatest gallantry a man can show; and I hope these facts may help you in your sad loss, together with the fact that he was spared all pain and suffering.

Captain Dubs's recommendation was accepted and Peachment's VC was gazetted on 18 November 1915:

For most conspicuous bravery near Hulluch on 25th September, 1915. During very heavy fighting, when our front line was compelled to retire in order to reorganize, Private Peachment, seeing his Company Commander, Captain Dubs, lying wounded, crawled to assist him. The enemy's fire was intense, but, though there was a shell hole quite close, in which a few men had taken cover, Private Peachment never thought of saving himself. He knelt in the open by his Officer and tried to help him, but while doing this he was first wounded by a bomb and a minute later mortally wounded by a rifle bullet. He was one of the youngest men in his battalion and gave this splendid example of courage and self-sacrifice.

Three days after the announcement Captain Dubs wrote a second letter to Mrs Peachment, telling her that he had made her son his orderly just before the battle in an attempt to prevent him having to go over the top. Plainly this was unsuccessful and Dubs was wracked with guilt. He confessed: 'I am afraid I feel very responsible for his death, because I might have sent him home a short time before when I found out his age, only he was so keen to stay.'

Peachment's VC was presented to his mother by George V at an investiture at Buckingham Palace on 29 November 1916. His body was never recovered, but he is commemorated on the Loos Memorial, alongside the names of more than twenty British and Commonwealth soldiers who died during the battle. His name has been carved into the 'Memorial to the Missing' at 'Dud Corner' Commonwealth War Graves Commission Cemetery at Loos.

Lord Ashcroft bought Peachment's VC and his other medals along with Captain Dubs's letters to Mrs Peachment. They are held at the Ashcroft Gallery at the Imperial War Museum.

A memorial service for Peachment had been held at Parkhills United Methodist Church, his school, on 17 October 1915. A bronze plaque commemorating him was unveiled there. But since that time he was largely forgotten and the plaque was later found in the backroom of The Fusilier Museum.

In October 2006, the plaque commemorating the only serviceman from Bury to win the VC was installed in St Anne's Church in Tottington. His VC was brought to Bury for the ceremony.

TEMPORARY LIEUTENANT
RICHARD JONES, 19
LOYAL NORTH LANCASHIRE REGIMENT
'Broadmarsh Crater', Vimy, France, 21 May 1916

Richard Jones was born in Honor Oak, near Lewisham in south east London, on 30 April 1897 and studied at Dulwich College from 1909 to 1914. When the First World War broke out he was seventeen years and four months old. He immediately volunteered for active service and was commissioned as a 2nd Lieutenant in the 8th (Service) Battalion of Loyal North Lancashire Regiment in October 1914. Two months later, he was promoted to temporary-lieutenant.

He went to France with the battalion in September 1915, where he was appointed Sniping Officer. In May 1916, three weeks after his nineteenth birthday, his battalion was in the line at Broadmarsh Crater, near Vimy in France.

On the night of 18 May the crater had been lost, so at 21.15 hours on the 19th, the 8th Loyals launched an attack to recapture it. Edward Underhill, a twenty-year-old subaltern, recorded the events in a letter to his parents:

We had our blooding the night before last, as we had to retake a crater which another battalion in the brigade had lost and couldn't retake. We sent a hundred men and three officers, and did it with ease. The Corps and Divisional commanders have congratulated us, and the Brigadier is very pleased. Poor little Tatam is missing. He was in charge of thirty bombers of C Company. Howard has a badly shattered thigh [2nd Lieutenant Cecil Cunningham Howard died of his wounds a week later], and one of my best sergeants is dead. But still a price must be paid. I'm awfully sorry about Tatam; he and I were pretty good pals, and had done a lot of work together this last tour, and I'm awfully sorry he's gone. But the men are splendid, and went for it like the good chaps they are. I was up all night with Ramsay looking after bomb supplies. [Captain Stuart Ramsay, DSO, died of his wounds on 3 June 1917.] We handled something like 1,000 boxes. I have never heard such bombing as was going on then. It sounded as though there was a sort of machine gun ejecting bombs as fast as it could go. Bennett is on leave, so I am OC C Company and very busy. [Lieutenant Ernest Bennett died on 12 August 1917.]

Underhill wrote to his parents again two days later to assure them that he was safe, but saying he had 'been through some awful times'. On 21 May, the Germans had counter-attacked. By early evening, Lieutenant Jones and his platoon were cut off by gas and shellfire. Their reserve of bombs had been destroyed. Little could be done.

Anticipating an attack from the north, Lieutenant Jones prepared his defences. But at 19.40 hours, a German mine exploded some thirty yards to the south. For around fifteen minutes, Jones's platoon managed to keep the Germans off the rim of the new crater, but then their supply of grenades ran out. Attempts to get more failed.

Taking up position between the two craters, Lieutenant Jones tried to keep the enemy back with rifle fire. He shot fifteen Germans before his ammunition ran out. Then he spotted some more grenades nearby, but as he picked one up he was shot through the head. The rest of the defenders were reduced to throwing lumps of flint and empty bomb boxes at the enemy.

The defenders had held out for over two hours since the beginning of the German assault but, at 22.00 hours, they were forced to abandon the post. Battalion headquarters had already given orders to launch a counter-attack at 02.00 hours the following morning. The Germans withdrew, leaving behind fresh entanglements of wire, holding up the British and cutting them down with machine guns and shellfire.

Underhill sent a detailed description of the action to his parents on 24 May, though it suffered at the hands of the censor:

They started on Sunday afternoon [21 May] with heavy bombardment of all sorts of shells. They gave the batteries, Mont St Eloy, the support and front line trenches showers of gas shells, which are the invention of the devil. The bombardment started about 3.30 pm. I was on the road, of which I sent you a postcard. Well, about 5 pm I got orders from my company to Cross Street, a trench about 500 yards from the front line. We got there without casualties, which wasn't bad. When we got there we walked into the gas shells and other shells, and for four hours we sat as much under cover as possible and were shelled. We only had two casualties in the company, and were very lucky. But the gas shells were beastly. One burst within five yards of me, and I was blind with tears for a bit, and nearly coughed my inside out, and my eyes were sore and ached terribly. Well, about nine, I sent for [news] and told that the Huns had broken through on the left. Cross Street is in our own battalion area when we're in the trenches, and the Hun had broken through on the next three battalion frontages. He had taken our outpost and retrenchment lines, which are only lightly held and not meant to be held in an attack, and also had take[n] our main line and support line, a depth of about 300 to 400 yards. I was told to occupy a second support line, known as Perrier, block a communication trench on my left known as Central, and hold the line at all costs, and watch my left flank. By this time there wasn't much shelling, what there was was a light barrage behind us, and it was pitch dark except for Hun flares, which were pretty continuous. Well, we dug in as best we could; the trench, all blown in. It was an eerie experience walking about like that, practically in the open with shell holes all round, in comparative silence after the terrific row before. About 12 we were told that the battalion would concentrate at 1 am and C Company would be on the left. We were to assemble in an old disused trench just in front and crawl as far as possible forward, and then go for the enemy with the bayonet and drive them out of our support and main lines. Well, of course, the front was too big a one for us at our then strength. We crawled forward under rifle fire and MG fire from two guns, and heavy shrapnel, and took the support line and most of several communication trenches, but were too weak to get to the main line. I never expected to get across that 150 yards of open untouched. There was one continuous stream of flares. The Huns never waited for us but ran. We found the trench very much knocked about, so set to work to dig for dear life. I got tools and bags from somewhere and we never dug so hard in our lives. It was then broad daylight and we had it quiet till 10, when the Hun started a few crumps and shrapnel and continued slowly till about 4 pm, when he set to work and we had two hours heavy shelling. We were relieved in the evening and came back to the road again, but I can tell you when I came out I was so fagged that I could hardly stand and my nerves were very rocky indeed. Everybody was pleased with what we had done on a front we had never seen before, in fact, a sort of blooming hero stunt. Then yesterday afternoon, while we were back here, the ball opened again and there was hell for several hours. And we had about four gas shells right round Company HQ, and my eyes aren't right yet.

Within a few days the battalion was sent to the rear to prepare itself for the Battle of the Somme. Lieutenant Jones was not to go with them. His body was never recovered.

The citation to his posthumous Victoria Cross read:

About 7.30 pm the enemy exploded a mine forty yards to his right, and at the same time put a heavy barrage of fire on our trenches, thus isolating the Platoon. They then attacked in overwhelming numbers. Lieutenant Jones kept his men together, steadying them by his fine example, and shot no less than fifteen of the enemy as they advanced, counting them aloud as he did so to cheer his men. When his ammunition was expended he took a bomb, but was shot through the head while getting up to throw it. His splendid courage had so encouraged his men that when they had no more ammunition or bombs they threw stones and ammunition boxes at the enemy till only nine of the platoon were left. Finally they were compelled to retire.

Richard Jones is one of the 35,000 British Commonwealth servicemen commemorated on the Arras Memorial, who died in the Arras sector between the spring of 1916 and 7 August 1918 and have no known grave. His Victoria Cross is kept at Dulwich College, south-east London.

FIRST CLASS BOY JOHN 'JACK' CORNWELL, 16

HMS *CHESTER*

Jutland, Denmark, 31 May 1916

The Battle of Jutland was the only major encounter between the Royal Navy and the German Grand Fleet during World War I and only the third naval battle between steel ships, the first two occurring during the Russo-Japanese War of 1904–05. The outcome was indecisive. The Germans sank more shipping – 113,300 tons against 62,300 tons – while the British retained control of the North Sea, for surface shipping at least. Some 2,551 German sailors were killed against 6,094 British – one of whom was a sixteen-year-old boy.

John Travers Cornwell was born in Clyde Cottage, Clyde Place, Leyton, Essex, on 8 January 1900. Known as Jack, he was the son of Eli and Lily Cornwell, née King, and had two brothers – Ernest, born in 1898, George, born in 1901, and a sister Lily, born in 1905. It was his father's second marriage and he also had a half-brother named Arthur, born in 1888, and a half-sister named Alice, born in 1890.

Jack's father had spent fourteen years in the Royal Army Medical Corps, serving in Egypt, the Sudan and South Africa. In civilian life, he worked as a nurse in a mental hospital; also as a milkman and a tram driver. The family was not well off and in 1911 Jack found himself in the care of the West Ham Poor Law Union, living in one of the children's homes in Romford Road, Forest Gate. Later, he was reunited with his family when they moved to 10 Alverstone Road, Little Ilford, Manor Park. Jack attended Walton Road School in Manor Park, where he was quiet and studious. A teacher said of him: 'We always felt we could depend on him.' He was also a keen Boy Scout in the Little Ilford Troop at St Mary's Mission, and won a special award for freeing a girl from a drain.

When Jack left school at fourteen, he wanted to join the Navy, but his parents would not sign the papers. Instead, he became a delivery boy for Brooke Bond & Co. and then worked as a dray boy with the Whitbread's Brewery Depot in Manor Park.

At the outbreak of World War I, Jack's father, then sixty-three, re-enlisted as a private in the 57th Company of Royal Defence Corps, the First World War's equivalent of the Home Guard. Jack was still determined to join the Royal Navy and, in August 1914, still only fifteen, he took references from his headmaster and his employer along to a local recruitment office, but was turned down on the grounds of age.

He tried again the following year and on 27 July 1915 he began training as Boy Second Class at Keyham Naval Barracks – HMS *Vivid* – at sixpence (2½p) a week. On 19 February 1916, he was promoted to Boy First Class and completed his training on HMS *Lancaster*, which was moored at Chatham. Then he joined a new light cruiser, HMS *Chester*, on the day it was commissioned at Cammell Laird's yard in Birkenhead on 1 May 1916.

By the 15th, HMS *Chester* had joined the fleet at Scapa Flow. On the 23rd, Jack wrote a final letter home to his parents. The *Chester* completed its battle drills on the 29th.

The German fleet under Admiral Reinhard von Scheer had left port and British naval intelligence informed Admiral John Jellicoe in Rosyth. He ordered the fleet to put to sea. Once Jellicoe found a German scouting party of forty ships under Admiral Franz von Hipper, he was joined by the fleet from Scapa Flow under Admiral David Beatty. The battle joined at around 15.48 hours on 31 May 1916, with the two sides lobbing shells at each other from a distance of about ten miles.

HMS *Chester* was stationed five ahead of the 3rd Battle Cruiser Squadron, which was twenty-five miles ahead of the main fleet. Lookouts reported distant gunfire and her captain ordered 'Action Stations' before setting off at full speed to investigate. At around 17.40, four German light cruisers came into sight. The *Chester* turned to open fire but could not match the firepower of the four enemy cruisers and was hit seventeen times in three minutes. Three out of her ten guns were disabled and one-fifth of the crew were either killed or wounded, including the entire crew of the forward 5.5-inch turret gun, which had been hit before it could be brought into action. Cornwell was stationed as sight-setter there, taking orders via headphones from Fire Control on the bridge and making any necessary range corrections to the gun sights. He was hit in the chest. Mortally wounded, he remained there awaiting further orders until the end of the action.

A report from the Commanding Officer of HMS *Chester* said: 'Boy (1st Class) John Travers Cornwell of the "Chester" was mortally wounded early in the action. He nevertheless remained standing alone at a most exposed post, quietly awaiting orders till the end of the action, with the gun's crew dead and wounded all round him.'

Other reports said he volunteered to go to the top of the turret to wipe the glass so that the rangefinder could line the target, and one said that he managed to ram home one last shell, close the breech and press the firing button and that this shell exploded on the German ship *Wiesbaden*, causing damage which led to her sinking.

The following day, the *Chester* was ordered back to the port of Immingham on the Humber, where the wounded were transferred to Grimsby and District Hospital. Jack was attended by Dr C. S. Stephenson, but he could not be saved and died of his wounds on 2 June 1916. He was sixteen years, three months old.

His body was brought back to East Ham in a naval coffin and his family buried him in a private ceremony at Manor Park Cemetery, in a communal grave marked only with a wooden peg with the number 323 on it.

However, in Admiral Beatty's account of the action, he drew attention to 'the instance of devotion to duty by Boy (1st Class) John Travers Cornwell who was mortally wounded early in the action, but nevertheless remained standing alone at a most exposed post, quietly awaiting orders till the end of the action, with the gun's crew dead and wounded around him. He was under 16½ years old. I regret that he has since died, but I recommend his case for special recognition in justice to his memory and as an acknowledgement of the high example set by him.' Jack was the only enlisted man picked out for commendation by Beatty.

The newspapers seized on this. It was a stirring tale of bravery, but also one of the scant regard the authorities paid the heroes who had fallen for the nation. The *Daily Sketch* printed a picture of the pauper's grave covered in flowers with the caption: 'England will be shocked today to learn that the boy-hero of the naval victory has been buried in a common grave. The flowers were sent by his schoolmates – they in their humble way paid the honour that the Admiralty failed to give the young hero'. The paper then promised that 'his memory and family are not forgotten'.

There was then a feeding frenzy among the press, who vied with each other to print pictures of friends and family posing beside the nameless grave. As First World War casualties mounted, this hit home among the general public. But Cornwell's commanding officer, Captain Robert Lawson, was outraged by the coverage.

'What was (and is, essentially) a clean, fine, simple story of devotion to duty has been besmirched by the paws of the Press,' he complained.

What's more, it was not the Navy's fault.

'If Mrs Cornwell had not elected to have his body moved from the hospital to her own house, there would have been a funeral with full naval honours,' he declared. 'As it was, she wished to take the body away for a private funeral, and the cost of the journey is paid by the Admiralty, but not, I believe, the cost of the funeral also. Perhaps poor Mrs Cornwell hardly understood all that, but felt she would like to have her neighbours at the funeral; then discovered that she couldn't afford to pay for a separate grave. Meanwhile, the pressmen discover this, and instead of helping quietly, publish half the story far and wide. Well, well. Many of his shipmates were more fortunate in resting in the North Sea, where not even a ghoulish pressman can disturb your mortal remains.'

However, in Parliament, Admiral Lord Beresford, MP for Portsmouth, urged that Cornwell should posthumously receive the Victoria Cross.

'An honour paid to Cornwell's memory would be an example to the boys of the Empire at their most susceptible age,' he said.

This was not enough for *The Spectator*, who wanted Jack Cornwell's portrait to be hung in every elementary school 'so that the lustre of his deed may shine where boys and girls are quick to catch the reflection of lofty and honourable conduct'.

But first it was suggested that his body be disinterred and buried with full military honours at Devonport. Mrs Cornwell opposed this. It was a consolation to her that he was buried nearby and she could visit his grave any time she felt like it. Nevertheless, on 29 July 1916, Jack Cornwell's body was exhumed and the coffin, swathed in the Union Jack, was drawn by gun carriage from East Ham Town Hall to Manor Park Cemetery, where her son was re-buried with full naval honours.

The Navy was represented by six boy sailors from HMS *Chester*, who had all taken part in the fighting at Jutland and carried wreaths from the ship's company, and Dr F.J. Macnamara MP, Financial Secretary to the Admiralty. At the graveside, he said: 'It has been written that what good men do is often interred with them. Not so here! This grave shall be the birthplace of heroes. Boy Cornwell will be enshrined in British hearts as long as faithful, unflinching devotion to duty shall be esteemed a virtue among us.'

A supplement to *The London Gazette* of 15 September 1916 carried a special notice that read:

The KING has been graciously pleased to approve the grant of the Victoria Cross to Boy, First Class, John Travers Cornwell, O.N. J.42563 (died 2nd June, 1916), for the conspicuous act of bravery specified below.

Mortally wounded early in the action, Boy, First Class, John

Travers Cornwell remained standing alone at a most exposed post, quietly awaiting orders, until the end of the action, with the gun's crew dead and wounded all round him. His age was under sixteen and a half years.

In the same month, The Jack Cornwell Memorial Fund was established to provide a ward in his name for disabled sailors at the Star & Garter Home at Richmond. His name was also adopted by other fundraising campaigns for the Navy and the war.

Every schoolchild in the British Empire was invited to give one penny towards the fund. In return for donations, there were commemorative stamps, which sold in their millions, along with postcards of his likeness. The distinguished artist Sir Frank Salisbury painted his portrait, though he had to use Jack's brother Ernest as a model. There was even a stained-glass window showing him in action in the City Hall of Kingston, Ontario, Canada.

Schools all over Britain celebrated Jack Cornwell Day on 21 September 1916, while local schools were invited to contribute towards the cost of a memorial stone and other charitable causes.

The Boy Scouts introduced the Cornwell Award, referred to as the Scout VC, given to boys as a badge of courage, and Lady Jellico unveiled a plaque at Walton Road School in memory of 'the imperishable boy Cornwell', as *National Review* dubbed him, 'a national hero'. The school was renamed the Jack Cornwell School in 1929, but demolished in 1969.

On 25 October 1916, Jack's father Eli died from bronchial catarrh while on active service. He was buried alongside his son. The following month, Jack's mother Lily received her son's VC from King George at an investiture at Buckingham Palace on 16 November 1916. He was the youngest person ever awarded a naval

VC. The medal was eventually presented on 'long loan' to the Imperial War Museum, where it was displayed, along with the 5.5-inch gun Cornwell was manning.

By the end of the war, his stepbrother was also dead and his mother was living in reduced circumstances and working in a sailors' hostel to supplement a very small pension awarded for her son. She was found dead on 31 October 1919, aged just forty-eight, and never lived to see the memorial erected on her son's grave.

Jack Cornwell has not been forgotten. In Manor Park, there is The Jack Cornwell Centre in Jack Cornwell Street, the Victoria Cross public house and Jack Cornwell VC House in Grantham Road. In Manor Park Cemetery, there is Cornwell Crescent and in Vicarage Lane, East Ham, there is The Cornwell VC Cadet Centre, where the Newham Sea Cadets are based. It is the only unit in Britain not to have the name of a T.S., or Training Ship, written upon the ribbon of their cap. Instead, they have 'J.T. Cornwell VC' printed upon it. A parade and memorial service is held in his honour by the Sea Cadets and The British Legion every year.

In 2001, the London Borough of Newham introduced the Jack Cornwell Bravery Award, which is presented annually in recognition of outstanding acts of bravery by the people of Newham.

PRIVATE WILLIAM
(BORN JOHN) JACKSON, 18
17TH BATTALION,
AUSTRALIAN IMPERIAL FORCE
Armentières, France, 25 June 1916

B etween March and June 1916, the 1st, 2nd, 4th and 5th
Australian Divisions were sent to France, where they were
deployed along the quiet Armentières sector. In the build-up to the
Battle of the Somme, which began on 1 July, they were ordered to
carry out as many raids as possible on the German lines. During
one of them Private William Jackson became the first Australian to
win a VC on the Western Front and the youngest Aussie to win the
highest gallantry award.

John William Alexander 'Billy' Jackson was born on 13 September
1897 at 'Glengower' station at Gunbar, a small settlement fifty
miles north of Hay, New South Wales. He was the fourth child
and eldest son of farm labourer John Gale Jackson and his wife
Adelaide Ann, née McFarlane. Billy Jackson was just eight years old
when his mother died. Two of his elder sisters were already dead,
one as the result of an accidental shooting. So Billy and his three
sisters – Elizabeth, Catherine and May – and two brothers – Albert

and Leslie – were then cared for by their grandparents, John and Elizabeth McFarlane. They already had fourteen children of their own, plus four children from John's first marriage.

During his teenage years, Billy Jackson – 'Jacko' to his friends – was well known for his daring, recklessness and strength. After leaving school he was employed by William Gibson of 'Carlowrie', then he enlisted in the 17th Battalion of the Australian Imperial Force at Liverpool, New South Wales, on 15 February 1915 at the age of just seventeen years and five months, one of the first volunteers from Gunbar. Army records show that he was five-feet ten inches tall and he weighed twelve stone. His eyes were grey, his hair and complexion fair, and his religion Presbyterian.

He joined B Company of the 17th Battalion of the 5th Infantry Brigade of the AIF (Australian Imperial Force). In May 1915, he sailed for Egypt, training at Heliopolis. On 12 August 1915, he was sent for 'special duty' in Alexandria, from where his battalion embarked. They landed on Gallipoli on 20 August, where he took part in the attack on Kaiajik Aghyl – Hill 60 – the following day.

At Gallipoli on 3 October 1915 he was admitted to a casualty clearing station suffering from diarrhoea. He also had a problem with his teeth, which prevented him eating the hard rations provided on Gallipoli. His condition was so serious that he was evacuated to Malta on the hospital ship *Assaye*. In Valletta, he was admitted to the St Elmo Hospital.

On 7 January 1916 he was put on board the *Esquibo* to be returned to Australia. But after three days at sea, he was offloaded at Cairo and admitted to the 1st Auxiliary Hospital, suffering from dysentery.

By 15 February, he was declared fit and rejoined his battalion on 8 March. Nine days later they embarked at Alexandria for the six-day voyage to Marseilles in France as part of the 2nd Division. They relieved the Northumberland Fusiliers at Bois Grenier, near Armentières, on 10 April.

Orders were issued to begin harrying raids on the German lines on 20 June. Jackson volunteered and at midnight on the night of 25–26 June he acted as a scout for a raiding party, which included nine officers and seventy-three men, on the forward trenches of the 231st Prussian Reserve Infantry Regiment. His party was led by Captain Keith Heritage of the 19th Battalion, who was killed in action one month later, and the raid had been planned by General W. Holmes, who was killed by shellfire in July 1917.

An artillery barrage had forced many of the Germans to abandon their positions. Despite this, the Australians faced withering machine-gun fire as they crossed four hundred yards of no-man's-land.

After the scout group had neutralised the enemy listening posts, the raiders, supported by a box barrage, entered the enemy trenches, encountering only token resistance. Engineers blew up two bomb stores, causing pandemonium, while the remainder of the party cleared the enemy trenches. After five minutes the Australians withdrew under heavy shelling and machine-gun fire.

Jackson returned safely, bringing a prisoner back with him for interrogation, but on learning some of the party had been hit, he said he didn't like the idea of leaving any wounded men out in no-man's-land. Despite the enemy barrage, he went back and rescued one of his wounded comrades.

Ignoring the intensifying bombardment, he went out on a second rescue mission, assisting Sergeant Hugh Camden of the 19th Battalion to bring in seriously wounded Private Alfred Robinson. The blast from an exploding shell knocked Camden unconscious, inflicted further wounds on Robinson, and blew Jackson's right arm off above the elbow.

Jackson said he 'didn't feel much, just a numbing sensation'. When he returned to the Australian lines, an officer applied a tourniquet using a piece of string and a stick. Disregarding his own condition he went back to rescue the other two injured men. He recovered one of them, then continued searching for another half an hour until he satisfied himself that all the wounded had been brought in, after which time he was sent to hospital.

During the raid thirty Germans were killed and four captured; the Australian casualties were fourteen wounded, though Private Robinson died of his wounds on 3 July 1916.

The hospital ship *St Patrick* took Jackson from Boulogne to England and on 30 June the rest of his right arm was amputated at the 3rd London General Hospital. He then spent time recuperating in the No. 1 Australian Auxiliary Hospital in the grounds of an estate known as Harefield Park, Middlesex, the No. 2 Australian Auxiliary Hospital, Southall, and the Queen Mary Convalescent Auxiliary Hospital, before returning to Australia.

Jackson was immediately awarded the Distinguished Conduct Medal, but this was cancelled and his name was put forward for a VC. The recommendation came from the general officer commanding (GOC) to the 5th Australian Infantry Brigade, who also praised Jackson for his ability as a scout, both with the raiding party and his own battalion.

The VC was gazetted on 8 September 1916, just five days before his nineteenth birthday. The citation read:

For most conspicuous bravery. On the return from a successful raid, several members of the raiding party were seriously wounded in No Man's Land by shell fire.

Private Jackson got back safely and, after handing over a prisoner whom he had brought in, immediately went out again under a very heavy shell fire and assisted in bringing in a wounded man. He then went out again, and with a sergeant was bringing in another wounded man, when his arm was blown off by a shell and the sergeant was rendered unconscious.

He then returned to our trenches, obtained assistance, and went out again to look for his two wounded comrades. He set a splendid example of pluck and determination. His work has always been marked by the greatest coolness and bravery.

By mistake he was given the Distinguished Conduct Medal as well, which was gazetted two weeks later, on 22 September 1916, though it was cancelled in *The London Gazette* of 20 October 1916. He was presented with his VC by George V at an investiture at Buckingham Palace on 18 November 1916. Both awards appeared in the *Commonwealth of Australia Gazette* on 14 December 1916 and his father was informed by the Department of Defence on 4 January 1917.

Jackson remained in England until 4 May 1917, when he was invalided back to Australia with 992 returning servicemen aboard TSS *Themistocles*, arriving in Sydney on 5 July 1917. The first recipient of the VC to return to Australia, he was hoisted shoulder-high at the reception held at the Anzac Buffet in the Domain in Sydney for the returning wounded soldiers.

There he was reunited with Sergeant Camden, who had managed

to find his own way back to the Allied lines. He had also been awarded the Distinguished Conduct Medal for the part he played in the rescue of the wounded that night. Together they travelled to Hay. Arriving there on 26 July 1917, they were met at the railway station by a large crowd before moving onto the Post Office Square, where Jackson was officially welcomed by Mr Butterworth, the Deputy Mayor of Hay.

'I have the greatest of pleasure in extending the welcome of the people of Hay,' said Butterworth, adding that, 'they did not want to deprive Gunbar of one iota of the glory but they were enjoying a degree of reflected glory from the fact that Jackson was always referred to as being from Gunbar, near Hay.'

Nevertheless, he said Jackson's deed 'was one of the incidents of this war, which so far as this district is concerned, will never be forgotten'.

Then Sergeant Camden told the crowd: 'Bill had gone out looking for him without his arm. Not looking for a VC but for a cobber.'

At Gunbar, the people of the district offered to show their appreciation by buying Jackson a farm. He declined, saying that the loss of his right arm would mean he could not work the land. Private Jackson VC and Sergeant Camden DCM, accompanied by Private George Salisbury and Private Stewart, both recipients of the Military Medal, went on a recruiting drive. Then on 15 September 1917, Jackson was discharged from the AIF.

Settling in Merriwa, New South Wales, Jackson became a dealer, buying and selling horses and skins. He left in 1927 to become the licensee of the Figtree Hotel at Figtree, a suburb of Wollongong. Later, he moved to Sydney where he would find work and marry.

During World War II he re-enlisted and served as a corporal, then acting sergeant in the Eastern Command Provost Company. But in December 1941, he was reprimanded for wearing his DCM ribbon. When it was suggested that he return his DCM, Jackson said he would continue to wear the ribbon and he would apply for a discharge and let the matter be decided in court rather than surrender the medal.

He took his discharge. Then the Army backed down. Although the War Office in London confirmed that the DCM had been cancelled, they did not know of an incidence of steps ever being officially taken to recover a medal. They also thought it undesirable to order Jackson to give it back. Jackson promptly re-enlisted in the 2nd Australian Labour Company, though he continued to sign all correspondence 'W Jackson VC, DCM'.

In 1956 he travelled to London with thirty-four other Australian VC holders for the Victoria Cross Centenary Celebrations. When he died in August 1959, he was buried with full Military Honours. The Members Bar in the refurbished Merriwa Returned Servicemen's League Club is named in his honour and, on 4 October 2003, a recreational area at Gungal, south of Merriwa, was officially opened as the Private Jackson Park.

PRIVATE JOHN CUNNINGHAM, 19

EAST YORKSHIRE REGIMENT

Ancre, Hebuterne Sector, France, 13 November 1916

The First Battle of the Somme was a costly and largely unsuccessful action on the Western Front which became a metaphor for the futility and indiscriminate slaughter of the war. It lasted from 1 July to 13 November 1916. On the first day alone there were 60,000 British casualties – 20,000 dead. Torrential rain in October turned the battlefield into a sea of mud, churned by regular bombardments. In all there were 650,000 German, 195,000 French and 420,000 British casualties. By the time it was called off, the Allies had advanced just five miles.

If that was not bad enough, the Allies made one final push in the Battle of Ancre from 13 to 18 November before the winter set in. Nineteen-year-old John Cunningham was with the 12th (Service) Battalion (3rd Hull), The East Yorkshire Regiment (The Duke of York's Own) of the 92nd Brigade, 31st Division that were on the left towards the north of the battlefield. Cunningham's battalion and the 13th East Yorkshires pushed forward soon after midnight on 13 November towards the village of Serre. Their snipers and Lewis gunners were to support the left flank when the main advance started a few hours later.

This time the artillery barrage was effective and the Yorkshire battalion reached the German front line and three hundred Germans were taken prisoner. However, enemy soldiers in the support trench fought back. Cunningham went with a bombing section up a communication trench to attack them. There they faced tough opposition and the rest of the section were either killed or wounded. Collecting all the bombs from the casualties, Cunningham went on alone and, when he had used up all the bombs he had, he went back to get some more. When he went up the communication trench again he encountered a party of ten Germans. He killed all ten, clearing the trench up to the new line.

John Cunningham was born in Scunthorpe, North Lincolnshire, on 28 June 1897, one of nine children. He was known in the family as Jack. When he was still a child, the family moved to Hull, where he went to school, though he did not do well. Like his father, he became a hawker – that is, a street trader – selling pots.

In 1915, at the age of seventeen, he enlisted in the 3rd Hull Battalion, known as the Hull Sportsmen, a 'pals battalion'. These were units of men who had joined up together in local recruiting drives. They were usually neighbours, workmates, or men who belonged to the same clubs.

In December, after training in South Dalton, outside Beverley in the East Riding of Yorkshire, the battalion were sent to Egypt to defend the Suez Canal. After that, they were sent to France in March 1916 with the 31st Division. Their first major action was in the first day of the Battle of the Somme, where they suffered 3,600 casualties and failed to reach any of their objectives.

Things did not get any better. Getting ready for the attack at Serre, Private Archie Surfleet, with the 13th East Yorkshires, wrote:

November 12th was the most thoroughly miserable day I ever remember. The morning broke dull, foggy and wet; everything was in a hopeless hubbub and bustle; even the mud seemed stickier and thicker. We had the usual fatigue parties, rolling the blankets in those bundles often, cleaning up camp as far are possible... and so on. Then Sergeant Raine came and told Bell and me that one of us had to be left at a place called Rossignol Farm until called for duty. It was a quiet moment, but without further talk, the sergeant said he would toss for it; poor Bell lost and Sergeant Raine told him he was 'for it'... to which Bell said 'San fairy ann.'... 'It doesn't matter', and now poor Bell is dead! God it seems awful...

With sad hearts we watched the main part of the battalion move off to the line. There was an artificial air of jollity about; a joke here, a coarse remark there, a wave of the hand to a pal... 'lucky devil staying behind' ... 'all the best, old man' ... 'get those bloody rations up early' ... 'We're going back for a rest after this' ... 'who the hell says we aren't a scrapping division' ... 'Send a postcard' ... all these and many more remarks, but it was the thinnest of veneers, a very feeble covering over the sense of grim reality which I feel the whole battalion was feeling. We stood there while the boys, in column of route, marched forward, slid down the hill, turned right and were gradually swallowed up in the mist and the mud and the confusion. There sounds died out; only a rumble of guns and the creaking of heavily laden limbers remained at the scene so desolate and miserable that one could not help feeling depressed…

At Ancre, while the 31st Division were initially successful, the 3rd Division on their right were overlooked by the enemy and fell back, leaving the 92nd Brigade's flank exposed, forcing them to pull back too.

The 12th's War Diary records:

All objectives were captured under twenty minutes with four casualties the barrage being excellent. Over 300 prisoners are captured, and sent back, less than 50% reaching our lines. The 3rd Division having failed on our right the position was a very difficult one; the trenches had been so blown about that it was impossible to make them really defensive. The Germans counter-attacked in force twice during the day from the left, but were annihilated by our Lewis guns. The whole day was spent fighting small parties, bombers and snipers. In the evening as there was a danger of being surrounded it was decided to withdraw, the last party withdrawing about 8.45 pm.

The German shelling had been so heavy that it was feared the forward troops might be cut off.

In the rear, news of the attack filtered back, as Private Surfleet recorded: 'Woke early on the morning of November 13th and heard the boys went over at 5.45 in thick fog and took the Germans first and second lines in this Serre sector fairly easily, surprising the Germans in their dugouts. Breakfast was an awful meal; news of losses, of wounded, of killed, kept coming through. Each time a man or an officer came up to the dressing station, the news of all he could tell spread like wildfire. Everything seems certain that there had been a big counterattack and that our losses have been terrible. So, too, have those of the other battalions who went over with our lads. Every moment we expect to be called upon to go up and reinforce them. During the morning, a draft of thirty new men arrive from England. Poor devils!'

Eventually the call came.

'It was five o'clock in the evening when Lieutenant John, who was in charge of us, dashed in and told us to get our fighting equipment on; we were to go up the line to help though no one seemed to know what the job was to be. My fingers trembled as I buckled my belt: a mixture of excitement and nervousness, but we were pretty well resigned to anything...'

Cunningham's VC was gazetted on 13 January 1917. The citation read:

For conspicuous gallantry and resource during operations. After the enemy's front line had been captured, Private Cunningham proceeded with a bombing section up a communication trench. Much opposition was encountered and the rest of the section became casualties. Collecting all the bombs from the casualties, this gallant soldier went on alone. Having exploded all his bombs, he returned for a fresh supply and again proceeded to the communication trench, where he met a party of ten of the enemy. These he killed and cleared the trench up to the enemy line. His conduct throughout the day was magnificent.

He was presented with his medal by George V at an open-air ceremony in Hyde Park, London, on 2 June 1917. Three-hundred-and-fifty decorations were presented that day, including four other VCs, with the Royal Flying Corps patrolling the skies above in case of an air attack by German bombers. The ceremony was filmed for the newsreels.

When Cunningham appeared before the King, there was a roar from the crowd. After the ceremony, he travelled back to Hull with his parents. Although the train arrived at Paragon Station at two o'clock on a Sunday morning, a huge crowd was waiting and Cunningham was carried home at shoulder height. He visited his old school and the newsreel of the investiture was shown at the Palace Cinema while he was on leave.

At a civic reception at the Guildhall, the Lord Mayor of Hull said: 'It was open to him, as well as to any of the rank and file, not only in the Army, but in civil life, by his zeal, industry, and determination, to achieve higher honours in the future. There was no doubt that his deed would be talked of for many years to come.'

Later, a plaque was unveiled at his primary school.

Returning to active service, Cunningham was badly wounded in the legs and lungs. Demobilised in 1919, he took to drink and was summonsed for beating up his wife. He wore his VC in court. The couple separated after just two years of marriage. Cunningham fell foul of the law again when he hit another crippled veteran over the head with a bottle during a fight, and in March 1922 he became the first of the Somme VCs to go to jail, for non-payment of maintenance to his wife and son.

He was in trouble with the law again in 1923 for beating a horse while drunk. In 1929, he was summonsed once more after the theft of some lino, though his two accomplices had swindled him out of his share and he did not turn up in court because he was attending a dinner for VC winners. He died in 1941 at the age of just forty-three.

SECOND LIEUTENANT
THOMAS MAUFE, 19
ROYAL GARRISON ARTILLERY

Feuchy, France, 4 June 1917

Thomas Harold Broadbent Maufe was unusual in that he did not win his VC fighting the enemy. His courageous act occurred at the 124th Siege Battery of the Royal Garrison Artillery at Fleuchy, some four miles from Arras, where a battle had stuttered to a stalemate the previous month at a cost of over a quarter of a million lives.

Again Captain J.P. Lloyd, serving with Military Intelligence, compiled the tale:

One evening in June Second Lieutenant Maufe and another officer were in the rear post of their battery, waiting to register a gun which was in a more advanced position. It was most vital that the gun should be registered, in view of certain operations times to commence on the following day. The enemy's shelling had been continuous all day, and now the storm was at its height. Suddenly all communication with the forward gun ceased: the telephone was mute. Second Lieutenant Maufe casually mention[ed] to the other officer that he was going to find out what had happened, and disappeared.

Meanwhile, the two officers who were on duty up at the firing point were cut off from the world. They could do nothing but wait until the shelling died down sufficiently to allow the linesmen to repair the break in the wire. Then suddenly Maufe broke in upon them. On his way up he had mended most of the breaks, but had run short of insulation tape. He asked for some more, and went out again.

He completed the repairs successfully, with shells falling all around him, and tested the circuit to see everything was working properly. Afterwards, feeling weary, he returned to the dugout, and lay down on the floor.

But he was not to rest for long. Some fifteen minutes later, there was a huge explosion just outside, an explosion which could only mean one thing. Second Lieutenant Maufe at once jumped up and ran outside, shouting: 'The dump has gone!' Steel helmet and gas respirator alike were forgotten in his haste. He had taken his tunic off when he laid down to rest.

When he got outside he saw that part of a dump belonging to a neighbouring battery had exploded, and had set fire to some boxes of straw packing at the edge of his own battery dump. Bareheaded and in his shirtsleeves, he dragged the boxes to a shell hole full of water and extinguished the flames.

He next turned his attention to the burning dump, and, followed by another officer and some men of his own battery, dashed to the rescue. He found that some matting which covered a number of fuses was still blazing fiercely. A couple of yards away was a large number of gas-shells, which were likely to explode at any moment. Entirely reckless of any risk to himself, he fetched water again and again for the men of the other battery, who were cut off by the fire from their own supply, and poured it on to the flames.

Without warning, in the midst of the confusion, another part of the dump blew up, stunning one officer, and burning another and several men in the debris. Second Lieutenant Maufe helped to extricate them, and personally attended to the wounded before they were taken down to the dressing station. By his resourcefulness and unflinching courage he undoubtedly saved many lives. Had it not been for him it is very possible that both dumps would have exploded with disastrous consequences to men and material.

Maufe was born in Ilkley in the West Riding of Yorkshire on 6 May 1898. Originally, his name was Muff and the family owned the Bradford department store Brown, Muff & Co Ltd., sometimes known as 'the Harrods of the North'. In response to their rising fortunes the family left Bradford and changed their name to Maufe, thereby inspiring the local ditty: 'In Bradford 'tis good enoof/To be known as Mrs Muff/But in Ilkley by the river Wharfe/'Tis better to be known as Mrs Maufe!'

After attending public school, he went on to the Royal Military Academy in Woolwich, south-east London, in October 1915. Four days after his eighteenth birthday, he was commissioned in the Royal Garrison Artillery and left for France, where he won his VC. The citation read:

On 4 June 1917 at Feuchy, France, Second Lieutenant Maufe, on his own initiative and under intense artillery fire repaired, unaided, the telephone wire between the forward and rear positions, thereby enabling his battery to open fire on the enemy. He also saved what could have been a disastrous occurrence by extinguishing a fire in an advanced ammunition dump caused by a heavy explosion, regardless of the risk he ran from the effects of gas shells in the dump. By this great promptitude, resource and entire disregard of his own personal safety, he set an exceptionally fine example to all ranks.

Ilkley awarded him a silver casket when he returned after the war and he unveiled the war memorial there. After graduating from Clare College, Cambridge, he went on to the Royal School of Mines in South Kensington and was involved in the mining and smelting of tin in Cornwall and Gravesend. Later, he became a director to Brown, Muff.

A reserve officer, Maufe resigned his commission in 1935, due to ill health. In World War II he joined the Home Guard as a private. During mortar practice in 1942, a grenade exploded in the barrel of the mortar, killing him and another man.

The *Ilkley Gazette* carried an obituary written by an old comrade. It read:

When he performed the deeds that were later rewarded by the Victoria Cross, I was serving in the same area on the Headquarters Staff of the Heavy Artillery under whose command was the battery in which Maufe was serving.

Maufe's gallantry was not chiefly the repair of telephone lines under fire – that was done hourly by scores of brave men – but his coolness in dealing with a fire in a forward ammunition dump. This dump had caused us much anxiety, being of necessity place[d] in a forward and exposed position.

The great peril was the presence of a number of gas shells. Had these been involved in the fire a whole area east of Arras would have become lethal for some considerable time and most probably have caused a temporary withdrawal in a vital sector. To attempt to deal with ignited ammunition is ever a terrible thing; when gas shells are included, it demands complete disregard of self and entire devotion to the welfare of others. Maufe did his task with calculated courage, and saved many lives.

Then, as since, his distinguishing characteristic was quietness. I remember that when we entertained him in our mess at Arras after he received his decoration he appeared terrified. The one subject on which he kept complete silence was himself, and it was typical of Maufe's modesty that many years later a fellow member with me of Maufe's club was astonished when I informed him that Maufe had received the Victoria Cross.

Having lived through many and great dangers he died as a result of an accident. High irony and sadness are here, but we remember that significantly he died in his own land preparing for its defence. Truly of him it shall be said that he lived by the artillery motto: '*Quo Fas et Gloria Ducunt*' (Whither Right and Glory Lead).

A stone bearing a brass plaque was erected near where Maufe and his comrade were killed. It read: 'To the honoured memory of Henry Galloway and Thomas Harold Broadbent Maufe, who gave their lives for King and country, 28th March 1942. This stone was erected by the Ilkley Company Home Guard'.

SECOND LIEUTENANT
DENNIS HEWITT, 19
HAMPSHIRE REGIMENT

Ypres, Belgium, 31 July 1917

F landers was a marshland that had been reclaimed over the centuries. In the west of it lies the town of Ypres, which lay on an important salient, or bulge, in the British line. It was fought over in the First Battle of Ypres, from 19 October to 22 November 1914, with the loss of nearly 70,000 men, and again in the Second Battle of Ypres, from 21 April to 25 May 1915, with the loss of another 100,000.

When preparing for the Third Battle of Ypres, also known as the Battle of Passchendaele in 1917, Field Marshal Douglas Haig was warned that a heavy bombardment of the area would turn the land there back into a swamp. But he was determined to beat the Germans by a purely British offensive before the Americans arrived, so he went ahead and ordered an offensive there anyway. It came as no surprise to the Germans, for security was not as good as it might be. The night before the attack, General William Robertson said: 'Everybody in my hotel knows the date of the offensive, down to the lift boy.'

The offensive began with a fortnight's intensive bombardment with 4.5 million shells being fired from three thousand guns and five tons of high explosive falling on every square yard of the front. This did no damage to the Germans, as they had pulled back. But it did smash the drainage system and the heavy rain predicted by the Meteorological Office turned the landscape into a sea of mud. The newly introduced tanks became stuck and men drowned. Others presented easy targets to the German machine-gunners perched on top of their concrete bunkers as they advanced along narrow duckboards. Meanwhile, the Germans managed to site their artillery on a firm footing on the few remaining ridges. Haig and his staff remained in a château well behind the lines and the Field Marshal did not bother to witness the devastation he had caused. In briefings, he spoke as if the attack had taken place in high summer.

However, at the outset, the British were surprisingly successful. Along the Messines Ridge nineteen huge mines were exploded simultaneously. These had been placed at the end of long tunnels under the German front lines. The capture of the ridge inflated Haig's confidence. Yet the flatness of the plain made stealth impossible. The Germans knew an attack was imminent and the initial bombardment served as a final warning.

While the right wing made little progress, the left achieved all its objectives. But this was partly due to the new German tactic of defence in depth. They left a thinly defended front line with heavier defences to the rear. When the advance slowed, they would counter-attack with specially trained troops.

Supported by newly introduced tanks which flattened the wire, the 39th Division broke through the German lines. By 08.00 hours, the 116th and 117th Brigades had captured the ruins of St Julien and crossed the Steenbeek River. With the 116th was nineteen-year-old Second Lieutenant Dennis Hewitt of the 14th (1st Portsmouth Pals) Hampshire Battalion. They crossed a farm track on no-man's-land, Admiral's Road, to the first objective of Caliban Trench, on the old German front line, and continued on towards Juliet Farm and beyond that to the village of St Julien. Having managed to clear the barbed wire entanglements in front of them, with the help of the Tank Corps, the 14th Hampshires advanced again. At this point Hewitt rallied his men and led an attack on the trenches protecting St Julien.

His unit leapfrogged the first wave two hundred yards beyond the Steenbeek. With the 11th Royal Sussex they were advancing forty yards behind a rolling barrage that was silencing all opposition. The 14th Hampshires continued their advance between the 13th Royal Sussex and the 17th Sherwood Foresters. But the flat plain was about to give way to higher ground. First came Pilckem Ridge, known as 'Black Line'. Two hundred yards further on, there was a slope overlooking the river, called 'Black Dotted Line', where the fortified farmhouses and pillboxes had remained undamaged by the bombardment. As the Allied advance approached, the front broke up into small actions.

After reaching Pilckem Ridge, Hewitt tried to regroup while waiting for the rolling barrage to move on. A shell burst near him. A fragment of shrapnel hit his haversack, igniting the flares he was carrying. These set fire to his uniform. The flames were extinguished, but Hewitt was terribly burned. He ought to have returned to have his wounds treated, but he refused to leave his men.

Instead he rallied them and led on to the next objective under heavy machine-gun fire. Despite his wound and his severe pain, he and his men reached the 'Black Dotted Line' and consolidated their position there. While inspecting the consolidation and encouraging his men, he was shot through the head by a sniper and died instantly. His body was never recovered and he is commemorated on the Menin Gate.

His VC was awarded posthumously. The citation read:

> For most conspicuous bravery and devotion to duty when in command of a company in attack. When his first objective had been captured he reorganized the company and moved forward towards his objective. While waiting for the barrage to lift he was hit by a piece of shell, which exploded the signal flares in his haversack and set fire to his equipment and clothes. Having extinguished the flames (by rolling in the mud) in spite of his wound and the severe pain he was suffering, he led forward the remains of the Company under very heavy machine gun fire, and captured and consolidated his objective. This gallant officer set a magnificent example of coolness and contempt of danger to the whole battalion, and it was due to his splendid leading that the final objective of his battalion was gained.

Born in Mayfair, London, Dennis George Wyldbore Hewitt was brought up in the family home, Field House in Hursley, near Winchester. His prep school was The Old Malthouse in Swanage, Dorset, and he went on to Winchester College. In 1915, he went to Sandhurst and was commissioned as a second lieutenant in the Hampshire Regiment on 1 April 1916.

Sent to the front in September 1916, he took part in the later stages of the Battle of the Somme. From 21 June 1917 the 14th Hampshires were billeted at Houlle, near St Omer, thirty miles behind Ypres. They were moved closer to the front and on 16 July

1917 the bombardment which preceded the Third Battle of Ypres began. On 29 July the battalion made their last move and crossed the Ypres-Yser Canal, making their way to their final position, ready for the attack.

Hewitt was awarded a posthumous VC for his gallantry that day. His body was left on the battlefield, buried 150 yards west of the St Julien-Poelcapelle road, although the grave was subsequently lost. It was marked with a wooden cross, but no other record was made. The original battlefield cross from the grave was taken to Hursley village church and placed alongside Hewitt's memorial. His old prep school has a war memorial in Langton Matravers Church, Dorset, and his name appears in the war cloister at Winchester College.

The battle dragged on until 10 November. British losses were put at 325,000 for an advance of five miles – that's less than an inch per man. Five months later, the Germans regained their lost ground without resistance.

PRIVATE HARRY BROWN, 19

10TH BATTALION, CANADIAN EXPEDITIONARY FORCE

Hill 70, Loos, France, 16 August 1917

With the Third Battle of Ypres still wreaking its inexorable toll, Field Marshall Haig asked the Canadian Corps to attack at Lens to the South. The object was not to gain any territory, but to draw German troops away from his doomed offensive. To take Lens and hold it, it would be necessary to take the Sallaumines Hill to the south-east and Hill 70 to the north. The Canadians were convinced that taking Hill 70 was the key. The British had taken it in September 1915, but had been unable to hold it. Retaking Hill 70 would earn the Canadians no less than six VCs.

The Commander of the Canadian Corps, Lieutenant-General Sir Arthur Currie, persuaded his superiors to make Hill 70 the objective of this limited offensive. The treeless crest would provide an excellent observation post over enemy lines. To the north it overlooked the Loos valley, to the south the shelled-out miners' cottages of Lens. Clearly the Germans would have to counter-attack, but General

Currie reasoned that they could inflict huge casualties on the countervailing forces with artillery.

To fool the Germans into thinking the attack was actually coming south of the La Bassée canal, the British First Army staged a poison gas attack north of Loos. On 15 August, gas shells and gas drums were fired into Lens. Burning gas drums were used to provide a smokescreen, but this also served to warn the Germans that an attack was imminent. They responded by firing gas shells into the Canadians' assembly areas. Nevertheless, the Canadians attacked in force at 04.25, just as dawn was breaking. For six minutes the artillery pounded the German trenches into pulp, then lifted to a hundred yards farther on. Shells ripped another line of devastation there for a further six minutes, and lifted again for another hundred yards' stride.

As the curtain of the Allied shells rose from the German front line, the Canadian infantry leapt from their jumping-off trenches and waded across no-man's-land. They found the Germans in the front-line garrison, shaken and dazed. Those who surrendered were taken prisoner; if they resisted, they were killed. The remaining enemy machine guns were outflanked and captured. Other emplacements were smothered by superior numbers.

Within twenty minutes two divisions had advanced six hundred yards, securing objectives beyond the Lens-Le Bassée highway. However, anticipating an attack, the Germans had moved up their reserves during the night.

Sergeant Frederick Hobson and some men of A Company of the 20th Battalion bombed their way along an enemy trench known as 'Nabob Alley', beating back the Germans. Having conquered about seventy yards of the trench, the Canadians established a post and waited for the gains to be consolidated. So far, the attack had been a success.

For the next three days, the Germans kept probing parts of the line. At 01.40 on the 18th, their artillery opened a heavy bombardment on the whole Canadian-Corps front. For half an hour shells were rained on every part of the line. The general bombardment slackened for a short time, while the line around the village of St Pierre received an avalanche of gas-shells. Then, at 04.12 hours, every gun the Germans had opened up on the front again.

Such a concentration of artillery took a terrible toll. As for the advance posts, where the majority of the Lewis guns were positioned, the men and guns there were simply obliterated. After twenty minutes, the headquarters of the 20th Battalion received a direct hit by a heavy shell and simply vanished. Every field-telephone wire leading to the posts was cut; every light extinguished. Despite the darkness and confusion, word came from the battalion to the right that the Germans were advancing across no-man's-land.

In his trench, Sergeant Hobson saw men in field grey swarming across the open ground. Only one of the Lewis guns was still operational, but as it was brought into action a German shell landed beside it. When the smoke cleared, only one man of the crew was left alive, and he and the gun were buried in debris. Hobson was no gunner, but he raced forward, grabbed an entrenching tool and hauled the dazed survivor out of the mud.

'Guess that was a close call,' said the man he rescued, Private A.G. Fuller.

'Guess so,' replied Hobson. 'Let's get the gun out.'

As the Germans rushed across the open ground, they began to dig frantically. Hobson was hit by a bullet, but took no notice of his wound. Together, he and Fuller got the gun up and into position, then opened up on the Germans, who were pouring down the trench. They managed to hold the enemy for precious minutes, then the gun jammed.

Hobson picked up his rifle.

'I'll keep them back,' he shouted to Fuller, 'if you fix the gun!'

Hobson ran towards the advancing enemy, wielding both bayonet and the stock of his rifle, using it as a club. No one knows how many Germans he killed in this fierce encounter, but dead and wounded were heaped in front of him when Fuller shouted that the gun was back in action.

Just at that moment, a German fired his rifle at the Canadian at point-blank range. As Hobson fell, Gunner Fuller pressed the trigger of the Lewis gun, finishing off the rest of the Germans. A few minutes later, reinforcements from B Company attacked the enemy's flank. As the Germans fled back across no-man's-land, the machine guns of B Company cut them down as they ran.

Sergeant Hobson was found dead where he had fallen. He was to receive a posthumous VC. The citation read:

During a strong enemy counter-attack a Lewis gun in a forward post in a communication trench leading to the enemy lines was buried by a shell, and the crew, with the exception of one man, killed.

Sjt. Hobson, though not a gunner, grasping the great importance of the post, rushed from his trench, dug out the gun, and got it into action against the enemy, who were now advancing down the trench and across the open.

A jam caused the gun to stop firing. Though wounded, he left the gunner to correct the stoppage, rushed forward at the advancing enemy and, with bayonet and clubbed rifle, single handed, held them back until he himself was killed by a rifle shot. By this time, however, the Lewis gun was again in action and reinforcements shortly afterwards arriving, the enemy were beaten off.

The valour and devotion to duty displayed by this non-commissioned Officer gave the gunner the time required to again get the gun into action, and saved a most serious situation.

Hobson was not one of our teenage heroes. He was forty-three when he died. He had previously served in the British Army during the Second Boer War with the Wiltshire Regiment, and enlisted in the Canadian Expeditionary Force in November 1914. His Victoria Cross is on display at the Canadian War Museum in Ottawa.

Next on the Canadian roll of honour at Loos was Private Michael James O'Rourke. He was a stretcher-bearer. Out of the sixteen stretcher-bearers with the 7th Battalion, two had been killed and eleven wounded. They had become a particular target for German snipers as they carried the wounded from the field. During the first three days and nights, O'Rourke had worked unceasingly rescuing the wounded, dressing their injuries under fire and bringing food and water to them. The area where he operated was continually subjected to the severest shelling and frequently swept by machine-gun and rifle fire.

Several times he was knocked down and partially buried by shell-bursts. Seeing a comrade who had been blinded stumble into the sights of a German sniper, O'Rourke jumped out of the trench and guided him home while being sniped at himself. To rescue a wound man, he went forward about fifty yards in front of the Allied barrage, under very heavy fire from enemy machine guns and snipers. Later, when the advanced posts retired to the line, he braved a storm of enemy fire of every description and brought in a wounded man who had been left behind. In all, he saved the lives of over forty men.

The citation of his VC read:

For three days and nights Mickey O'Rourke, who is a stretcher bearer, worked unceasingly in bringing in wounded to safety, dressing them and getting them food and water. During the whole period the area he worked was subjected to severe shelling and swept with heavy machine gunfire and rifle fire. On several occasions he was knocked down and partially buried by enemy shells.

Seeing a comrade who had been blinded rambling ahead of our trench, in full view of the enemy who were sniping him Pvt. O'Rourke jumped out of his trench and brought the man back being heavily sniped while doing so. Again he went forward about 50 yards in front of our barrage and under heavy and accurate fire from enemy guns and snipers brought in a comrade.

On a subsequent occasion when the line of advanced posts was retired to the line, to be re-coordinated, he went forward under heavy fire of every description and brought in wounded men left behind.

He showed throughout an absolute disregard for his own safety going wherever there were wounded succoured and his magnificent courage and devotion in continuing his rescue work in spite of exhaustion and incessant heavy fire of every description he inspired all ranks and undoubtedly saved many lives.

It was for these acts, in which he showed an absolute disregard for his own safety, that O'Rourke gained the highest award – one of the comparatively few men who have been given the Victoria Cross in this war for saving life under fire.

Years later, when asked about his Victoria Cross, O'Rourke said: 'Sure, I don't know what the fuss is all about, it was me job you see to take out the wounded. There was a lot of machine gun and sniper fire. I could not do anything else but keep on goin', you know what I mean...'

He had already won the Military Medal the Battle of the Somme in September 1916 for bravery at Mon Ouet Farm. The citation read:

In the absence of orders he initiated a counter attack against the advancing army, who had arrived within bombing distance of our trenches. He led the men in his immediate sector over the parapet, maintained his position well in advance, successfully bombing the enemy from several points of vantage. He endeavoured to hold on to No Man's Land.

O'Rourke gave his own account in *The Daily Province* of 10 January 1918:

The Germans many of them got into a sap [trench] very early in the morning. I bombed them for three hours until the supplies of bombs ran out. Then I lay in the hellhole sniping. A Lewis Gunner came up and I sent for ammo but while I was waiting he was killed. I got another Gunner from the 4th Battalion but the same fate awaited him. Finally I came in contact with a German in a sap. Our respective conditions were such that I could see him but he could not see me. I

located a bomb and threw it with the desired effect intended.
I took his rifle and a lot of bombs called potato markers which
also I sent into the enemy positions.

Born in Limerick, Ireland, in 1879, Michael James O'Rourke served
in the Royal Munster Fusiliers before emigrating to Canada, where
he had worked as a miner and served in the militia in Revelstoke,
British Columbia. Having enlisted in the Canadian Expeditionary
Force in 1914, he did not have a distinguished service career, being
disciplined several times for drunkenness and the use of abusive
language. Serving in France for over twenty-seven months, he was
hit by shrapnel in the thigh and gassed, though he was one of the
few from the 7th Battalion to survive.

While recuperating in California, he was diagnosed with shell
shock. However, he was denied a pension as his problems were
'exacerbated by his drinking habits and the vices that the life of
miner, living in camps and mining towns, would entail'. Finally,
he won a pension in 1920 after the personal intervention of the
Governor General of Canada, Field Marshal Julian Byng, 1st
Viscount Byng of Vimy.

Because he was living the life of a down-and-out, O'Rourke's
medals were stolen. He suddenly found himself, as the second
most decorated man in Canada, shipped off to Buckingham Palace
for the tenth anniversary of the Armistice, all expenses paid. The
attention embarrassed him and he eked out the rest of his life as a
longshoreman.

The final objective was taken at 16.00 hours on 17 August by
two fresh battalions, the 5th and the 10th. Although the 10th
were in the second wave of the assault, they had not had an easy
time of it. A, B and C Companies had attacked the redoubt on

the left of Hill 70, known as the 'Chalk Pit'. A Company was met with intense enemy machine-gun fire. Within two hundred yards of the pit, they were forced to take cover in shell-holes for a time. After a short rest in this position, they were carried forward by the impetus of the advance, reaching a trench seventy-five yards beyond Chalk Pit, where the German occupants were either killed or captured.

The position was being consolidated when Sergeant J. Wennevold and a party of men of C Company went out to reinforce a post to the right of the new battalion front to protect the flank from a counter-attack. They tried to dig in, but the soil was hard and chalky, and they could make little impression. After a night of hard labour, their tools were blunt, their backs ached, their hands were sore and the trench was barely two feet deep. This proved little protection against the hurricane of fire the Germans poured on them with machine guns and field guns. Men were killed and wounded faster than others could take their places. They managed to hold on for most of the day. Then they spotted the Germans preparing for an attack on the right.

By this time every wire to headquarters had been cut by the enemy artillery. They knew that if the Germans were allowed to attack, the companies in the trench would be annihilated and the vital position lost. Without support, the situation was desperate. A runner had to get through to tell the Allied artillery to smash the German attack. Nineteen-year-old Private Harry Brown and another runner undertook to deliver the message.

The Germans were already bombarding the area behind C Company's position to prevent reinforcements getting through. The messengers had to run through this curtain of fire that churned the ground ahead of them. They had not gone far when the messenger with Brown was killed. So Private Brown went on alone, knowing that if he failed, his comrades would be wiped out to a man.

As he made his way to the rear, he was plastered in flying debris and fell into still-smoking craters, managing to drag himself out. He was hit and wounded, his arm shattered. Bleeding and exhausted, he sat down, dazed and uncomprehending, but finally forced himself to get to his feet again. Somehow, he staggered onwards towards the support lines.

An officer standing in a dugout was peering out at the devastation when he saw a dark figure stumbling through the maelstrom. It was a young soldier – hatless, pale, dirty and haggard, with one arm hanging limp and bloody by his side, and his uniform torn and stained. When he reached the steps of the dugout, seeing the officer, he tried to descend. But his strength was exhausted and he fell down the short stairway, utterly spent.

The officer lifted him gently and brought him into the dugout and laid him down. Then Brown handed over his precious slip of paper.

'Important message,' he whispered.

Fortunately, the telephone line between the dugout and the Allied batteries was still intact.

Private Harry Brown fell into unconsciousness. He died the following day in a dressing station after having his arm amputated.

He was awarded a VC posthumously. The citation read:

For most conspicuous bravery, courage and devotion to duty. After the capture of a position, the enemy massed in force and counter-attacked. The situation became very critical, all wires being cut. It was of the utmost importance to get word back to Headquarters. This soldier and one other were given the message with orders to deliver the same at all costs. The other messenger was killed. Private Brown had his arm shattered but continued on through an intense barrage until he arrived at the close support lines and found an officer. He was so spent that he fell down the dug-out steps, but retained consciousness long enough to hand over his message, saying 'Important message.' He then became unconscious and died in the dressing station a few hours later. His devotion to duty was of the highest possible degree imaginable, and his successful delivery of the message undoubtedly saved the loss of the position for the time and prevented many casualties.

Harry Brown was born on 10 May 1898 in Gananoque, Frontenac, Ontario. After leaving school, he became a farmer. At the age of eighteen, he enlisted in the Canadian Mounted Rifles in London, Ontario. Before he left to go overseas, he made a will, leaving everything to his mother. He was buried at the Noeux-les-Mines Communal Cemetery and his decorations are held at the Governor General's Foot Guard's Museum, and the Canadian War Museum in Ottawa has a memorial and a portrait of him.

The Germans were making another counter-attack the following day. By then, the 2nd Battalion relieved the 3rd Brigade in the trenches that ran down from the Chalk Pit, down Hugo Trench to Hurray Alley. The German bombardment continued with ferocious intensity. The line was very thinly held. At daybreak on the 18th, the whole strength of the battalion was down to just 614.

The German artillery laid down another terrific bombardment that lasted for forty minutes. When it lifted, the Germans attacked, using flamethrowers. On the left wing the Germans succeeded in entering the trenches held by No. 4 Company. But a bombing party was sent, the enemy were driven out again, leaving behind a *flammenwerfer* and a considerable number of dead.

Both company commanders had been killed and Captain O'Kill Massey Learmonth found himself in command of Nos. 2 and 3 Companies as Acting Major. Although the German advance had been checked within a few yards of the Canadian trenches, some of the enemy had found shelter to a certain extent in a small wood. To rout them, a bombing party from No. 3 Company was sent forward. They bombed the Germans out of the wood and down a trench named Horse Alley, driving them into the open, where the Canadian snipers and machine-gunners could cut them down.

According to the Canadian War Records Office publication *Thirty Canadian VCs*: 'Throughout the whole of the attack Learmonth showed what his Commanding Officer has named a "wonderful spirit". Absolutely fearless, he so conducted himself that he imbued those with whom he came into contact with some of his personality. When the barrage started he was continually with his men and officers, encouraging them and making sure that no loophole was left through which the enemy could gain a footing. When the attack was launched against the thin Canadian line, Learmonth seemed to be everywhere at once. When the situation was critical, he took his turn at throwing bombs. He was wounded twice, but carried on as if he were perfectly fit and whole. He was wounded a third time, his leg this time being broken, but still he showed the same indomitable spirit. Lying in the trench, he continued to direct his men, encouraging them, cheering them, advising them.'

At 06.15 hours the battalion headquarters received word that Learmonth was badly wounded and was being carried out of the line on a stretcher. But, by then, the enemy attack had been repulsed and Learmonth had stayed at his post until he had seen the job done. At headquarters, lying on his stretcher, he gave valuable information to the officers there before he was taken to hospital. He died there shortly afterwards, aged just twenty-three.

The citation of his VC read:

> For most conspicuous bravery and exceptional devotion to duty. During a determined counter-attack on our new positions, this officer, when his company was momentarily surprised, instantly charged and personally disposed of the attackers. Later, he carried on a tremendous fight with the advancing enemy. Although under intense barrage fire and mortally wounded, he stood on the parapet of the trench, bombed the enemy continuously and directed the defence in such a manner as to infuse a spirit of utmost resistance into his men. On several occasions this very brave officer actually caught bombs thrown at him by the enemy and threw them back. When he was unable by reason of his wounds to carry on the fight he still refused to be carried out of the line, and continued to give instructions and invaluable advice to his junior officers, finally handing over all his duties before he was evacuated from the front line to the hospital where he died.

The first three days of the battle for Hill 70 had yielded four VCs. Another two would be awarded before the operation was over, six days later.

Thirty-year-old Company Sergeant-Major Robert Hanna was with B Company when the 29th Battalion moved up on the night of the 18th and were in position when the second stage of the offensive began at 04.35 on the 21st.

At 01.00 hours, the companies had begun to move into the

assembly positions. At 03.15 the scouts reported that the tapes had been laid. By then the companies were in position but the enemy was nowhere to be seen. But about 04.10 the German artillery began to shell the front of the parapet. The intensity of the barrage increased towards 04.30, when a sudden deluge of 'fish-tails' – mortar bombs known for their distinctive fins – descended on the trenches.

Accompanying this bombardment was another kind of bomb, a kind they had not come across before. It was square in shape, exploded with a great flame and sent out a dense, suffocating smoke. One of these dropped in the trench occupied by D Company, wounding practically every man in a platoon.

While attempts were being made to clear the debris, Sergeant Croll, who was stationed near the corner of Nun's Alley and Commotion trench, heard the word passed along: 'Heine has broken through the 25th and is coming down the trench'.

Croll collected five unwounded men and kept the advancing Germans at bay by bombing them until reinforcements arrived from the 28th Battalion and drove the enemy out.

Major Grimmett, who was in command of A Company in support, heard the bombing and realised that something had gone wrong with D Company, so he sent forward a platoon under Captain Abbott. By this time, the Canadians' opening barrage had begun and was moving forward. Following it, Abbott's platoon took up the fight, carried it into Nun's Alley and established a block there.

The other companies – B, C and the remainder of D – had also gone forward behind the barrage. One platoon of D company, which attempted an attack over open ground on Nun's Alley, was wiped out almost to a man by machine-gun fire. C Company, which was attacking in the centre, was also badly mauled. The left platoon was cut down by German machine-gun fire before it reached its objective. The right platoon had almost reached its objective – Cinnebar trench – when it ran into a strong enemy machine-gun post surrounded by barbed wire. Already wounded, Lieutenant Carter was killed in an attempt to drive the Germans out of this stronghold.

On the extreme right, Lieutenant Sutherland got into Cinnebar trench and gave the order for rapid fire on a party of Germans who were advancing over open ground. While picking up a rifle he was hit by a sniper's bullet and mortally wounded. Sergeant Stevens, who then took command, was lifting Sutherland's rifle when he too was shot through the head. A corporal took the sergeant's place. A moment later, he too was killed. The remainder of the men fought on desperately until a platoon of the 28th Battalion came to their aid.

In the meantime B Company had reached the objective in Cinnebar trench. Believing that all was well with C Company to their left, Lieutenant Gordon, the commander of B Company, was about to send off the pre-arranged signal when it was discovered that the signal cartridges were wet. Before others could be found, word was brought that C Company was under intense attack and all the officers had been killed. Lieutenant McKinnon was sent with a bombing party to the aid of C Company, but he was killed just as he joined the fight.

Gordon then went along to the relief of the company on his left, after ordering Lieutenant Montgomery to get a party of snipers outside the trench so that they could take a toll on the enemy. Gordon was badly wounded in the arm and Montgomery was soon afterwards killed by a German sniper. The leadership of the company then fell upon Sergeant-Major Hanna.

Hanna saw that the crux of the position was a German post protected by a heavy wire and armed with a machine gun. He collected a party of his men and led them against the post amid a hail of rifle and machine-gun fire. Rushing through the wire, he bayoneted three of the Germans, brained a fourth and seized the machine gun. The redoubt was captured.

The Germans arrived in force and counter-attacked. Hanna, who was now short of bombs, managed to defend the position. Again and again the enemy tried to rush him, but he and his handful of men held it until they were relieved later that day. Next day, the battalion frontage was taken over by another Canadian unit and the 29th went back to the rear.

Hanna received his VC from George V at Buckingham Palace on 5 December 1917. The citation read:

For most conspicuous bravery in attack, when his company met with most severe enemy resistance and all the company officers became casualties. A strong point, heavily protected by wire and held by a machine gun, had beaten off three assaults of the company with heavy casualties. This Warrant Officer under heavy machine gun and rifle fire, coolly collected a party of men, and leading them against this strong point, rushed through the wire and personally bayonetted three of the enemy and brained the fourth, capturing the position and silencing the machine gun. This most courageous action, displayed courage and personal bravery of the highest order at this most critical moment of the attack, was responsible for the capture of a most important tactical point, and but for his daring action and determined handling of a desperate situation the attack would not have succeeded. C.S./M. Hanna's outstanding gallantry, personal courage and determined leading of his company is deserving of the highest possible reward.

Born in Ukraine, Filip Konowal had served in the Russian Imperial Army before emigrating to Canada. He was an Acting Corporal in the 47th (British Columbia) Battalion when he arrived at Hill 70 in France on 22 August.

Corporal Konowal was in charge of a mopping-up section while the main attack swept on. His job was to search the rabbit warren of bombed-out houses and tunnelled foundations where many Germans with machine guns were left, a constant danger to following waves of soldiers. The buildings along the Lens-Arras Road proved particularly difficult to clear. While the main body of troops had passed through on their way to the objectives beyond, a couple of buildings still held Germans and German machine guns, and there was heavy firing upon the rear of the advancing men. Entering one of these houses, Konowal searched for the Germans. Finding no trace of anyone living, he dropped daringly into the cellar below. Three men fired at him as he landed, but he miraculously escaped, unharmed. They then fought it out in the dark with rifle fire and bayonets. The odds were three to one. Emerging into the daylight, Konowal had bayoneted all three of the gun crew. He then moved on, ever alert to the close rifle-crack that might be a sniper.

There was a large crater to the east of the road. From the Canadian bodies piled around its edge, it seemed obvious that a German machine gun had been positioned there. Halting his men, Konowal advanced alone. Upon reaching the lip of the crater he saw seven Germans endeavouring to move their machine gun into a dugout. He opened fire at once, killing three. Then charging down into the crater, he finished off the rest with his bayonet.

The following morning, troops of the 44th Battalion were held up by a machine-gun emplacement in a tunnel. Corporal Konowal had proved his metal at subterranean fighting, and his party succeeded in entering the tunnel. Throwing two charges of ammonal (an explosive) ahead of him, Konowal dashed forward in the darkness, engaged the machine-gun crew with the bayonet, overcoming and killing them all. Altogether he killed sixteen men in the two days of battle.

During the action, Corporal Konowal had gunshot wounds to the face and the neck. He was invalided back to England. After ten days in hospital, he was appointed to command duty with the Russian Military Attaché in London and promoted to acting sergeant. He received his VC from George V at Buckingham Palace on 5 December 1917. The citation read:

> For most conspicuous bravery and leadership when in charge of a section in attack. His section had the difficult task of mopping up cellars, craters and machine-gun emplacements. Under his able direction all resistance was overcome successfully, and heavy casualties inflicted on the enemy. In one cellar he himself bayonetted three enemy and attacked single-handed seven others in a crater, killing them all. On reaching the objective, a machine-gun was holding up the right flank, causing many casualties. Cpl. Konowal rushed forward and entered the emplacement, killed the crew, and brought the gun back to our lines. The next day he again attacked single-handed another machine-gun emplacement, killed three of the crew, and destroyed the gun and emplacement with explosives. This non-commissioned officer alone killed at least sixteen of the enemy, and during the two days' actual fighting carried on continuously his good work until severely wounded.

Konowal also received the Russian Cross of St George, 4th Class and went on to serve with the Canadian Siberian Expeditionary Force from October 1918 to June 1919. He was left with a crippled hand and the partial paralysis of the left side of his face.

Soon after leaving the Army, he killed an Austrian man for insulting the Canadian flag and pleaded insanity. After nine years in asylums for the insane, he enlisted in the Governor-General's Foot Guard in Ottawa and travelled to London in 1929 for a dinner at the House of Lords. Then he became a janitor at the Canadian House of Commons. Meanwhile, the wife he had left behind in Ukraine had disappeared into a Soviet labour camp.

He attended a Garden Party with George VI, who visited Canada in 1939, and was at the dedication of the Canadian War Memorial. Ukrainian veterans raised the money for him to attend the VC centenary celebrations in London in 1953. When he died in 1959, Konowal was buried with full military honours. His VC was bought by the Canadian War Museum in Ottawa in 1969.

CORPORAL ERNEST EGERTON, 19

SHERWOOD FORESTERS

Bulgar Wood, Ypres, Belgium, 20 September 1917

As the meat-grinder of Passchendaele ground on, the 17th Sherwood Foresters advanced towards enemy posts in Bulgar Wood, south-east of the Menin Road, followed by the 16th (Chatsworth Rifles). There was a thick mist. Officers advanced using compasses. Among the men there was a certain amount of confusion as the two units got mixed up, but the mist kept the number of casualties down.

Captain P.E. Burrows, MC, commanding the 16th's Support Company, located enemy machine guns and led an attack. He took the strongpoint, capturing two machine guns and thirty prisoners. It was then taken over as the 16th's Headquarters.

At 07.00 hours, the 16th pressed on to a second objective. The rolling barrage fell short, causing casualties, but they succeeded in taking the enemy by surprise.

However, as the mist lifted, Major J.R. Webster, at the command post, spotted that the advancing troops had missed a strongpoint bristling with machine guns and snipers. It was a clear threat and had to be taken, despite the dangers.

Major Webster wrote later: 'An attack was quickly organized, covered by the fire of one of the attached Vickers Guns of the 57th Brigade. A party was sent to take the dug-out from the north side, which was led in a most gallant manner by Corporal Egerton of my Support Company. Several of the enemy were shot, 29 prisoners, including one officer were taken here.'

In fact, only one man was responsible. Nineteen-year-old Ernest Egerton had run forward alone, so fast that the rest of the company could not keep up. According to Captain Lloyd of Military Intelligence:

On the morning of the 20th of September 1917, the 16th Sherwood Foresters rose from their trenches, and marched behind the rolling thunder of bursting shell against the German defence in Bulgar Wood, which is near Poelcapelle. They took the first line, and the two leading waves of the battalion went forward through the smoke of the barrage to the heart of Bulgar Wood. But, as must often happen, in the heat and confusion of battle, they left a nest of Germans behind them, untouched. When the storm had passed over their heads, these men came up out of their underground sanctuary, a chain of deep dug-outs, cunningly hidden away among the litter of splintered trunks and tree roots in the south-west corner of the wood.

So it was that, when the third wave entered the wood, confidently, looking for no danger; suddenly, from close in front of them, came the evil chatter of a machine gun and a quick gust of bullets that beat them to the ground.

A Vickers answered the challenge, and, as the German gunner swung his weapon round in search of his next foe, a corporal of the Sherwoods, named Egerton, saw his chance and took it. Jumping to his feet with a shout of 'Come on, boys,' he ran with all his might towards the dug-outs, and his companions followed him as best they could across a tangled wilderness of maimed branches and treacherous shell-holes. The Germans saw him coming but they did not kill him. When Egerton was but ten yards away, the nearest of them flung his rifle to his shoulder, but he died before his finger could touch the trigger. The corporal shot another as he stood poised to throw a bomb. The machine gunner was already dead, and lay huddled behind the silent gun. One of his fellows tried to take his place, but Egerton was upon him, and he too died quickly. The reckless daring of the corporal's action had taken all the steel out of the Germans, and, when the remainder of the party came running to the scene, they saw that it was useless to resist any longer and surrendered to a man. Twenty-nine of them, including one officer, did the Sherwoods take from that place, before they formed up again and passed on in search of new adventures in Bulgar Wood.

Ernest Albert Egerton was born on 10 November 1897 at Longton, Staffordshire, the third of four sons. After attending Queen's Street, Cooke Street and Blurton Church Schools, he entered Florence Colliery at the age of sixteen, working as a haulage hand. On his eighteenth birthday, he enlisted in the 3rd North Staffordshire Regiment at Shelton recruiting office. His two older brothers also served in the Army. The eldest, Thomas Edward, was medically discharged from active service by December 1917. The second eldest, William Charles, an acting corporal in the Rifle Brigade, was killed in action on 17 August 1917, aged twenty-eight. His youngest brother, Harold, was too young to serve in the war.

After hearing of William's death, Ernest wrote to his parents: 'I am sorry to hear about Will's death. I can tell you it upset me very much; I could not say anything all day. We have just been into action again. We took a large number of prisoners. I am pleased to say I have come through another battle quite safely. Well, I had a bit of revenge, I accounted for a few Germans, I can tell you.'

After training at Wallsend-on-Tyne, Ernest Egerton was posted to the 1st North Staffordshires in France, and transferred to the 16th Sherwood Foresters in October 1916. Promoted to lance-corporal on 21 February 1917 and corporal on 23 August 1917, he came through the fighting on the Somme and at Ypres unscathed.

Later, he gave his own account of what had happened at Bulgar Wood.

'It was in September,' he said, 'I felt lost at first. I was in a shell-hole in front of some concrete dugouts, and someone with a machine gun was causing heavy casualties on our left flank, which included some North Staffords. I could see the damage they were inflicting, so I took it into my head to go forward. I kept running from shell hole to shell hole until I got to the back of this particular concrete dug out, and having gone so far, I could see three men with a machine gun. I first shot the man who was firing the gun: then I shot the second, who was waiting with another belt of cartridges, and I also shot the third man, who was a bomber. By that time I was supported by other men who had followed me up, and 29 Germans, including an officer, came out of their dug outs holding up their hands and surrendered.'

Major Webster said it was 'the most reckless piece of gallantry I ever saw'.

Egerton did not see it that way.

'I did not think of getting done in,' he said. 'I went over with the hope of coming back.'

At the time, he was thinking of the death of his brother, who had been killed in action.

'I went over with the intention of killing a few, to have revenge in the name of my brother's wife,' he said. 'It was my object from the time I heard of his death to get revenge. I was longing to get into action and pay back a debt, and now in a measure, I feel I have done it.'

Major Webster wrote: 'I shall never forget 20 September; it was the greatest day of my life. The dash of the men was simply amazing and nothing could stop them. They came out with their tails right up and every man had stories to tell of the Bosche they had killed.'

The 16th Sherwood Foresters fought alongside the 16th Rifle Brigade that day. In the 16th (Prince Consort's Own) was another VC winner, Sergeant William Burman, who was just two-and-a-half months older than Corporal Egerton.

William Francis Burman was born in Stepney, in London's East End, on 30 August 1897. Educated at Stepney Red Coat School, he joined the cadet force there. At seventeen, he enlisted in the Rifle Brigade. Sent to France, he was promoted to sergeant when he was still only eighteen.

Ten days after his twentieth birthday, his company were advancing across no-man's-land towards the German trenches when suddenly, from a group of shell holes some thirty yards away, a machine gun opened fire. Men were falling all around him, but Sergeant Burman continued, apparently with no thought for his own safety.

Shouting 'Wait a minute, lads,' he signalled to his platoon to take cover and dashed forward alone across the broken ground towards the machine gun. The Germans saw him coming and swung the muzzle round to meet him as he ran. But they were not quick enough and their bullets flew wide.

Before they could recover, he was on them with his bayonet. Of the three in the shell hole, none survived.

The way was now clear and the survivors of the company continued their advance as Sergeant Burman rejoined his platoon, carrying the machine gun. For the rest of the day, they used it with great effect on its former owners.

Soon after he had a second chance to distinguish himself. His company had driven the Germans out of their trenches, but the battalion of their right was still pinned down by heavy machine-gun and rifle fire from the flank. But Sergeant Burman could see where the fire was coming from and, without waiting for orders, he called out for two volunteers. His call was answered immediately.

The three men left the trench and ran out into the open towards a low hedge a little distance away, firing their rifles as they did so. The Germans did not realise this was a new danger until Sergeant Burman and his small party had worked round behind them and were shooting at them from the rear. Six Germans were killed before the remainder – thirty-one of them including two officers – decided to surrender to the three Englishmen.

Corporal Egerton received his Victoria Cross from King George V at Buckingham Palace on 5 December 1917. The citation read:

On September, 1917 south-west of Ypres, Belgium during an attack, visibility was bad owing to fog and smoke. As a result, the two leading waves of the attack passed over certain hostile dugouts without clearing them. Enemy rifles and machine guns from these dugouts were inflicting severe casualties. Corporal Egerton at once responded to a call for volunteers to help in clearing up the situation. He dashed for the dugouts under heavy fire at short range. He shot a rifleman, a bomber and a gunner. By which time, support had arrived and 29 of the enemy surrendered.

He was given a tumultuous welcome in his home town. Among the many letters of congratulation was one from the Duke of Devonshire, as the unit took its name from his family seat at Chatsworth. At an official reception the staff at Florence Colliery presented him with an inscribed silver cigarette-case and war bonds worth £85.

Sergeant Burman got his VC on 19 December 1917. The citation read:

When the advance of his company was held up by a machine-gun at point-blank range, Sergeant Burman shouted to the men next to him to wait a few minutes and going forward to what seemed certain death killed the enemy gunner and carried the gun to the company's objective, where he used it with great effect. Fifteen minutes later it was seen that about 40 of the enemy were enfilading the battalion on the right. Sergeant Burman and two others ran and got behind them, killing six and capturing two officers and 29 other ranks.

Egerton was badly gassed during the enemy's spring offensive the following year. After a spell in hospital in France, he returned to his unit and was promoted to Sergeant on 11 May 1918. He left the battalion on 20 August and returned to England for officer training, though he eventually declined a commission and joined the 3rd Sherwood Foresters as a sergeant-instructor. He was discharged on 25 April 1919 on medical grounds. The gassing had caused tuberculosis and he was only given a few months to live. However, he trained as a gamekeeper and working out in the fresh air led to a great improvement in his health. He served in the Home Guard in World War II and lived to the age of sixty-eight.

Burman also survived in the war. In 1929, at the dinner for VC winners, he found himself sitting next to HRH the Prince of Wales.

'Naturally, I was excited but I soon found that I had no need to be embarrassed,' he said. 'The Prince soon put me at my ease and we had a long chat. In fact, it was like talking to your brother. When he heard that I was a chauffeur, we discussed cars and he asked me which I liked best.'

He lived to the age of seventy-seven. Modest the end, when asked about the action that won him the VC, he said: 'I couldn't help it. It was a case of going on or going back. I couldn't go back.'

PRIVATE THOMAS HOLMES, 19

2ND BATTALION, CANADIAN
EXPEDITIONARY FORCE

Passchendaele, Belgium, 26 October 1917

By October 1917, there had been two failed attempts to take the heavily fortified Bellevue spur during the Third Battle of Ypres. The New Zealanders had made the first attempt. Then, on 12 October, the Australians were repulsed. After nearly three months fighting, Field Marshall Haig had begun to give up on the idea of making a breakthrough. Instead, he planned to secure a defensible line for the winter and to divert the enemy's attention from preparations for a large-scale engagement fifty miles to the south at Cambrai, where large formations of tanks would be used, to great effect, for the first time.

The Canadian Corps were brought up from Lens. The attack was to begin on 26 October. Heavy rain had been falling for two days before the 4th Canadian Mounted Rifles waded up to their positions in the front line, between Wallemolen and Bellevue. All the dykes and ditches of the low country there were full and overflowing. Even the ground that had been firm and solid had now turned into a dangerous swamp.

Nevertheless, the men pushed on through the darkness, slipping and splashing. There were long halts. With few landmarks left intact, it was easy to get lost. Finally, by 05.00 of the 25th, they were in position. During the day, the weather cleared. The sun and wind considerably improved the ground. In the clear weather, the men were able to seen their objectives for the following day's attack. They had some misgivings. There seemed entirely too much water around the low hills and copses they had to cover. And, though the wire had been broken in places, the pillboxes along the crest of the spur were still largely intact.

Nineteen-year-old Private Thomas Holmes was with the 4th Canadian Mounted Rifles (CMR), who were on the extreme left of the Canadian Corps front, with the 43rd (Cameron Highlanders of Canada) and 58th Battalion of the 9th Brigade on the right. Their objectives were Woodland Copse and Source Farm. It was hoped they could consolidate a strong line upon Wallemolen Ridge, all with a view to the establishment of a good jumping-off line for the capture of Passchendaele town itself.

While the clear weather had greatly improved the ground, it also made visibility much better. From the high ground, the German artillery and riflemen had an easy task shooting upon the Canadians' hastily improvised communication lines. The persistent bombardment became very severe indeed. Gallant attempts were made to supply the soldiers in the front line with munitions, but regularly parties were wiped out and supplies dispersed by the incessant shells. Eventually enough ammunition made it through, but the men went into action the following day, carrying empty water bottles.

Soon after 05.00 on the 26th, C and D Companies of the 4th CMR advanced from the front line, with A and B Companies in close support. The barrage opened up at 05.40. So did the heavy rain, making the ground slippery and difficult. Almost at once, concentrated machine-gun fire erupted from a line of pillboxes across the flanks of the low hills. Each of these small fortresses had to be stormed, using bayonets.

They did not take long to clear, and after a few minutes of close bayonet work the Canadians swept through. On the Wallemolen-Bellevue line, they found stout resistance. To the north-east of Wolf Copse, there was a German pillbox, its own strong defences supplemented by machine guns mounted close to the building on each side. The men had to advance against their fire, at times up to their waists in water. It was not possible to advance quickly, and one man after another from the small attacking force disappeared into the mud.

Reinforcements from A Company came up on the right, and a series of gallant attempts were made to rush the enemy's position, which was holding up the entire advance. Each time the men failed to reach the pillbox, and were forced to take whatever cover was possible, some fifty yards from it.

It was then that Private Holmes advanced alone. Ignoring the concentrated fire of the two guns, he made his way forward until he reached a point where he could throw his bombs. Coolly, he hurled the grenades, knocking out the two guns one after another, and killing or wounding every man around them. But this result was not sufficient for him, and he returned to his comrades for more ammunition. Taking another bomb from a friend, Holmes ran forward alone again. This time he got close to the pillbox itself to throw the grenade into the entranceway. The enemy soldiers who had not been killed or wounded in the blast – nineteen in all – came out with their hands up, surrendering. The Canadian advance could continue.

Thirty Canadian VCs (a book compiled by various authors and the Canadian War Records Office) says:

Making his way forward, indifferent to the concentrated fire of the two guns, Holmes reached a point from which he could throw his bombs. Then, with marvellous coolness, he hurled his missiles, with such precision that he succeeded in knocking out each gun, one after the other, killing or wounding every man about them. But this result was not sufficient for him, and he returned to his comrades for more ammunition. Securing another bomb from a friend, once more Holmes ran forward alone, this time getting close to the pill-box itself. Landing his bomb within the entrance of the concrete fort, he caused such an explosion in the confined space that the unhappy survivors of the garrison crawled out and surrendered. One does not know how Private Holmes escaped the sweeping fire that was poured upon him, but there is no doubt that his gallant action saved a critical situation, and allowed our men to push forward and establish a strong line in advance of their intermediate objective. Here they held back counter-attack after counter-attack, subjected to intense bombardment and heavy machine-gun fire from the high ground on the right, until later in the day the gallant capture of Bellevue Spur by the 43rd and 52nd Battalions cleared the situation, and permitted the consolidation of a strong line.

A Company's commander, Major Harold Archibald Scott, was taking cover with his company when the troops in the enemy pillbox opened fire. He witnessed the incredible heroism of one of his men and wanted to ensure he was decorated, but did not know who exactly had carried out the attack. He sent Private Herbert Hawley forward to identify the hero. But when Hawley returned he discovered that Major Scott had just been killed. Other men had also witnessed the action and recommended Holmes for an award.

Born in Montreal, Quebec, on 17 August 1898, and raised in Owen Sound, Ontario, Thomas William Holmes lied about his age when he enlisted in the 147th Battalion, Canadian Expeditionary Force, in December 1915. He claimed to be eighteen, the minimum age to see service overseas. He was described as 'a frail, delicate youth with a contagious smile'. At the time of his enlistment he was five foot five inches tall, with fair hair and blue eyes. He had no military experience, still lived at home and worked on a chicken farm.

After sailing to Europe with the 147th Battalion, Holmes was sent to a reserve battalion before being moved onto the 4th CMR. He was wounded in the left arm during the fighting at Vimy Ridge in April 1917 and had only just returned to the battalion before the fighting at Passchendaele began. At the time of the award of his Victoria Cross, Holmes was reportedly the youngest Canadian to receive the Empire's highest military honour.

Gazetted on 11 January 1918, the citation read:

For most conspicuous bravery and resource when the right flank of our attack was held up by heavy machine-gun and rifle fire from a 'pill-box' strong point. Heavy casualties were producing a critical situation when Pte. Holmes, on his own initiative and single-handed, ran forward and threw two bombs, killing and wounding the crews of two machine guns. He then returned to his comrades, secured another bomb, and again rushed forward alone under heavy fire and threw the bomb into the entrance of the 'pill-box', causing the nineteen occupants to surrender. By this act of valour at a very critical moment Pte. Holmes undoubtedly cleared the way for the advance of our troops and saved the lives of many of his comrades.

Discharged as a sergeant at the end of the war, he returned home to a hero's welcome. However, his time in the trenches undermined his health and he suffered from tuberculosis. His VC was stolen by burglars in 1935. A replacement presented to his sister nine years after his death in 1950 was also stolen, but was eventually returned, minus its ribbon.

While Private Holmes's action had allowed the 4th CMR's advance to continue, the 58th Battalion on the right began to stall. By 06.30 hours, men of the Cameron Highlanders were seen against the skyline going over the crest of Bellevue Spur. The German artillery fire had been immediate and heavy, and formidable pillboxes on the top and flanks of the hill maintained steady fire upon our troops, causing many gaps in the waves of infantry stumbling and slipping upon the muddy slopes. Soon B and C Companies, who were leading the attack, found themselves without officers.

D Company, led by Captain D.A. Galt and Lieutenant Robert Shankland, made good progress up the hill, until checked by the heavy fire of a machine gun in a strong emplacement to the right front. With a few men, Captain Galt attempted to capture it, while Lieutenant Shankland continued the advance with the remainder of the company. He reached the crest of the hill, where close fighting won the 43rd more ground. The pillboxes were captured, but a trench some fifty yards beyond them checked the advance again, and the weary survivors of the attack dug themselves in as best they could.

On the right, the 58th Battalion was held up by determined resistance and the concentrated fire of many machine guns at Snipe Hall. Unable to make good their objective, the wounded began drifting back in twos and threes to the comparative safety of the jumping-off line. Nevertheless a few held out with Shankland's company on the crest, making a rough and disjointed line of shell-holes across the hill top.

The Germans poured a stream of lead onto this line. At no time before had the men experienced such relentless shelling. The exploding shells threw up mud and water that clogged the Canadians' weapons. Despite this Lieutenant Shankland held his battered line for four hours along the crest of the Spur, keeping his men together and in good spirits. He also recruited the soldiers of other companies who were without officers, holding the position that had cost so much to win against a heavy counter-attack.

Shankland had established rough connection with the 8th Brigade to his left but now they were forced to withdraw, while his right flank was completely exposed. German troops were advancing from the direction of Snipe Hall, and had enfiladed his line and threatened to cut him off altogether.

After a careful survey of the whole position, Shankland handed over the command to the Machine-gun Officer Lieutenant Ellis, who, though wounded, had refused to leave the line while his guns were in action. Shankland then made his way back to Headquarters and handed in a report, giving a clear summary of a critical situation, and enabling steps to be taken that previous lack of information had rendered unwise.

In view of this valuable information, a new plan was devised. While the men of the 52nd and 58th Battalions drove back the enemy on the flanks, Shankland headed back through the mud and shellfire to his own company on the hilltop.

Meanwhile the Germans had attempted to rush this precarious position and had been beaten back by the Allied force's machine-gun fire with heavy losses. The advance of the 52nd Battalion drove many of the Germans back across the field of fire of Shankland's company, who were on the crest of the Spur. Eventually, the flanks were firmly established and the Canadians consolidated the new line. The objective of the attack had been accomplished, though they had not penetrated as far into enemy country as they had hoped.

Lieutenant Shankland was awarded the VC. His citation read:

Having gained a position at Passchendaele on 26th October 1917, Lieutenant Shankland organized the remnants of his own platoon and other men from various companies to command the foreground where they inflicted heavy casualties on the retreating Germans. He later dissipated a counter-attack, allowing for the arrival of support troops. He then communicated to his HQ a detailed evaluation of the brigade frontage. On its completion he rejoined his command, carrying on until relieved. His courage and his example undoubtedly saved a critical situation.

After the war, Shankland, an immigrant from Scotland, stayed on in the militia. In World War II, he went overseas with the battalion as Officer Commanding Headquarters Company. At the age of fifty-three, he was too old for combat duty. Promoted to lieutenant colonel, Shankland was appointed camp commandant of the Canadian Army Headquarters in England, in December 1940.

Twenty-one-year-old Lieutenant (Acting Captain) Christopher

Patrick John O'Kelly was with the 52nd Battalion, who were in support during the attack on Bellevue spur. At first, everything seemed to be going well, but by 08.30 the situation had changed. Weary parties of survivors were straggling back in twos and threes to the jumping-off line and the 52nd Battalion knew that their services would soon be required.

Colonel Foster, the Commanding Officer, went forward to the front line and returned with news of a critical situation. On the right the 58th had encountered terrible machine-gun fire and had been unable to make any progress, while some forty men of Lieutenant Shankland's company of the 43rd had fought their way to the crest of the spur and were roughly entrenched themselves, being able to advance no further. But they were still holding out after four hours of steady fighting and under heavy close-quarter fire from pillboxes on the ridge. What's more they were in constant danger of a flanking move by the enemy on either side.

Lieutenant O'Kelly, commanding A Company, was ordered to go to their assistance, advancing on the left flank of the 43rd Battalion to fill the gap between the 8th and 9th Brigades.

Drenched by the steady rain and pounded by the enemy's shells, the men of the 52nd were keen to get into action. They moved forward rapidly through the German barrage on the flank without heavy losses and made good progress up the low northern slope. When they reached the crest of the spur they found that the men of the 43rd were doing such an effective job that they had prevented the Germans from paying very much attention to the manoeuvres of the 52nd.

Even so, the machine-gun positions along the top of the hill caused a number of casualties, but no delays. As Lieutenant O'Kelly's men swept over the brow, they caught the flank of the enemy advancing against the 43rd, driving the Germans before them and shooting them down as they ran. For a moment it was almost a successful rout. But then the fire from the pillboxes grew heavier.

Canadian troops rushed pillbox after pillbox, with small parties of men trying to get close to the walls of each fort, while sections to the rear bombarded every opening and loophole with bullets and rifle-grenades. This made it difficult for the Germans to take aim, allowing the forward assailants the chance of taking the dead ground close beneath the walls and hurling bombs inside through any aperture. The effect of quite a small bomb going off in the confined space of a pillbox was terrible. Usually one was enough to compel the survivors to surrender.

Even so, taking these hilltop forts was a costly business. Often, the attackers would get caught in the open in the zone of fire of a machine gun and would be practically wiped out. However, on more than one occasion, the attack was brought to a successful conclusion by two or three survivors, who forced the surrender of thirty or forty defenders.

Through all this fighting Lieutenant O'Kelly led these assaults, selecting the point and method of attack with cool precision. He also never lost sight of his main objective – to gain ground and consolidate the ridge. Finally, his force was joined by B Company of the 52nd, and together they continued the advance.

The buildings of Bellevue Farm proved excellent cover for the retiring Germans and there was stubborn fighting around the ruined outhouses before the Canadians got through. Half a mile of ground was captured and consolidated. The Canadians reached the Wallemolen-Bellevue Road.

The German artillery continued shelling even though there were pockets of German soldiers among the Canadians. And when the new line formed the German shelling became intense before the inevitable counter-attack developed at two points of the Allies' thinly-held line.

Nevertheless, O'Kelly's men felt that they had saved the day and the men of the 52nd had no intention of giving up a foot of the ground they had won. They rained down such heavy fire that the counter-attack was shrivelled and dispersed two hundred yards from their line.

During the night Lieutenant O'Kelly's men went forward again and raided several strongpoints that might have hampered the advance of their men in the next phase of the offensive. That day alone, the 52nd Battalion had captured nine officers, 275 men and twenty-one machine-guns – and had saved a very critical situation indeed.

Lieutenant O'Kelly's VC citation read:

For most conspicuous bravery in an action in which he led his company with extraordinary skill and determination. After the original attack had failed and two companies of his unit had launched a new attack, Capt. O'Kelly advanced his command over 1,000 yards under heavy fire without any artillery barrage, took the enemy positions on the crest of the hill by storm, and then personally organised and led a series of attacks against 'Pill-boxes', his company alone capturing six of them with 100 prisoners and 10 machine guns. Later on in the afternoon, under the leadership of this gallant officer, his company repelled a strong counter-attack, taking more prisoners, and subsequently during the night captured a hostile raiding party consisting of one officer, 10 men and a machine gun. The whole of these achievements were chiefly due to the magnificent courage, daring and ability of Capt. O'Kelly.

Born in Winnipeg, Manitoba, O'Kelly was nineteen when he joined the Canadian Expedition Force from St John's College, where he was an undergraduate in October 1915. He was sent overseas as a lieutenant. Reaching the trenches in March 1917, he soon won a reputation as a daring leader, winning a Military Cross for charging a trench in the Avion-Méricourt sector.

He came through Passchendaele unscathed, though a reporter who interviewed him later said: 'He was very young. His manner was quiet and somewhat grim, as if he had looked too closely into a hundred faces of death.'

After the war he became a prospector and, in 1921, rejoined the Winnipeg Rifles as a major. On 15 November 1922, O'Kelly was drowned during a storm on Lac Seul, near Kenora, Ontario. His body was never found. He was just twenty-six.

LANCE-CORPORAL
ROBERT MCBEATH, 19
SEAFORTH HIGHLANDERS
Ribecourt, near Cambrai, France, 20 November 1917

During the British advance near Cambrai on 20 November 1917, the Seaforth Highlanders and the battalion to their right were held up by heavy machine-gun fire, when they were only a short distance from the railway line to the west of the village of Ribecourt, which was their objective. The fire appeared to be coming from some houses at the western end of a village to their right.

The company commander called for a Lewis gun to deal with these German machine guns. Nineteen-year-old Lance-Corporal Robert McBeath immediately volunteered and went off alone with his Lewis gun on his shoulder, carrying a spare tray of ammunition and a revolver.

As he approached the village he saw a German machine gun in action. Working his way to within twenty yards of the gun, he shot the gunner with his revolver. There were four other machine guns near the same spot – and Lance-Corporal McBeath was now fully 150 yards away from the nearest man of his company. But he never thought of going back. He managed to attract the attention of a tank, and with this formidable ally at his side he charged down upon the astonished gun crews. The Germans turned tail, and fled for shelter in a deep dugout.

But Lance-Corporal McBeath would not be deprived of the fruits of his victory. He promptly dived down into the dugout after them. He was halfway down the steps when the last German turned and fired at him. The bullet grazed McBeath's head, and buried itself in the woodwork of the steps. McBeath returned fire with his revolver and the German fell dead. Inside the dugout he found thirty men and three officers huddled together. Later, it was discovered that this was a battalion headquarters.

Captain Lloyd, who was with Military Intelligence, said: 'MacBeath [sic], however, at that moment, had little respect for the dignity of the German Staff, and drove his terrified prisoners before him through another doorway and up into the trench above.'

There would soon be confirmation of McBeath's extraordinary heroism.

'By this time a second man of his battalion had come up,' Captain Lloyd recorded, 'and he was just in time to see the exodus from the dug-out. L/C MacBeath [sic], after showing his captives their way to the rear, placed the newcomer as sentry over the entrance to the dug-out, and himself entered it once more. He searched it thoroughly, and shot two Germans who were still lurking in its recesses and showed some fight.

'His search concluded, he returned to his company. A sergeant who arrived on the spot shortly afterwards saw strange things around the dug-out. He could read, as well as if he had been there himself, the incidents of MacBeath's [sic] whirlwind charge. Lying dead around the first machine gun were four Germans. The gunner lay dead with his weapon still at his shoulder and his finger on the trigger. The four remaining machine guns were surrounded by a litter of empty cartridge cases and one of them had a half-empty belt still in the feed-block. The trampled earth outside the dug-out showed the haste with which the Germans had bolted for cover from the onslaught of the Scotsman. Half-way down the stairs the white scar of newly splintered wood told how narrow had been the corporal's escape.

'It was entirely owing to MacBeath's [sic] courage and resource that both battalions were enabled to continue their advance and capture their objectives. His conduct, not only on that day, but also on the following days, during which the battalion was heavily engaged, was beyond all praise.'

The brigade's War Diary recorded: 'Lance-Corporal McBeath has already lost three brothers in the war and he is absolutely regardless of his own safety so long as he can kill Germans.'

And there was plenty of opportunity. Once Ribecourt had been taken, the Seaforths and the 9th Norfolk Battalion moved on the village of Flesquières, a thousand yards beyond.

'Here very heavy fighting took place,' wrote Douglas Haig. 'The stout brick wall skirting the Chateau grounds opposed a formidable obstacle to our advance, while German machine guns swept the approaches. A number of tanks were knocked out by direct hits from German field batteries in position beyond the crest of the hill. None the less, with the exception of the village itself, our second objectives in this area were gained before midday. Many of the hits upon our tanks at Flesquières were obtained by a German artillery officer who, remaining alone at his battery, served a field gun single-handed until killed at his gun. The great bravery of this officer aroused the admiration of all ranks!'

By the time the Seaforths reached Flesquières, they found it abandoned. They moved on until they could look down on Cambrai. It was still in German hands, but they had crossed the Hindenburg Line, the Germans' last great line of defence.

Lance-Corporal McBeath's VC was gazetted on 11 January 1918. The citation read:

For most conspicuous bravery when with his company in attack and approaching the final objective, a nest of enemy machine-guns in the western outskirts of a village opened fire both on his own unit and on the unit to the right. The advance was checked and heavy casualties resulted. When a Lewis gun was called for to deal with these machine-guns, L/Corpl. McBeath volunteered for the duty, and immediately moved off alone with a Lewis gun and his revolver. He located one of the machine-guns in action, and worked his way towards it, shooting the gunner with his revolver at 20 yards range. Finding several of the hostile machine-guns in action, he, with the assistance of a tank, attacked them and drove the gunners to ground in a deep dugout. L/Corpl. McBeath, regardless of all danger, rushed in after them, shot an enemy who opposed him on the steps, and drove the remainder of the garrison out of the dug-out, capturing three officers and 30 men. There were in all five machine-guns mounted round the dug-out, and by putting them out of action he cleared the way for the advance of both units. The conduct of L/Corpl. McBeath throughout three days of severe fighting was beyond praise.

Robert McBeath was born on 22 December 1898 in Fraserburgh, Caithness, but was brought up in Kinlochbervie, Lairg,

Sutherlandshire by his adoptive parents. He went to Inshegan School there. At sixteen, he enlisted as a private in the 1st/5th Seaforth Highlanders on 12 August 1914 and was promoted to lance-corporal on 24 July 1917.

He was presented with his VC by George V at Buckingham Palace and was awarded a farm under a scheme set up by the Duke of Sutherland. But this did not suit him. After a Garden Party for VC winners at Buckingham Palace in June 1920, he emigrated to British Columbia, joining the Vancouver City Police on 12 August 1921. On 9 October 1922, he and a colleague stopped a car. The driver shot them both dead. McBeath was just twenty-three years old.

SECOND LIEUTENANT
ALAN 'BABE' MCLEOD, 18
NO. 2 SQUADRON, ROYAL FLYING CORPS
Arras, France, 27 March 1918

In World War I, young heroes also took to the air. One such was Alan McLeod, born on 20 April 1899 in Stonewall, Manitoba, to Scottish immigrant parents. It seems he was a daredevil from the outset. At the age of nine, he removed a trap from the foot of a stray dog and did not see why everyone made such a fuss about it. In January 1909, the *Stonewall Argus* reported:

Master Alan McLeod was observed to perform a feat the other day which called for some endurance and some nerve on the part of so young a lad. It also gave evidence of his kindly disposition. A dog passed along the street and was seen to have a trap on its foot. A gentleman tried to catch it, but did not succeed. Alan started after it and after following it for nearly half a mile and coming up with it several times succeeded in stopping it and removing the trap. He let the dog go and returned the trap to the constable. Asked how the dog behaved he explained that it showed its teeth at first, but he got it to understand after a little. Not the least praiseworthy feature was his seeming unconsciousness that he had done anything but what any boy would do.

McLeod was fascinated with all things military from an early age. At fourteen he went on militia training with the 34th (Fort Garry) Horse with a detachment from Stonewall. When World War I broke out in 1914, he tried to enlist, but at fifteen he was still too young.

Having failed to pass muster in Winnipeg, at seventeen he tried to join the cadet wing of the Royal Flying Corps in Toronto, but when the recruiting officer saw his birth certificate he was told to wait until his next birthday. Finally, he received word to report for a medical examination on 23 April 1917. His last day of school fell on his birthday; his classmates and teachers gave him a rousing send-off.

The next day he was sent for training at Long Branch in Deseronto, Ontario. He made his first flight on 4 June in a dual-control Curtiss JN-4 – a 'Jenny' biplane. It lasted just ten minutes.

Three days later, he took over control once the plane was at a safe height, and his first flight was on 9 June, after just two hours fifty-five minutes' instruction. It was on an Avro 504 – the first plane to be shot down by the Germans in World War I. Then he moved on to Camp Borden, Ontario, where he joined No. 42 Wing for advanced training.

Writing home on 19 June 1917, he said: 'I arrived at Camp Borden yesterday. It is an awful hole. I guess I'll get used to it but it's lonely here, just a mass of sand and tents… we are sleeping in tents without floors, there are lots of us in a tent, we have no dressers or wash stands, we have to walk about ¼ mile to the building to get washed... we have to get up at 3.45 am and there is no time to spare till noon and we just have two hours for dinner, then in the afternoon after dinner, we work till 4.30 then have a lunch and fly till 8.15, then we have supper and after supper, there are lectures from 9–10.30, then we go to bed. We have lots of drill and have to polish our buttons and boots or get Cain. We can have a weekend pass once a month... I just hate this place.'

Even so, he stuck at it. On 31 July he was given his wings – still with only fifty hours' flying time – and was commissioned second lieutenant on 19 August 1917. The following day, he embarked for England on board the SS *Metagama*. Menaced by U-boats, they put into port in Ireland for a few days on the way.

Arriving in England on 1 September, he went on a short refresher course in Winchester before reporting to 82 Squadron at Waddington in Lincolnshire. The squadron was equipped with the heavy Armstrong Whitworth FK8 biplane known as the 'Ack-W' or 'Big Ack'.

Over thirty feet in length and with a wingspan of just over forty-three feet, the FK8 was typically used for reconnaissance, artillery spotting and light bombing. Its single engine gave it a top speed of ninety miles an hour and a range of 240 miles, and it could climb to an altitude of 13,000 feet. Along with its pilot and observer or gunner, the Ack-W could carry a mere 150 pounds of bombs. It was typically fitted with a fixed forward Vickers machine gun and a Lewis machine gun on a swivel mount. Somewhat ungainly in appearance, it was sturdy, reliable and not very agile. McLeod said it had 'the aerodynamics of a cow', though it was popular with pilots.

The squadron was moving to France in November, but McLeod was not allowed to go with them as he was not yet nineteen. Instead, he was transferred to 51 Squadron as a night fighter defending London against German air raids.

He was sent to the Home Defence Squadron flying the FE2b – the Royal Aircraft Factory Farman Experimental 2b two-seater pusher biplane known as 'Fees'. The propeller was at the back because they had not yet perfected the gearing to allow a forward-facing machine gun to fire between the blades. On the FE2b, the gun was mounted in a nacelle, or housing, on the front of the plane.

Going into action in an FE2b was described by American ace Frederick Libby: 'When you stood up to shoot, all of you from the knees up was exposed to the elements. There was no belt to hold you. Only your grip on the gun and the sides of the nacelle stood between you and eternity. Toward the front of the nacelle was a hollow steel rod with a swivel mount to which the gun was anchored. This gun covered a huge field of fire forward. Between the observer and the pilot a second gun was mounted, for firing over the FE2b's upper wing to protect the aircraft from rear attack. Adjusting and shooting this gun required that you stand right up out of the nacelle with your feet on the nacelle coaming [raised lip]. You had nothing to worry about except being blown out of the aircraft by the blast of air or tossed out bodily if the pilot made a wrong move. There were no parachutes and no belts. No wonder they needed observers.'

There were other dangers. Night flying was in its infancy and there was always the constant risk of a mid-air collision, either with the enemy or another British plane. For the next two months, McLeod flew the black-painted fighters over the skies of London at night in search of German Zeppelins and Gotha bomber aircraft.

Once he was shot down, but managed to land the aircraft safely and considered the event amusing rather than life-threatening. His enthusiasm for combat came to the attention of his commander, who pulled some strings, and McLeod finally found himself being sent to the front.

On 29 November 1917, he reported to the Pilot's Pool at St Omer and was posted to No. 2 Squadron at Hesdigneul. When he arrived, his commanding officer said: 'What's this, a nursery? The kid can't be more than fifteen.'

He became known as 'Babe', though others called him 'Buster' or 'Bus'. He was attached to B flight, where he was assessed by Lieutenant Higgins, senior observer with the squadron, who passed him fit for combat. Again he was flying Whitworth FK8s, on photo-reconnaissance, night bombing and artillery-spotting missions, and proved himself to be a first-class pilot.

He made his first flight over France on 30 November 1917. On 19 December he and his observer, Lieutenant J.O. Comber, had a 'Scrap with 8 huns' – [German Albatros scouts] – claiming that '1 spun away'.

The most dangerous missions were for the artillery. The pilot had to fly steadily over the enemy positions and report where the Allied rounds were landing. This meant they were a sitting target for enemy anti-aircraft fire or fighters. Even small arms fire from German riflemen aiming to take a pot shot was a danger.

While there was little he could do about that, when enemy fighters came up after him, he turned and took them on, believing attack was the best form of defence. Once when an enemy Albatros was on his tail, McLeod grew annoyed that his gunner was not firing on him. After a rapid exchange of hand signals, he understood that the observer's gun had jammed. Dodging the bullets, McLeod performed a series of daring manoeuvres that shook his pursuer. After he had landed safely, he discovered that the gun had not jammed at all: the safety catch was still engaged and the observer had simply forgotten to release it.

McLeod was not just a danger to enemy airmen; Germans on the ground had reasons to fear him too. On 3 January 1918, he spotted a concentration of enemy troops near La Bassée in Flanders and went in, guns blazing.

On 14 January, he was mentioned in despatches when he attacked a German observation balloon accompanied by observer Lieutenant Reginald Key, an Englishman from Northampton. This was considered a very dangerous business as balloons were frequently ringed with anti-aircraft guns. It was a hazardous act using a fast, manoeuvrable fighter plane, but in a lumbering machine such as an Armstrong Whitworth FK8 it was almost foolhardy. Knowing the height of the balloon, gunners would also know the height to the attacking aircraft and set the fuses of their shells appropriately. McLeod had discovered a way to deal with this. He would climb high above the flak, then dive on the balloon, pulling up level with it at the last moment, allowing the observer to rake it with machine-gun fire.

As the hydrogen-filled bag exploded and the spotter crashed to earth, McLeod turned for home, only to be set upon by three Albatros scouts. McLeod then turned to engage them. Getting into a position where his observer could return fire, they downed one of them; the other two fled.

Two days later, McLeod and Key were near La Bassée again, directing artillery fire, when they were shot at by an anti-aircraft battery and small-arms fire from surrounding buildings. Ignoring the heavy bombardment, McLeod dived on the guns, dropping bombs, while Key raked them with machine-gun fire. Having silenced them, he attacked a column of enemy soldiers, before resuming his duties artillery spotting.

The guns he had taken out had been menacing airborne artillery spotters for some time and, when he got back to the airfield, he was granted two weeks' leave. He took this in London, though he might have been safer in France. On his second night in England, the Germans dropped a bomb near the Savoy Hotel, which killed forty-nine people and injured 147.

When McLeod returned to France, Key was moved to another squadron, but he later wrote a testament to McLeod: 'Alan would take on anything, and I was willing to go anywhere with him. He was the finest pilot I have ever flown with, devoid of fear, and always merry and bright. We were in many scraps together and often after getting out of a very tight corner by sheer piloting, with six or seven Huns on our tail, he would turn to me and laugh out loud.'

McLeod's new observer was Lieutenant William Hammond, who had already won the Military Cross. At the beginning of the German Spring Offensive in 1918, their squadron was ordered to fly south to the Amiens battle area and bomb the enemy troop concentrations advancing near Bapaume. The threat of a German breakthrough had them flying day and night.

At the same time, Baron von Richthofen's fighter squadron, Jasta 11, moved into the area. Von Richthofen had already built a formidable reputation and, to distinguish himself, had his Albatros painted red – earning himself the nickname 'The Red Baron'. The rest of his squadron followed suit, painting their aircraft in bright colours, and were known by the Allies as 'The Flying Circus'. They were to occupy Lechelle airfield, directly across the front line from No. 2 Squadron's base at Hesdigneul.

On the morning of 27 March 1918, B Flight took off to bomb and strafe German infantry in the area of Bray-sur-Somme. They flew into a thick fog and McLeod lost touch with the rest of the formation. For two hours they flew blind before finding a break in the cloud. Spotting the airfield at Avesnes-le-Comte where 43 Squadron was based, they put down. As they were still carrying a heavy load of bombs, the small skid that supported the tail broke and they had to wait for another to be delivered and put on.

At 13.00 hours, the plane was repaired and refuelled. Taking off again, they headed for the target area. But the weather had got no better. McLeod was about to abort the sortie and head for home when he spotted a German observation balloon in the distance.

He began his attack, as usual, from a height. As he dived towards the balloon a Fokker Triplane came into view. McLeod switched his attack to the enemy fighter. Hammond sprayed it with bullets and the Fokker went into an uncontrollable tailspin and crashed outside the village of Albert.

However, eight Fokker Triplanes from Baron von Richthofen's 'Flying Circus' had witnessed the engagement and came in for revenge. As McLeod put it in a letter to his parents later: 'We went quite a piece over the line and were just going to drop my bombs when all of a sudden a whole flock of Bosch came out of the clouds on us there must have been 8 or 10 anyway, I foolishly stayed to scrap [with] them.'

As the German planes attacked, the first was felled in flames. The rest came in from all angles. Two more were downed. But the numerical advantage and superior manoeuvrability of the Fokker triplanes soon proved too much for the lumbering Armstrong Whitworth.

Leutnant Hans Kirschstein managed to get below McLeod and raked the FK8 from nose to rubber, seriously wounding Hammond twice.

A second Fokker attacked from the beam, hitting McLeod in the leg and wounding Hammond a third time. Nevertheless, he still managed to level his machine gun and hit the second Fokker in the fuel tanks. It exploded in flames.

Leutnant Kirschstein banked steeply, turning his Spandau machine guns on McLeod's plane. He hit the FK8 in the fuel tank. Flames burnt away the superstructure between the cockpits and the cockpit floor, melting knee-length flying boots and burning the hem of McLeod's leather coat.

McLeod and Hammond were forced to quit their cockpits. Had they worn parachutes in those days, they would have jumped. Hammond clung onto the gun mount, sitting on the coaming with his feet on the bracing wires at the side of the fuselage to prevent himself being swept away in the slipstream. McLeod put the plane into a side-slip to direct the flames away from Hammond and to prevent him from being burnt alive. He kept on firing, hitting two other aircraft.

When the fire came too close, McLeod swung a leg out of the cockpit. With one foot on the lower left wing, the other on the rudder pedal, and his hands on the smouldering control column, he steered the plane towards the Allied lines.

The FK8 was now bound to crash. A Fokker triplane followed them down and Hammond managed to down him with a final burst on his machine gun.

McLeod's plane crashed in no-man's-land during heavy fighting. Though wounded, he managed to drag Hammond from the wreckage before the bombs exploded. A German machine-gunner raked them with fire and they took refuge in a foxhole. There, McLeod was wounded again, this time by shrapnel.

Eventually, they were rescued by South African troops. In the relative safety of their outpost, McLeod collapsed. For the next five hours they were trapped there until the German barrage lifted. Then they were moved to a dressing station under cover of darkness.

After being treated at Étapes Hospital, they were evacuated to the Prince of Wales' Hospital in London. As McLeod's life hung in the balance, Hammond had his leg amputated.

The official citation for the award of the Victoria Cross to Second Lieutenant Alan Arnett McLeod, Royal Air Force, was gazetted on 1 May 1918. It read:

> While flying with his observer, Lieutenant A.W. Hammond, M.C., attacking hostile formations by bombs and machine gun fire, he was assailed at a height of 5,000 feet by eight enemy triplanes which dived on him from all directions, firing from their front guns. By skilful manoeuvring he enabled his observer to fire bursts at each machine in turn, shooting three of them down out of control. By this time Lieut. McLeod had received five wounds, and while continuing the engagement a bullet penetrated his petrol tank and set the machine on fire.
>
> He then climbed out on to the left bottom wing, controlling his machine from the side of the fuselage and by side-shipping [sic] steeply kept the flames to one side, thus enabling the observer to continue firing until the ground was reached.
>
> The observer had been wounded six times when the machine crashed in 'No Man's Land' and 2nd. Lt. McLeod, notwithstanding his own wounds, dragged him away from the burning wreckage at great personal risk [from] heavy machine-gun fire from the enemy's lines. This very gallant pilot was again wounded by a bomb while engaged in this act of rescue, but he persevered until he had placed Lt. Hammond in

comparative safety, before falling himself from exhaustion and loss of blood.

Lieutenant Hammond got a bar for his MC. He later emigrated to Canada and served in the Royal Canadian Air Force in World War II, as did Reginald Key.

With twenty-seven aerial victories to his credit, Leutnant Kirschstein was awarded the *Pour Le Mérite* medal, known as the 'Blue Max'. He was killed in an air accident while flying as a passenger in July 1918. The inexperienced pilot stalled at 150 feet.

McLeod's father sailed over from Canada to accompany his son, then on crutches, to receive his VC at an investiture at Buckingham Palace on 4 September. He was the youngest airman to receive the medal.

Fellow pilot Billy Bishop, the first Canadian airman to be awarded the Victoria Cross, hosted a champagne dinner at the Savoy Hotel afterwards. He had won his VC at the grand old age of twenty-three. Gazetted on 11 August 1917, his citation read:

For most conspicuous bravery, determination, and skill. Captain Bishop, who had been sent out to work independently, flew first of all to an enemy aerodrome; finding no machines about, he flew on to another aerodrome about three miles southeast, which was at least 12 miles the other side of the line. Seven machines, some with their engines running, were on the ground. He attacked these from about fifty feet, and a mechanic, who was starting one of the engines, was seen to fall. One of the machines got off the ground, but at a height of 60 feet, Captain Bishop fired 15 rounds into it at very close range, and it crashed to the ground. A second machine got off the ground, into which he fired 30 rounds at 150 yards range, and it fell into a tree. Two more machines then rose from the aerodrome. One of these he engaged at a height of 1,000 feet, emptying the rest of his drum of ammunition. This machine crashed 300 yards from the aerodrome, after which Captain Bishop emptied a whole drum into the fourth hostile machine, and then flew back to his station. Four hostile scouts were about 1,250 feet above him for about a mile of his return journey, but they would not attack. His machine was very badly shot about by machine gun fire from the ground.

The co-host at this Savoy dinner was Arthur Richardson, who had won the VC in the Boer War. Born in Southport, Lancashire, in 1872, he had emigrated to Canada as a youth and was the first solder to be awarded the VC while serving with the Canadian unit under British command. Gazetted on 14 September 1900, the citation read:

On the 5th July, 1900, at Wolve Spruit, about 15 miles north of Standerton, a party of Lord Strathcona's Corp, only 38 in number, came into contact, and was engaged at close quarters, with a force of 80 of the enemy. When the order to retire had been given, Sergeant Richardson rode back under a very heavy cross-fire and picked up a trooper whose horse had been shot and who was wounded in two places and rode with him out of fire. At the time when this act of gallantry was performed, Sergeant Richardson was within 300 yards of the enemy, and was himself riding a wounded horse.

McLeod and his father left England when he was well enough to travel. When they arrived on Winnipeg on 30 September 1918, thousands of Winnipeg citizens and hundreds from Stonewall were there to give the hero a fitting reception. Stonewall declared a civic holiday in his honour. A modest man, McLeod said he did not wish people to be 'thinking that I'm suffering from a swelled head instead of wounds'.

He was promoted to captain and said he was looking forward to returning to the front once he had recuperated. However, in October, he contracted the Spanish flu. Already weakened by his wounds, he got pneumonia in Winnipeg General Hospital on 6 November 1918 and died.

His funeral was held on Saturday, 9 November. Thousands lined the street as his body was borne on a gun carriage draped in the Union Jack. He was buried in Kildonan Presbyterian Cemetery with full military honours. The pallbearers were six officers of the Royal Air Force. The guard of honour consisted of a hundred officers and men of the 1st Depot Battalion and fifty men of the Engineering and Construction unit. The firing party were troopers of the Fort Garry Horse, as was the bugler who played 'The Last Post'.

Although his death had been front-page news in the *Manitoba Free Press* of 7 November, the coverage of his funeral was relegated to page ten as, that day, the newspapers were reporting the Armistice in Europe and the *Free Press*'s front page headline was: 'Huns Quit; War Is Over'.

McLeod's medals and letters were donated to the Canadian War Museum, but his VC had been on loan and displayed in the Bishop Building, Headquarters of 1 Canadian Air Division in Winnipeg. His name can be seen on many military bases across Canada, as well as on streets, buildings, conference rooms, and even an air annex museum. No. 301 Royal Canadian Air Cadet Squadron ('Alan McLeod, VC' Squadron) was officially re-formed in Stonewall in May 2009.

RIFLEMAN KARANBAHADUR
RANA, 19

3RD QUEEN ALEXANDRA'S
OWN GURKHA RIFLES

El Kefir, Egypt, 10 April 1918

Born on 21 December 1898 in the village of Litung in the Baghlung district of Nepal, Karanbahadur Rana joined the 2nd Battalion of the 3rd Queen Alexandra's Own Gurkha Rifles at the age of sixteen. In 1914, soon after the Declaration of War, the battalion was sent to France as part of the Garhwal Brigade of the 7th (Meerut) Division, an infantry division of the British Indian Army.

Their first large-scale action came at La Bassée on 12 October, during the initial phase of the war known as 'Race to the Sea', before the lines of trenches were established. The battalion was involved in the defence of Festubert in November and of Givenchy in December. Soldiers from the sub-continent then spent the winter in France.

In March, the 2nd Battalion then took part in the Battle of Neuve Chapelle, followed by the battles of Festubert and Aubers in May. In September, at the Battle of Loos, Kulbir Thapa of the 2nd Battalion became the first Gurkha to win a VC. The citation read:

For most conspicuous bravery during operations against the German trenches south of Mauquissart. When, himself wounded, on the 25th September, 1915, he found a badly wounded soldier of the 2nd Leicestershire Regiment behind the first line German trench, and, though urged by the British soldier to save himself, he remained with him all-day-and-night. In the early morning of the 26th September, in misty weather, he brought him out through the German wire; and, leaving him in a place of comparative safety, returned and brought in two wounded Gurkhas one after the other. He then went back in broad daylight for the British soldier and brought him in also, carrying him most of the way and being at most points, under the enemy's fire.

This was all the more daring as it was reported that Germans were scouring the battlefield shooting or bayoneting the wounded. Both the officers of the 39th Garhwal Rifles and the 2nd Leicesters recommended him for the award. Kulbir Thapa received his VC from George V at Buckingham Palace. After he had recovered from his wounds, he rejoined his battalion in Egypt, where they were defending the Suez Canal, on 4 January 1916. He was promoted to Naik, or corporal, the following day.

The unit then joined the campaign in Palestine, fighting in the Battle of Gaza on the night of 1–2 November 1917 and the Battle of Mughar Ridge – also known as the 'Action of El Mughar' – on 13 November. They also took part in the capture of Jerusalem in December.

The 7th Indian Division was with XXIst Corps to the south of Gaza. In April 1918, they were involved in an attack on an enemy position on the top of a rocky slope at El Kefir. While the defenders were hidden by scrub, the attackers were on open ground, and visible to the machine-gunners above.

Karanbahadur Rana was with No. 2 Lewis gun section of B Company, who had already lost their commanding officer and suffered heavy losses, while No. 1 Lewis gun section had been wiped out. It was clear that they had not knocked out the enemy machine gun. During the action, Karanbahadur Rana also rescued their company commander, Lieutenant Frederick Barter, who had won his own VC with the Royal Welsh Fusiliers at the Battle of Festubert when he was twenty-two. The citation read:

> For most conspicuous bravery and marked ability at Festubert on 16th May, 1915. When in the first line of German trenches, company sergeant Major Barter called for volunteers to enable him to extend our line and with eight men who responded he attacked the German position with bombs, capturing 3 German officers and 102 men along with 500 yards of their trenches. He subsequently found and cut eleven of the enemy's mine leads, situated about 20 yards apart.

During the attack at El Kefir, Lieutenant Barter had fallen down and was feigning death. According to the brigade's War Diary, at 12.45: 'Lieut Barter turned up at the ridge; he had been lying within 30 yds of a German gun for $5\frac{1}{2}$ hours pretending to be dead. The machine gun was put out of action by a Lewis gunner No 4146 Rfm Karanbahadur Rana enabling Lieut Barter to get away. After No. 1 had been shot dead this man No. 2 pushed No. 1's body off and killed or wounded the whole machine gun crew and escort.'

For this action, nineteen-year-old Rifleman Karanbahadur Rana won the VC. The award was listed in *The London Gazette* on 21

June 1917 and in *The Gazette of India* on 6 December 1918. The citation read:

> For most conspicuous bravery, resource in action under adverse conditions, and utter contempt for danger. During an attack he, with a few other men succeeded under intense fire, in creeping forward with a Lewis gun, in order to engage an enemy machine gun which had caused severe casualties to officer and other ranks who had attempted to put it out of action. No. 1 of the Lewis gun opened fire, and was shot immediately. Without a moment's hesitation Rifleman Karanbahadur pushed the dead man off the gun, and in spite of bombs thrown at him, and heavy fire from both flanks, he opened fire and knocked out the enemy machine gun crew; then, switching his fire on to the enemy bombers and riflemen in front of him, he silenced their fire. He kept his gun in action, and showed the greatest coolness in removing defects which on two occasions prevented the gun from firing. During the remainder of the day he did magnificent work and when a withdrawal was ordered, he assisted with covering fire until the enemy were close on him. He displayed throughout a very high standard of valour and devotion to duty.

Lieutenant Barter was awarded the Military Cross for the action at El Kefir. It was gazetted on 26 July 1918 and the citation read:

> For conspicuous gallantry and devotion to duty when ordered to make a flank attack. He led his two platoons up a precipitous hill, and turned the enemy's flank. Then, placing one platoon with two Lewis guns to command the enemy's line of retreat,

he gallantly led an attack with the other platoon from the rear
and flank, killing or capturing practically the whole garrison.

Karanbahadur Rana was promoted to Naik. In August 1919, he
travelled to London for the investiture at Buckingham Palace.
Around two thousand men of the Indian Army marched from
Waterloo Station to the Palace through streets thronged with
cheering crowds. They assembled on the west lawn, where they
were inspected by the King, before Karanbahadur Rana received his
decoration.

Addressing the troops, George V said: 'It is with feelings of pride
and gratification that I welcome here in my home this representative
contingent of British and Indian officers and men of my Army
in India, and I am especially glad that this meeting should take
place when we are celebrating peace after victory. I deeply regret
that unavoidable circumstances prevented your joining the troops
of the Empire and of our Allies in the Victory Procession on 19
July. I thank the British troops for their magnificent services in
the field. I gratefully recognise the prompt and cheerful response
of the Territorials to their country's call, their patient endurance of
a prolonged separation from their homes, and the sacrifices they
made in giving up their occupations in civil life. When temporary
trouble arose in India they, in common with their comrades from
Mesopotamia, who were on their way home, of their free will
remained at their posts (though home-coming was at hand). The
exemplary conduct of all has filled me and their countrymen with
admiration. I heartily thank all my Indian soldiers for their loyal
devotion to me and to my Empire, for their sufferings, cheerfully
borne, in the various campaigns in which they have served in lands
and climates so different from their own. At times their hearts must

have been sad at the long separation from their homes; but they have fought and died bravely. They have rivalled the deeds of their ancestors; they have established new and glorious traditions which they can hand on to their children for ever. I am glad to see among you representatives of the Imperial Service Troops, and I thank the Princes of the native States of India and their subjects for their noble response to the call made by me for the defence of the Empire and for the cause in which the Allies have fought and conquered. I know you will all unite with me in gratitude to God for the victory we have achieved. I trust you will enjoy your visit to India. May you return in safety, and take with you to your homes and villages my personal message of thanks and goodwill.'

Colonel Edmund Costello, commanding, called for 'Three cheers for our King an Emperor'. Then he called for three more 'for our Queen Empress'. Colonel Costello had won his own VC at the age of twenty-three during the Malakand Frontier War with the 24th Punjab Infantry. The citation read:

> On 26 July 1897 at Malakand on the Indian Frontier, Lieutenant Costello went out from the hospital enclosure and with the assistance of two sepoys, brought in a wounded lance-havildar who was lying 60 yards (55 m) away, in the open, on the football ground. This ground was at the time over-run with swordsmen and swept by a heavy fire from both the enemy and our own men who were holding the sapper lines.

Karanbahadur Rana left the Indian Army in the 1930s and returned to his village in Nepal. In 1971, a journalist from the magazine *Weekend* found him, reporting that: 'The former rifleman, who had lost an eye in the war is always at home in Litung in Nepal... he is a wizened man of 80 with one eye and he doesn't go far these days from the dark of his tiny mud hut. But as he sits among the chickens and pigs that share his home Karanbahadur can recall the time when his home was the toast of the pink-gin sipping colonels who were around when the rifleman's conspicuous bravery and utter contempt for danger won him the Victoria Cross.'

Two years later, he died. His VC and other medals are now held at the Gurkha Museum in Winchester.

PRIVATE JACK THOMAS COUNTER, 19
KING'S REGIMENT (LIVERPOOL)
Boisleux St Marc, France, 16 April 1918

Jack Thomas Counter was born on 3 November 1898 at Blandford Forum. One of three children, he was educated at Blandford National School, then went to work at International Stores in the town. At the age of seventeen, he joined the Army in February 1917 and was posted to the 1st Battalion, The King's Liverpool Regiment and served with them in France.

In March 1918 the Germans launched their Spring Offensive on a fifty-mile front opposite the British Third and Fifth Armies. This was Germany's last-gasp attempt to defeat the Western Allies before the overwhelming might of the United States was fully deployed against them. For the moment they had the advantage because nearly fifty divisions had been freed from the Russian front after the Bolshevik revolution led to the Brest-Litovsk peace treaty being signed on 3 March.

The main attack was an attempt to break through Allied lines, outflank the British and defeat them, forcing the French to surrender. Over the following days and weeks the Allies were forced to retire before the German onslaught, giving up ground. Though the British fought fiercely they were on the back foot. The Germans only paused briefly to re-form and bring fresh troops forward to replace casualties before launching further attacks.

The King's Liverpool Regiment were part of the 6th Brigade, 2nd Division and the brigade had been deployed on the left of the British sector to the south of Arras. The trenches opposite the villages of Boyelles and Boisleux-St Marc were occupied by the 1st Battalion. A sunken road ran between the two villages, which provided good cover for the enemy as they approached to attack the battalion.

On the morning of 16 April, the British front line was subjected to a heavy artillery barrage, before it lifted onto the support and reserve positions. The shelling of the front line had caused heavy casualties and the Germans were able to break through the line in numerous places. In the chaos of battle, battalion headquarters found themselves cut off from the front line. To get reliable reports of the situation, headquarters had to send men down the sunken road and across a forward slope of some 250 yards in full view of the enemy. Battalion HQ had sent a party of runners to get to the front line, but all had become casualties. Aware of the risk and the likelihood of death, Private Jack Counter volunteered to try to get to the front line and bring back information.

Captain Lloyd, with Military Intelligence, takes up the tale:

Early on the morning of the 16th of April 1918, near Boisleux St. Marc, the Germans attacked the 1st Battalion of the King's Liverpool Regiment.

Machine guns and rifle pelted death into the ranks, as they

crossed no-man's land, but nothing could stay that tide of men which flowed slowly over the broken ground, and poured at last into the British trenches.

Here and there a post held out, like some sullen rock, surrounded by a sea of enemies. So it was with No. 8 platoon of B Company. With Germans in front of them and on each side of them they battled on, fighting grimly, hoping that help would come to them. They could send no news of their desperate plight back along the sunken road that climbed the ridge behind them, for every inch of it was swept by German machine guns.

At 9.30, No. 7, the reserve platoon of B Company, had marched up to the support trenches that ran along the crest of the hill 250 yards behind. Two hours later the company-commander sent word to the officer in charge of No. 7. platoon, bidding him at all costs to get in touch with No. 8. Platoon, and to find out whether they still held their ground astride the sunken road.

So from the support trenches went out 6 men and an NCO, and began that perilous journey along the sunken road. No sooner had they shown themselves above the crest than they were a target for every machine gun in the German lines. The NCO was killed, one man was wounded, and the others could go no further for the storm of lead that beat down between those steep banks.

Then one man went out alone and gambled with death upon the sunken road. And he died. A second followed him, and he, too, fell, as the first man had fallen, when he came to the crest of the ridge. But, as is the habit of the British soldier, a third man volunteered to sacrifice himself, then a fourth, and a fifth; but the Germans saw them, and they all died there in turn on the sunken road, beneath the eyes of their comrades.

Five men had gone out, and five men had died, but there was still another man who was not afraid to go the way that his comrades had gone. This was Private Jack Thomas Counter, a soldier who was not yet 19 years old.

It was then two o'clock. The Germans caught sight of him as he came over the ridge. Private Counter saw all the road in front of him lashed with bullets, but never flinched. Keeping close to one of the high banks, he lay flat on his face, and dragged himself, foot by foot, down the road. Twice, where the road was stopped by entanglements of barbed wire, he had to cross it to crawl through a gap on the further side. He was very near to death many times, but he came to his goal unharmed at the last.

It was a wonderful thing that he reached the front line at all. It was a miracle that he came back. But he did so, and by the same way, an hour later, and he brought back with him news that was worth much to his side.

Action on the information that he brought, his colonel that evening launched a counter-attack, and drove the Germans back to their trenches once more.

By 18.30 that evening, all the British positions had been retaken and the line restored. This was all due to Private Counter's daring and he was awarded the VC.

It was gazetted on 23 May 1918 and the citation read:

For most conspicuous gallantry and devotion to duty. It was necessary for information to be obtained from the front line in which the enemy had effected a lodgement. The only way was from the support line along a sunken road and thence down a forward slope for about 250 yards with no cover in full view of the enemy and swept by their machine-gun and rifle fire. After a small party had tried unsuccessfully (the leader having been killed, another wounded before leaving the sunken road) it was thought that a single man had more chance of getting through. This was attempted five times, but on each occasion the runner was killed in full view of the position from which he had started. Private Counter who was near his officer at the time and had seen the five runners killed one after the other then volunteered to carry the message. He went out under terrific fire and succeeded in getting through. He then returned carrying with him vital information with regard to the estimated number of enemy in our line, the exact position of our flank and the remaining strength of our troops. This information enabled his commanding officer to organise and launch the final counter-attack, which succeeded in regaining the whole of our position. Subsequently this man carried back messages across the open under a heavy artillery barrage to company headquarters. Private Counter's extraordinary courage in facing almost certain death, because he knew that it was vital that the message should be carried, produced a most excellent impression on his young and untried companions.

Private Counter received the medal from George V at an investiture at Buckingham Palace on 28 June 1918. Returning to Blandford with his father later in the day, they were welcomed at the railway station by a guard of honour mounted by local volunteers, the town band, borough officials and enthusiastic citizens. After a short speech of welcome the local hero and his father were driven in an open landau to Blandford's Market Square, where a platform had been erected in front of the municipal buildings for an official reception before a cheering crowd.

The Mayor expressed the town's pride in Private Counter's exploits in France and read out the official citation. He was then made Private Counter, the first Honorary Freeman of Blandford Forum, and presented with £100 in War Saving Certificates and a gold watch and chain, inscribed by the International Stores.

The Mayor also read out a letter from the chairman of the International Stores, which said: 'We hear with very great pleasure of the honour that has been conferred upon Jack Counter, and we are pleased to join in the public testimonial that is being presented to him to commemorate his gallant deed. As prior to the war he was in the service of this company we desire to present him with the accompanying gold watch as recognition of his bravery and shall be very glad if you will be so good as to present it to him with our best wishes for the future.'

Jack replied: 'Mr Mayor and fellow citizens, it is with great pleasure I receive the honorary freedom of my native town, also the War Saving Certificates and the watch and chain. I may say that in what I was able to accomplish I was only doing my duty as a soldier of the King. I thank you one and all for your kindness to me this evening.'

After a lengthy applause and the playing of the National Anthem, the procession was reformed and Jack and his father were escorted to their home in Dorset Street.

Returning to his regiment Jack Counter VC was promoted to corporal. He was alleged to have said that he only accepted it to get out of 'spud bashing'. After the Armistice, his regiment went to Jersey, where he was demobilised in 1922. Deciding to stay on the island, he took a job as a postman at the St Ouen Post Office, working there for three years. In 1925, he was seconded to the Post Office at Sudbury Common, Middlesex, but returned to Jersey four years later.

He joined the Jersey branch of the British Legion in 1930, regularly taking the role of standard bearer. Throughout the German occupation of the Channel Islands during World War II, he continued to work as a postman in St Helier and was later awarded the Imperial Service Medal.

While being a quiet, unassuming man, he attended numerous VC functions, including a Garden Party for VC recipients given by George V at Buckingham Palace in 1920; a VC Reunion Dinner at the House of Lords in 1929; the World War II Victory Day Celebrations at the Dorchester Hotel in 1946; the VC Centenary held in Hyde Park in 1956 and a Garden Party given by Queen Elizabeth II at Buckingham Palace in 1962.

On 17 September 1970, Jack Counter went back to Blandford Forum to visit his sister-in-law. There he suddenly collapsed and died. He was seventy-one. His ashes were returned to Jersey and interred with his wife and daughter in St Andrew's Churchyard, First Tower, St Helier.

The following year, his likeness appeared on a 7½d stamp issued by Jersey Post Office to commemorate the fiftieth anniversary of the founding of the British Legion. His name is inscribed on memorial plaques inside and outside St Andrew's Church and a block of flats at St Saviour's for the elderly was named 'Jack Counter Close'. A Blue Plaque was erected on the house in Dorset Street, Blandford, where he had lived and a road in the town is also named after him.

His VC and other medals are on display at the Jersey Museum at St Helier.

ABLE SEAMAN ALBERT MCKENZIE, 19
HMS *VINDICTIVE*
Zeebrugge, Belgium, 22–23 April 1918

While the war along the Western Front remained a stalemate, the two sides tried to starve each other out. Germany was effectively cut off from international trade by the Royal Navy's hold on the North Sea. However, the German Navy retaliated with submarines. U-boats were sent out into the Atlantic to sink ships bringing food and materiel to Britain.

In 1917, the Admiralty drew up plans to block the entrances to Zeebrugge and Ostend in Belgium, which the Germans were using as submarine bases. Early attempts to close the ports had failed and Operation Hush, an attempt to make an amphibious assault behind the lines on the River Yser, just three miles south of Ostend, was thwarted by the Germans.

At Zeebrugge the objective was the mouth of the Bruges Canal as the U-boat pens were some way inland. The aim was to sink a number of blockships there and at the same time damage the port installations as much as possible. But it was well defended with a dozen heavy guns – some 5.9-inch – anti-aircraft guns, machine guns and a garrison of a thousand. The Germans had removed the buoys that marked sunken hazards and the whole harbour was protected by a 1½-mile mole, the longest in the world at the time. Any attempt to sail blockships round it and through Zeebrugge harbour into the canal entrance would draw the fire of five guns. The plan was to create a diversion by attacking the mole.

This would be done by a raiding party from HMS *Vindictive*, a twenty-year-old, three-funnelled, coal-burning light cruiser. She would be accompanied by two Mersey ferries, the *Daffodil* and *Iris II*. The ferry boats were used as they have a very shallow draught and, it was hoped, they could ride over and clear any mines.

The *Vindictive* was fitted with flamethrowers, mortars, pom-poms and Lewis guns, along with armour plating and fenders to protect the hull when she ran alongside the mole. She was to be commanded by Commander Alfred Carpenter, a staff officer who had the one advantage of having worked in detail on the plan for the huge structure with its architect Vice-Admiral Roger Keyes. Carpenter then had to be promoted to acting captain as the commander of the assault was Captain Henry Halahan, DSO.

The assault would be made by 730 men from the 4th Royal Marine Battalion. With them would be eight officers and two hundred sailors recruited from the Grand Fleet in Scapa Flow. Divided into three seaman storming companies, each fifty-strong, they would be commanded by thirty-two-year-old Lieutenant-Commander Arthur Harrison, a rugby international and gunnery officer from HMS *Lion*. The other fifty sailors would join twenty-two marines in a demolition party to wreck the dock facilities and enemy installations.

In the end, there would be eighty-six officers and 1,698 men on board 142 vessels – seventy-three bound for Zeebrugge and sixty-seven for Ostend. They set out from Dover on 11 and 14 April, but had to turn back on both occasions due to bad weather. Finally, they made it across the Channel on 22 April, arriving off the Belgian coast at around 11.00 hours. The wind was blowing towards the land and there was a light rain.

Still a mile from the harbour, the armada prepared to deploy. The coast was regularly shelled by monitors, heavily armoured ships used for coastal bombardment, so the enemy were not alerted then when the barrage started that night. At the same time, the fleet began making smoke to hide their movements. At 23.30, Coastal Motor Boats raced forward to torpedo any enemy shipping. Only then did the Germans realise they were under attack, and put up a star shell to illuminate the scene.

At the same moment, the wind changed direction, robbing the *Vindictive* of its cloak of smoke.

'At once the guns on the mole opened fire. From our dark bay we could see their quick flashes on our port bow, and there was a faint popping in the sea all round the ship,' wrote Lieutenant Edward Hilton-Young, who had been commanding the rear gun of the *Vindictive*. 'More accustomed to the crash which a shell makes when it bursts ashore, I did not realize at the time that this was the noise of shells that had missed us and were bursting in the sea. During the next few minutes we had by far the greater part of our heavy casualties. There were swift, shaking detonations close by, and one blinding flash of blue light right in our eyes. It was at this moment that Captain Halahan and Colonel Elliot were killed on the landing-deck a few feet away; but at the time my attention was so wholly fixed in listening impatiently for the first shot from the top, in order that the six-inch guns might begin too, that I hardly noticed what was going on. It was afterwards that I remembered the eruptions of sparks where the shells struck, the crash of splintering steel, the cries, and that smell which must haunt the memory of any one who has been in a sea-fight – the smell of blood and burning.'

Casualties were particularly heavy among the landing party.

'No sooner had the second burst, the enemy scored a direct hit on our after funnel, practically blowing it to pieces,' wrote Leading Seaman Childs. 'It seemed like hell let loose. The shrapnel and pieces of funnel caused havoc among the men, and the air was full of the cries of the wounded and dying. The Huns were hitting us every round they fired. At this time my sandbag dugout was demolished by two shells that hit us, taking away both sides, but not touching the front. These two shells wounded seven of us (myself only slightly), the only one of our crew not being wounded being AB Lodwig of A Company's Lewis gun.'

Nineteen-year-old Able Seaman Albert McKenzie was wounded too.

Despite the terrible damage, the *Vindictive* ploughed on at full speed. With the mole only feet from the ship's side, Captain Carpenter turned hard to starboard, putting her parallel and throwing her engines to full speed astern. At 00.01 on 23 April, the ship bumped the mole, taking the blow on two fenders and on the bulge on the port side of the forecastle. The bump was slight and the fenders remained intact. Carpenter then gave the order to let go the starboard anchor.

While the *Vindictive* had reached the mole just one minute behind schedule, she was a quarter of a mile from her intended landing point. The starboard anchor jammed, so the port anchor was lowered, but this made it difficult to hold the ship against the mole.

Two gangways were swung out precariously from the *Vindictive* and the landing party began to disembark as best they could as the vessels lurched to and fro. Adding to their misery, they were now being raked with machine-gun fire.

'We'd had things called "brows" constructed – a sort of light drawbridge with a hinge in the middle,' wrote Captain Carpenter. 'These were lowered away, but the current was so strong against the mole, and the *Vindictive* bounced up and down so nimbly, that the men had the devil of a job to drop the ends of these brows on the wall. All this time, naturally enough, the Huns were blazing at us with everything they'd got.'

A few minutes later the *Daffodil* arrived. She had also been badly shot up. The *Iris* then arrived at the mole around a hundred yards away at around 00.15 and dropped her starboard anchor.

'We went astern on it to bring us close in,' wrote nineteen-year-old Petty Officer G. Warrington, commander of a flamethrower party on board. 'There was an eight-knot current running along the wall, and the great hook fixed to the derrick was not strong enough to hold us in position.'

Lieutenant-Commander George Bradford, a navy boxer, led the party ashore. Bradford had three brothers in the Army. Between them they had won one VC, two MCs and a DSO. Two of the three were now dead.

George was not to be outdone. He leapt onto the mole. Already injured, he lay there for a few minutes. Then he shouted up to those on deck to throw a grappling iron to make them fast. Accounts differ, but at some point he was hit and fell into the sea.

His VC was awarded posthumously. The citation read:

For most conspicuous gallantry at Zeebrugge on the night of the 22nd–23rd April, 1918. This Officer was in command of the Naval Storming Parties embarked in *Iris II*. When *Iris II* proceeded alongside the Mole great difficulty was experienced in placing the parapet anchors owing to the motion of the ship. An attempt was made to land by the scaling ladders before the ship was secured. Lieutenant Claude E. K. Hawkings (late *Erin*) [having recently served on HMS *Erin*] managed to get one ladder in position and actually reached the parapet, the ladder being crushed to pieces just as he stepped off it. This very gallant young officer was last seen defending himself with his revolver. He was killed on the parapet. Though securing the ship was not part of his duties, Lieut.-Commander Bradford climbed up the derrick, which carried a large parapet anchor and was rigged out over the port side; during this climb the ship was surging up and down and the derrick crashing on the Mole. Waiting his opportunity he jumped with the parapet anchor on to the Mole and placed it in position. Immediately after hooking on the parapet anchor Lieut.-Commander Bradford was riddled with bullets from machine guns and fell into the sea between the Mole and the ship. Attempts to recover his body failed. Lieut.-Commander Bradford's action was one of absolute self-sacrifice; without a moments [sic] hesitation he went to certain death, recognizing that in such action lay the only possible chance of securing *Iris II* and enabling her storming parties to land.

Lieutenant-Commander Bradford died on his thirty-first birthday. Lieutenant Hawkins, who was with him, was also killed.

To keep the *Vindictive* hard against the mole so the men could get off, Carpenter ordered the *Daffodil* to push against her. This meant that the men on board the *Daffodil* could not get ashore directly, though some of them scrambled over the *Vindictive*.

'Suddenly the thing happened for which we had been, semi-consciously, waiting,' said Captain Carpenter. 'There was a tremendous roar, and up went a huge tower of flame and debris and bodies into the black sky! My fellows cheered like mad, for they knew what it meant.'

One of the ancient submarines that had been sent with the armada had blown up the three-hundred-foot steel viaduct that connected the mole to the causeway along the shore. Hundreds of German soldiers had been standing on it, watching the *Vindictive*, *Iris* and *Daffodil* being pummelled.

'They paid for their curiosity,' said Captain Carpenter.

The submarine, *C3*, was commanded by twenty-six-year-old Lieutenant Richard Sandford. He had called the crew up onto the bridge, then rammed the submarine into the superstructure of the viaduct. The Germans above thought there was no escape for the crew and they were to all intents and purposes already prisoners. But as the crew climbed into the skiff, Sandford went below to light three timed fuses. The men on the skiff waited with bated breath. According to Leading Seaman Cleaver:

> The shouting on the mole above increased. There was the clatter of rifles. At last we saw the figure of our commander. He was hurrying along the deck towards us bending low.
>
> 'Come on, sir,' we yelled in chorus. There was a fusillade of rifle bullets from the mole that whizzed menacingly past our heads. 'Everything OK,' said Lieutenant Sandford as breathlessly he jumped aboard the skiff. He told us afterwards that his delay

was due to difficulty in lighting the fuses. He had also seen that all the lights were out.

It was now that we were faced with a fresh problem. Roxburgh announced that the propeller of the skiff was permanently out of action. It was an awful situation. In less than three minutes the first of the fuses to be lit if it functioned would reach the charge in the bows and destroy the viaduct and every living thing in the vicinity.

'The oars!' shouted someone. Bendall and Harner grabbed them from the bottom of the skiff and began to pull madly away from the mole. Less than two minutes to go now probably. And still the rifles cracked and bullets whistled all around. 'They couldn't hit a pussy cat,' said Lieutenant Sandford derisively. And at that moment he sank back, wounded in the leg. What frantic strokes Bendall and Harner were making. One hundred yards! One hundred and fifty yards!

Bendall rolled over with a groan. He was wounded in the thigh. I took his place with the oars. By this time the boat had been hit several times and was leaking badly. Roxburgh and Lieutenant Howell-Price were having a busy time with the hand pumps. Had it not been for them the boat would undoubtedly have sunk. And then it was as though Heaven came to meet Earth in one momentary upheaval… *C3* and the viaduct were no more. Great chunks of masonry fell in the water all around us. The boat rocked and swayed as though possessed. Flames shot up to a tremendous height. In their glare was visible a great break in the mole.

Sandford was hit in the hand and leg. Others were injured, but none of the crew were killed. They were picked up by a picket boat offshore and survived.

Lieutenant Sandford was awarded the VC. The citation read:

On 22/23 April 1918 at Zeebrugge, Belgium, Lieutenant Sandford commanding HM Submarine *C.3*, skilfully placed the vessel between the piles of the viaduct which connected the Mole with the shore, before laying his fuse and abandoning her. He disdained to use the gyro steering which would have enabled him and his crew to abandon [sic] the submarine at a safe distance, but preferred to make sure that his mission would be successful.

Eleven days after the Armistice, Sandford's last command, the submarine HMS *G11*, was wrecked on the rocks off Howick, Northumberland. The following day he died of typhoid fever at Eston Hospital in North Yorkshire.

The survivors from the explosion on the viaduct were stunned.

'Many of the seamen and Marines had landed on the mole and were making fine play with the astonished Germans,' said Carpenter. 'Some went right to the head of the Mole and found the guns deserted. One gun, I must tell you, had not even been uncovered, which is clear proof that the garrison was taken by surprise. Others were chasing the enemy all down the Mole towards the viaduct, which they were never to cross, and some went into the shed and dealt with such people as they found.'

The *Vindictive* was still under fire. Its only defence was a steel nest of guns above the bridge. This was the only weapons platform that was above the level of the mole. In it were Lieutenant Rigby and twenty-seven-year-old Sergeant Norman Finch. They were armed with a Lewis gun and a two-pounder pom-pom, and engaged two destroyers on the other side of the mole and swept the breakwater.

'The men in the fighting-top were also doing fell work,' said Captain Carpenter. 'All along the mole, you see, and close under the fifteen-foot parapet, there are dug-outs or funk-holes. At first the Huns popped into these, but by-and-by it occurred to them that they would certainly be found and spitted if they stayed there, so the bright idea occurred to them of nipping across the mole and dropping down the side into their own destroyers lying there. An excellent scheme but for our fellows in the fighting-top, who picked them off with their Lewis guns as they ran.

'Those chaps in the fighting-top had to pay for it, though, in the end. They were attracting a lot of attention, and the Huns were constantly trying to drop a shell among them. They succeeded at last, I'm sorry to say, and laid out every man jack but one – Sergeant Finch. He was wounded badly, but dragged himself out from under the bodies of his pals and went on working his little gun until he couldn't work it any longer.'

Lieutenant Hilton-Young was in the starboard battery.

'I heard the guns there still bursting out at regular intervals into their mad barking,' he recalled. 'But soon there came a crash and a shower of sparks, and silence followed it. They are all gone, I said to myself; but in a minute or two a single gun in the top broke out again, and barked and barked. Then there was another crash, and the silence of the top became unbroken. Words cannot tell with what a glow of pride and exultation one heard that last gun speak. It seemed impossible that there should be anyone left alive in the top after the first shell struck it, and when the gun spoke again it seemed as if the very dead could not be driven from their duty. We learned afterwards that the first shell killed Rigby and all his crew except the sergeant. The sergeant was severely wounded, but he managed to get a gun back into action before the second shell struck, wounding him again, and putting his gun out of action.'

Wounded in the hand and leg, Sergeant Finch found himself under a heap of bodies.

'We all went down in a bunch,' said Finch, 'and I had a job to get out from underneath.'

Sergeant Finch tried to get one of his wounded pals down onto the deck, but was too dazed to be of much use. He was eventually rescued by Commander Edward Osbourne and Leading Seaman Childs.

His VC was gazetted on 23 July 1918. The citation read:

For most conspicuous gallantry. Sergeant Finch was second in command of the pompoms and Lewis guns in the foretop of Vindictive, under Lieutenant Charles N. B. Rigby, R.M.A. At one period the Vindictive was being hit every few seconds, chiefly in the upper works, from which splinters caused many casualties. It was difficult to locate the guns which were doing the most damage, but Lieutenant Rigby, Sergeant Finch and the Marines in the foretop, kept up a continuous fire with pompoms and Lewis guns, changing rapidly from one target to another, and thus keeping the enemy's fire down to some considerable extent. Unfortunately two heavy shells made direct hits on the foretop, which was completely exposed to enemy concentration of fire. All in the top were killed or disabled except Sergeant Finch, who was, however, severely wounded; nevertheless he showed consummate bravery, remaining in his battered and exposed position. He once more got a Lewis gun into action, and kept up a continuous fire, harassing the enemy on the mole, until the foretop received another direct hit, the remainder of the armament being then completely put out of action. Before the top was destroyed Sergeant Finch had done invaluable work, and by his bravery undoubtedly saved many lives. This very gallant sergeant of the Royal Marine Artillery was selected by the 4th Battalion of Royal Marines, who were mostly Royal Marine Light Infantry, to receive the Victoria Cross under Rule 13 of the Royal Warrant dated 29th January, 1856.

Finch left the Royal Marines as a Quartermaster Sergeant in 1929. In World War II, he rejoined as a Store Keeper Officer with the rank of lieutenant and served until 1945, later becoming a Divisional Sergeant Major the Yeoman of the Guard. His Victoria Cross is on display at the Royal Marines Museum, Eastney Barracks, Southsea, Hampshire.

Teenage hero Able Seaman McKenzie and Leading Seaman W. Childs had been recruited together from HMS *Neptune*. They had trained together and found themselves in the same four-man Lewis-gun team. McKenzie was No. 1, while Childs was No. 3 ammunition carrier. The other two men were Able Seaman Frank White and Ordinary Seaman E. Ryan from HMS *St Vincent*. With a team of wire cutters, rifle grenadiers and bomb throwers, they formed No. 1 Section of B Company under the command of Lieutenant Chamberlain.

Once ashore, they were to support A Company in their assault on the 4.1-inch gun battery that threatened the blockships' approach. But Lieutenant Chamberlain was already dead and his second-in-command badly wounded. Childs and McKenzie were already injured and Childs had been knocked silly when a bullet struck his helmet. Nevertheless, when someone yelled 'Over the top', they ran for it.

McKenzie was a strapping lad but, carrying his Lewis gun, ammunition, spare parts and a gas mask, he was weighed down with a hundred pounds of gear. The men ran towards the end of the mole, dropping down after fifty yards to fire upon some heavy guns.

Ahead, Lieutenant-Commander Adams was leading A Company towards enemy positions at the mole head. They were met with machine-gun fire and several men were hit. Adams went back to get his Lewis-gun team, but found them all dead except for Able Seaman William Lodwick, and the Lewis gun was out of ammunition.

Childs and McKenzie were quickly seconded. As Adams headed down the mole again, McKenzie supported him with heavy busts of fire – to little effect. A Company were down to six men, while B Company consisted only of Childs, McKenzie who had been wounded again, and three others. The Lewis gun had been smashed and they were pinned down by machine-gun and pom-pom fire.

Lieutenant-Commander Harrison arrived. He had been wounded in the face and his jaw was shattered. Adams went to try and find some Royal Marines. Then he heard the *Vindictive* siren, recalling the landing party. He headed back to look for stragglers, finding only one – Leading Seaman George Bush, an Australian. Bush told him that Harrison had led another rush towards the end of the mole and had been killed by machine-gun fire. Bush thought he was the sole survivor of the party, but Able Seaman Harold Eves, though badly wounded, had also survived. Both Bush and Eves were awarded the Distinguished Service Medal.

Lieutenant-Commander Harrison was posthumously awarded the VC. The citation read:

For most conspicuous gallantry at Zeebrugge on the night of the 22nd–23rd April, 1918. This officer was in immediate command of the Naval Storming Parties embarked in 'Vindictive'. Immediately before coming alongside the Mole Lieut.-Commander Harrison was struck on the head by a fragment of a shell which broke his jaw and knocked him senseless. Recovering consciousness he proceeded on to the Mole and took over command of his party, who were attacking the seaward end of the Mole. The silencing of the guns on the Mole head was of the first importance, and though in a position fully exposed to the enemy's machine-gun fire Lieut.-Commander Harrison gathered his men together and led them to the attack. He was killed at the head of his men, all of whom were either killed or wounded. Lieut.-Commander Harrison, though already severely wounded and undoubtedly in great pain, displayed indomitable resolution and courage of the highest order in pressing his attack, knowing as he did that any delay in silencing the guns might jeopardize the main object of the expedition, i.e., the blocking of the Zeebrugge-Bruges Canal.

McKenzie and Childs had made it back to the *Vindictive* and McKenzie wrote to his brother about the action.

'Well, we got within about fifteen minutes' run of the mole, when some marines got excited and fired their rifles,' he said. 'Up went four big star shells, and they spotted us… They hit us with the first two shells and killed seven marines. They were still hitting us when we got alongside… I tucked the old Lewis gun under my arm and nipped over the gangway aft… I turned to my left and advanced about 50 yards and then lay down. There was a spiral staircase which led down into the mole, and Commander Brock fired his revolver down and dropped a Mills'. You ought to have seen them nip out and try to get across to the destroyer tied up against the mole, but this little chicken met them half way with the box of tricks, and I ticked about a dozen off before I clicked. My Lewis gun was shot spinning out of my hands, and all I had left was the stock and pistol grip which I kindly took a bloke's photo with who looked too business-like for me with a rifle and a bayonet. It half stunned him, and gave me time to get out my pistol and finish him off. I then found a rifle and bayonet, and joined up our crowd who had just come off the destroyer. All I remember was pushing, kicking and kneeing every German who got in the way. When I was finished I couldn't climb the ladder, so a mate of mine lifted me up and carried me up the ladder, and then I crawled on my hands and knees inboard.'

Childs said that McKenzie's Lewis gun was 'doing glorious work' when it was hit. They threw the remaining ammunition drums in the sea. Childs grabbed and McKenzie drew his revolver.

'This was better than nothing,' said Childs, 'so we opened fire on some Germans who were escaping from shelters underneath us, and were trying to reach the destroyers on the opposite side of the mole. Had these Germans remained where they were they would in all probability be alive now, but panic reigned among them, and they were shot down or bayoneted. We now advanced further, and came across a concrete sentry box. In here were some Germans who made a rush for it. In making a point with my bayonet at one of them, my blade finished up like a corkscrew.'

Another of the men making his way back to the *Vindictive* was thirty-year-old Captain Edward Bamford. He had joined the Navy in 1905 at the age of seventeen and had served as a gunnery officer before transferring to the 4th Royal Marines. He had been on the *Chester* at Jutland with Jack Cornwell, winning a DSO. His younger brother Arthur enlisted as a private in the Grenadier Guards and was killed near Loos on 11 October 1915.

Edward was commanding B Company of the 4th Royal Marines. His first words to them when he took command were: 'Well, fellows, if you will be right with me, I'll be right with you.'

B Company were to follow C Company ashore and secure the ammunition dumps, shelters and sheds along the mole until A Company moved through them to secure the rest of it. As it was A Company failed to get ashore from *Iris II* and the *Vindictive* was a quarter of a mile west of where she should have been. In the rapid reorganisation, B Company found themselves leading the attack.

Bamford went ashore with No. 5 platoon, commanded by Lieutenant T.F.V. Cooke.

'With Lieutenant Cooke's platoon I moved along the upper promenade of the mole, to quiet some snipers who were disturbing the landing of the remainder,' said Captain Bamford. 'We came abreast the spot where the *Iris* was trying to get alongside, and hailed her. She replied with loud cheers, but it was clear she would never get close enough to the mole to land her men, and when I last saw her she had shoved off and was being badly shelled with tracer shell. Lieutenant Cooke was shot in the head at my side, just before 12.15 am, when the submarine blew up the shore end of the mole…'

Other accounts say this happened some five minutes later.

'…The blockships could now be seen stealing across the harbour towards the canal entrance,' continued Captain Bamford, 'and did not appear to be receiving much attention from the Huns. I climbed down the scaling ladders abreast *Vindictive*, having withdrawn the men from the right, and crossing the mole collected men of the 7th and 8th Platoons, and with a few of the 5th started an assault against the batteries at the seaward end of the mole. This was interrupted by the general recall (Ks on the siren), and we returned to the ship, crossing the mole in small parties, so as not to clog the ladders, which were under heavy fire from the shore batteries.'

Their losses were heavy. Nevertheless, the battalion's adjutant, Captain Arthur Chater, recalled that Bamford's 'totally unperturbed manner had the most reassuring effect on all who came in contact with him that night'.

The German losses were heavy too. Marine James Feeney with the 7th Platoon said: 'There was a group of bodies at the foot of the ladders – all Germans – who tried to knock the ladders, and among them three men in white ducks. The light was wonderful. I don't believe there was ever such a firework display. The German star shells, that light up the sea and land for miles, were terrible in their effective grandeur. I ran across to the dump-house opposite the ship, and took cover by lying on the ground. The ground floor of the dump-house was raised about 2½ ft over the roadway, and had a pathway like as if carts were loaded there, like at a railway goods store. We had a grand chance of chucking bombs in the doors of this dump-house, as we had splendid cover.'

Chater caught up with Bamford there.

'Together we discussed the situation,' said Chater. 'Our battalion plan had been based on the assumption that *Vindictive* would be put alongside some 400 yards from the end of the mole. All those men who belonged to units, which were to have attacked the fortified zone, therefore, now found themselves at No. 3 shed. No attack on the fortified zone had yet been made. As this was our principle objective, we decided to organise an attack along the mole. This entailed attacking a prepared position across some 200 yards of flat pavement devoid of any form of cover.'

It was clear to Bamford that it was his duty to lead the charge though he knew there was little chance of survival.

'Captain Bamford came up, and said, quite cool, "Fall in, B Company",' Marine Feeney said. 'I fell in with McDowell, and Sergeant Brady took charge of us. There were only sixteen there, and Captain Bamford was leading us along, when he looked back to see how many he had, and apparently he thought we were insufficient, as he told the sergeant to retire to the ship.'

Actually, though they were few in number, it was the siren from the ship that led him to return. This was no easy task as Bamford's men were caught out in the open. They ran the gauntlet through a fire-swept zone, scrambled up the ladders to the parapet, fell over the railings, leapt onto the heaving gangways and landed back on board, Feeney said, 'nervous and funky from looking at the dead and listening to the dying'. Miraculously, Bamford made it back too. It was clear that they had achieved none of their objectives and had lost a lot of men, seemingly for nothing.

Captain Bamford won the VC for the action on the mole. The citation appeared in *The London Gazette* on 23 July 1918. It read:

For conspicuous gallantry at Zeebrugge. April 1918. This officer landed on the Mole from 'Vindictive' with Nos. 5, 7 & 8 platoons of the Marine Storming Force in the face of great difficulties. When on the Mole under heavy fire, he displayed the greatest initiative in the command of his company, and by his total disregard of danger, showed a magnificent example to his men. He first established a strong point on the right of the disembarkation, and when that was safe, led an assault on a battery to the left with the utmost coolness and valour. Captain Bamford was selected by the officers of the R.M.A. & R.M.L.I. detachments to receive the Victoria Cross under Rule 13 of the Royal Warrant, dated 26 January 1856.

Bamford survived the rest of the war and died of pneumonia on board HMS *Cumberland* on 30 September 1928 on his way to Hong Kong, where he was Instructor of Small Arms and Musketry Officer. He was buried in Bubbling Well Road Cemetery in Shanghai, which was destroyed during the Cultural Revolution of 1966–76.

What Bamford did not know when he managed to get back to the *Vindictive* was that, although the landing party had not wreaked the havoc they had intended, they had created enough of a diversion for the three blockships to reach the mouth of the canal.

The ancient cruisers – the *Thetis*, *Intrepid* and *Iphigenia* – filled with concrete were supposed to lodge themselves in the canal, then blow their bottoms out. The *Thetis* was to take the lead and ram the lock gates. But as the guns on the mole had not been taken out, the slow-moving vessel, weighed down by its load of concrete, invited concentrated fire. Hit along the waterline, she snagged on the steel netting that defended the entrance to the canal.

Shielded by the *Thetis*, the *Intrepid* sailed into the canal and manoeuvred into position. Following her was the *Iphigenia*, which had been hit twice. Steering blind through the smoke that now enveloped the canal, she rammed into a barge. Her twenty-two-year-old captain, Lieutenant Edward Billyard-Leake, said: 'As soon as I was clear of the barge I went ahead on both engines and sighted the *Intrepid* aground on the western bank with the gap between her bows and the eastern bank. I endeavoured to close this gap but collided with the port bow of *Intrepid* while turning.'

The force of the collision threatened to shove the *Intrepid* out of position, so her captain blew her scuttling charges immediately. Under heavy machine-gun fire, Lieutenant Billyard-Leake then manoeuvred the *Iphigenia* into position, gave the order 'Abandon ship' and scuttled her. The men from the three ships were now in boats in the water, raked by machine guns and shrapnel.

Following close behind the three blockships was Motor Launch *ML282*, commanded by Lieutenant Percy Dean of the Royal Navy Volunteer Reserve. He was forty and had been rejected by the Army as unfit.

In the midst of the maelstrom, he pulled up alongside the *Iphigenia's* overloaded cutter, which was dangerously low in the water.

'The majority of the crew managed to get into the motor launch, which then went astern,' said Lieutenant Billyard-Leake. 'The remainder pulled round the stern and the ML came up and picked them up. I was the last to leave the cutter and to the best of my knowledge only three hands were left in her, one of whom was killed.'

The *Intrepid's* skiff also pulled alongside and the survivors scrambled on board. By then, there were over a hundred men crammed on her foredeck. Only the intervention of an officer who got them to spread out stopped *ML282* capsizing. With the motor launch threatened with sinking, Lieutenant Dean stopped any more men getting on board from the *Iphigenia's* cutter and tied it to the stern.

Oily water lapped over the bows of the motor launch as it made its way slowly back across the harbour under intense fire. One after the other, three steersmen standing beside Lieutenant Dean were hit, two fatally.

Suddenly, the enemy gunners were distracted by a distress flare; it had been fired by the captain and six officers on board a life raft. The flare attracted fire on them and they jumped overboard. Lieutenant Dean turned back in what seemed like a futile attempt to rescue them. Despite the intense fire from all the guns around the harbour, he managed to pick up the six officers. The captain, Lieutenant Stuart Bonham-Carter, was missed, but he managed to grab a rope and was towed through the water for some way until one of the crew noticed him. By then he was exhausted and let go of the rope.

Luck was with him, though. A star shell burst overheard. In the bright light, Lieutenant Dean spotted his head above the water. Returning to get him, the steering gear jammed and Dean had to steer the boat using the engines.

As they had to run under the guns at the end of the mole, Dean went in so close that the guns could not be depressed enough to fire on the launch. He recalled looking up to see the frustrated German gunners immediately above him, while the crew fired revolvers at them.

Once clear of the harbour the *ML282* still had to make it home. There was a fire in the aft and the fumes had suffocated some of the men they had rescued. It was suggested they put in at Flushing and accept interment in neutral Holland. But the fire was extinguished and they pressed on.

They came upon HMS *Warwick*, Keyes's flagship for the operation, and transferred the survivors. *ML282* made it back to Dover. Dean was the only man on board who had not been killed or wounded. He was awarded the VC. The citation read:

For most conspicuous gallantry. Lieutenant Dean handled his boat in a most magnificent and heroic manner when embarking the officers and men from the blockships at Zeebrugge. He followed the blockships in and closed 'Intrepid' and 'Iphigenia' under a constant and deadly fire from machine and heavy guns at point blank range, embarking over 100 officers and men. This completed, he was proceeding out of the canal, when he heard that an officer was in the water. He returned, rescued him, and then proceeded, handling his boat throughout as calmly as if engaged in a practice manoeuvre. Three men were shot down at his side while he conned his ship. On clearing the entrance to the canal the steering gear broke down. He manoeuvred his boat by the engines, and avoided complete destruction by steering so close in under the mole that the guns in the batteries could not depress sufficiently to fire on the boat. The whole of this operation was carried out under a constant machine-gun fire at a few yards range. It was solely due to this officer's courage and daring that ML282 succeeded in saving so many valuable lives.

Dean was later promoted to Lieutenant-Commander and was elected MP for Blackburn in the General Election of 1918.

When Lieutenant Dean docked in Dover, he found that the *Vindictive* had reached home too, even though she had five-foot holes torn in her sides. On board was Captain Carpenter, who had escaped death twice as the *Vindictive* pulled clear of the mole. A shell landed among boxes of Stokes bombs, causing a fire that his chief quartermaster stamped out. Another shell burst near him, causing a deep flesh wound in his shoulder – though he described it as 'very slight'. Other gashes in his cap, uniform and binoculars case showed that he had been very lucky to survive.

He was awarded the VC. Gazetted on 23 July 1918, the citation read:

> For most conspicuous gallantry. This officer was in command of 'Vindictive'. He set a magnificent example to all those under his command by his calm composure when navigating mined waters, bringing his ship alongside the mole in darkness. When 'Vindictive' was within a few yards of the mole the enemy started and maintained a heavy fire from batteries, machine guns and rifles on to the bridge. He showed most conspicuous bravery, and did much to encourage similar behaviour on the part of the crew, supervising the landing from the 'Vindictive' on to the mole, and walking round the decks directing operations and encouraging the men in the most dangerous and exposed positions. By his encouragement to those under him, his power of command and personal bearing, he undoubtedly contributed greatly to the success of the operation. Capt. Carpenter was selected by the officers of the 'Vindictive', 'Iris II', and 'Daffodil', and of the naval assaulting force to receive the Victoria Cross under Rule 13 of the Royal Warrant, dated the 29th January, 1856.

Carpenter retired from the Navy as a vice-admiral in 1934. During World War II he commanded the Wye Valley section of the Gloucestershire Home Guard.

After the Zeebrugge Raid, Carpenter was asked by Keyes to make recommendations for conspicuous gallantry, but he refused to do so. The matter was settled by ballot. One officer and one rating would be selected. Though he refused to participate, Carpenter won by a single vote.

The sailors from the *Vindictive*, *Iris* and *Daffodil* also held their ballot and chose the critically wounded Albert McKenzie to represent them.

His VC was gazetted on 22 July 1918 and the citation read:

> The King has been graciously pleased to approve the award of the Victoria Cross to Able Seamen Albert Edward McKenzie O.N. J 331736 (Ch) Royal Navy for most conspicuous gallantry. This rating belonged to B Company of the seamen storming party. On the night of the operation he landed on the Mole with his machine gun in the face of great difficulties and did very good work, using his gun to the utmost advantage. He advanced down the Mole with Lt Commander Harrison, who with most of his party was killed, and accounted for several of the enemy running from shelter to a destroyer alongside the Mole. This very gallant seaman was severely wounded while working his gun in an exposed position. Able Seaman McKenzie was selected by the seaman of the Vindictive, Iris and Daffodil and of the naval assaulting force to receive the Victoria Cross under rule 13 of the Royal Warrant dated 29th January 1855.

After the *Vindictive* had docked in Dover, McKenzie was taken by train straight to the Royal Naval Hospital in Chatham, Kent. He was treated for his wounds and began to make a good recovery.

By the summer, he was up and about on crutches and was well enough to travel to London – apparently the hero of Zeebrugge was to have his portrait painted by order of the Navy Board.

Albert Edward McKenzie had been born on 23 October 1898 at 10 Alice Street, Bermondsey, south-east London, the youngest of a large family. He was still an infant when his father, a photographer, died and his widowed mother moved to Shorncliffe Road, off the Old Kent Road in Bermondsey. Educated at London County Council schools in Webb Street, Bermondsey, and Mina Road, Southwark, he attended St Mark's Sunday School in Camberwell. This parish would supply 4,286 men for the country's armed forces, the largest number of any London parish. More than five hundred of 'St Mark's Little Army' would lose their lives before the end of the war.

Enlisting in the Royal Navy at the age of fifteen, he joined the training ship *Arethusa* at Greenhithe in 1913. Just five-foot two, he was an athlete and won numerous trophies for football and boxing. He left the *Arethusa* as a Boy Second Class in June 1914 and made Boy First Class by Christmas. Promoted to Able Seaman on 23 April 1916, he served on minesweepers, patrol boats and convoy escorts until he was sent to the battleship HMS *Neptune* with the Grand Fleet at Scapa Flow.

In 1918, Lieutenant Arthur Chamberlain was looking for volunteers for a 'secret stunt'. The first he picked was Leading Seaman Childs. By then the lightweight boxing champion of the 4th Battle Cruiser Squadron, MacKenzie, who had just spent seven days in the brig for some unknown offence, also volunteered. They were told that they would be lucky to return alive. He was one of eight lads from the *Arethusa* to sail on the *Vindictive*. The other seven won DSMs.

On 31 July 1918, Albert went to Buckingham Palace with his sister and mother, who had already lost one son in the war. Along with all the other Zeebrugge heroes, McKenzie was presented with his VC by George V. After his investiture he went back to his mother's house in Shorncliffe Road to a hero's welcome. The house was a blaze of colour with flags and bunting. On the doorstep, he was welcomed by the Mayor of Southwark, who said McKenzie was the first London sailor to win the VC – and the first to be awarded it by the votes of his comrades. The Mayor then held up Albert's bloodstained uniform and smashed wristwatch for the crowd. His mother was given War Bonds and an illuminated address.

Late in 1918 Albert McKenzie was still recovering from his wounds at Chatham Naval Hospital. Despite developing septic poisoning in his wounded foot, his recovery was progressing well. But he was still vulnerable to infection and when the world influenza pandemic hit on October 1918 he had little resistance. He developed pneumonia and died on 3 November, ten days after his twentieth birthday and one week before the Armistice. His body was taken from Chatham back to London for a magnificent funeral.

T.J. Macnamara MP, Financial Secretary to the Admiralty, and Captain Carpenter VC of the *Vindictive* were present and a message from the King and Queen was read to the mourners. It said: 'In the special circumstances of Able Seamen Albert Edward McKenzie's lamentable death and the fact of his being a VC and the first London sailor to receive that most honourable reward, you are authorized to express at the public funeral at St Mark's Camberwell the sympathy of their Majesties with the widowed mother and family. Their majesties were grieved to hear of his untimely death and to think that he had been spared so short a time to wear the proud decoration which he so nobly won.'

Captain Carpenter told Albert's mother: 'The splendid example which your boy set at Zeebrugge will be accorded a high place of honour in the navel records of the British Empire.'

Dr Macnamara added: 'Mrs McKenzie has lost a son but the nation has found a hero.'

Albert McKenzie was buried in Camberwell Old Cemetery. The plot was donated by the local council '…in consideration of the gallant services rendered to his King and country by Seamen McKenzie VC son of Eliza – By Resolution of Public Services Committee November 1918'. A year later, the Mayor of Southwark added a headstone, which bore the legend: 'Albert McKenzie died nobly; we perpetuate his name; God bless him!'

McKenzie's VC is on display in the Imperial War Museum.

Though Able Seaman McKenzie's sacrifice was indeed noble, the raid had not been a success. The blockships had not been positioned correctly. The Germans simply removed two piers along the western bank of the canal, dredged a fresh channel through the silt around the sterns of the *Iphigena* and *Intrepid*, and within a week submarines were entering and leaving again.

In the raid, the Royal Navy had lost 227 dead, 356 wounded and one destroyer sunk; Germany losses were eight dead, sixteen wounded. However, in the press, the Zeebrugge raid trumpeted as a huge success and it raised the morale of a war-weary nation.

On the same night as the raid on Zeebrugge, more young men were sent to Ostend to block the canal there too. The fleet arrived off the port shortly before midnight. But when they went in, a strong wind blew the smokescreen back at the advancing cruisers, blinding their commanders. In the face of withering fire, HMS *Brilliant* ran aground and HMS *Sirius* ran into the back of her. The survivors abandoned ship while the scuttle charges were set, leaving the blockship stuck fast one-and-a-half miles east of where they should have been.

Commanding *ML276*, Lieutenant Rowley Bourke, a thirty-two-year old Canadian who had been rejected by the Canadian Army because of his poor eyesight, went in three times under heavy fire from machine guns and the shore battery to take off the last of the men, including the captain of the *Brilliant*, Commander Alfred Godsal, and his first lieutenant, twenty-four-year-old Victor Crutchley. With another thirty-eight officers and men on board and towing a crippled launch, Lieutenant Bourke got his motor launch back to Allied-held Dunkirk after twelve hours on the bridge without a break and was awarded the DSO.

The attack had been a disaster. Nevertheless, the Navy were determined to try again the following month. Despite the damage she had sustained at Zeebrugge, the *Vindictive* would be patched up and given one last outing, this time as a blockship with two hundred tons of concrete and rubble on board. Godsal was given command, again with Crutchley as first lieutenant. Lieutenant Bourke volunteered to command the rescue launch again, but *ML276* was still being repaired and *ML254* under Lieutenant Geoffrey Drummond, who had been in charge of one of the smoke units on the first raid, was selected instead. However, when the operation was delayed, *ML274* was back in action and came along as a standby boat.

The armada set out in near-perfect weather on the evening of 9 May. However, just before midnight, the second blockship, *Sappho*, blew a boiler and limped back to Dunkirk. Nearing Ostend, Drummond served the men of *ML254* a tot of whisky.

'We didn't have rum for some occult reason,' he said. 'Then I ordered gas masks and started putting my own on, which stuck and blinded me for a few moments. During that time there was a crash and we had been rammed by another ML. I sent a hand forward to see if the fo'c's'le had been damaged. He, wishing to carry on, gave me a report that all was well. I don't think from after events that this can have been quite true. However, we did; but by that time all trace of the fleet was lost. I saw a double flashing light and made for it. However, I very soon found by my watch that it was too far east and I turned straight inshore and was lucky enough to spot the eastern smoke unit. Knowing the bearing they were working on I was able to set a course for my proper station on the position of the Stroom Bank buoy. Just as I got there the *Vindictive* loomed up, going all out. I wrenched my helm over and rang for full speed, but it was all we could do to keep her in sight.'

At 01.35 on 10 May, the smokescreen started. Eight minutes later, the bombardment began and torpedoes fired from the motor launches demolished the ends of the piers marking the entrance to the canal. Then the signal was given for ten heavy bombers of the newly formed Royal Air Force to start dropping incendiaries.

Suddenly the weather closed in. The sky was overcast and, just as Godsal was beginning his run in, a thick sea fog came up. He sailed past the entrance to the harbour twice without seeing it. On a third pass, he spotted it, but a shore battery also spotted the *Vindictive* and began heavy, accurate fire. Shells repeatedly crashed into the superstructure.

Entering the harbour, Commander Godsal stepped out on deck to check their position. A shell burst near him and he was never seen again. Momentarily dazed by the blast, Lieutenant Crutchley took command.

'I ordered the port telegraph to full speed astern to try to swing the ship across the channel,' he said. 'She grounded forward on the eastern pier when at an angle of about three points to the pier. As the ship stopped swinging and at the time I considered that no more could be done, I ordered the ship to be abandoned.'

The *Vindictive* was now stuck on a sandbank, only partly blocking the entrance to the channel. The propellers, already damaged at Zeebrugge, were unable to pull her off. Engineer Lieutenant-Commander William Bury, *Vindictive*'s engineer at Zeebrugge, was below in the stokeholds.

'There was a fearful din on the upper deck,' he said. 'The machine-gun bullets were making a noise like pneumatic caulkers. Several of our people never got further than the escape doors, and all made for the cutters, which were just touching the water. Seeing that the ship was not slewing, and also there was a danger of the falling funnels and things cutting the electric leads, I made my way aft, to the dynamo-exploders, and fired the after mines. Several portions of the port engine shot up into the air, and the poor old ship sat down on the mud with a loud crash, at an angle of about 30 degrees to the pier, where her bows touched, and on a fairly even keel. Then I got down the sea gangway and into a cutter, which was all splintered by a pom-pom or something, and to my intense surprise and relief, saw there was a motor launch alongside, and scrambled over her bows somehow.'

Seeing the *Vindictive* through the murk, Drummond moved in with *ML254* and immediately became a target for the shore batteries.

'All the shells that didn't hit exploded on the bottom,' he said. 'On one occasion I was blown off my feet by a shell bursting alongside. The fireworks were amazing and very pretty; the star shells were red, green, blue and yellow. And then there were the "flaming onions" as we called them [small calibre projectiles calibrated together in groups of twenty-five on the same trajectory]. I got one string along my bridge. It took off the back of my right handrail, broke everything there, signal lamps, switches, etc., but by the mercy of Providence the compass and its light and the telegraph handles and chains were untouched. Shortly after that, a four-inch burst just by the mast. Number One [Lieutenant Gordon Ross, Bourke's replacement and another Canadian] at that moment had left his torpedo-mat fort to get some trays of Lewis gun ammunition, which we had stacked by the mast, and it killed him outright, also the relief coxswain standing alongside me, chipped the coxswain's hand and I got 2½ inches of copper driving band into the back of my left thigh.'

As *ML254* passed the pier head, Drummond was hit again. A piece of shrapnel lodged in his chest. Weak from loss of blood, he had to rip open the canvas roof of the bridge and put his head out to see, operating the controls with his feet.

Crutchley blew the forward scuttling charges, then, as bullets sparked around him, he went to look for Godsal. Once he was sure that no one was left alive, he jumped down onto Drummond's *ML254*, which was so overloaded with survivors her bows were almost awash.

As *ML254* turned to go, someone called out that there was a man in the water. Drummond stopped abruptly. At that moment, *ML276* came round the stern of the *Vindictive* and crashed into him.

With the crew choking on the artificial fog, *ML276* had been following the *Vindictive* in, only to lose her in the smokescreen. Then they glimpsed her 'surrounded by columns of water' made by the shells falling all around her.

'We dash across to her, lose her, find her again, again to lose her in a maze of turnings in the patchy smoke,' said Sub-Lieutenant James Petrie. 'Crash! A grinding forward and a terrific impact throws us to the deck. We have "rammed" the eastern arm of the pier but fifty yards from the beach. As we back out a shell explodes on our forecastle and our splendid coxswain goes west.'

Petrie took the wheel, before manning the Lewis gun to take out the lights of the lighthouses the shore batteries were using to get range on the attackers.

After dumping onto *ML254*, Bourke shouted across, asking if anyone was left behind from the *Vindictive*. Crutchley replied that everyone was safe. Bourke did not hear him and ploughed on anyway.

'I thought someone might have been overlooked so went into the harbour and turned, shouting to see if I could get a reply,' Bourke said. 'We thought we heard someone but could not be sure and then, as we heard nothing, started out of the harbour, and again we thought we heard someone, so put back. We could not, however, locate where the shouting came from and thought it might be the wily Hun trying to detain us till we were quite done in, so started out again.'

Bourke returned three times through heavy fire. His boat was shot to pieces, once taking a direct hit by a six-inch shell. Nevertheless, on the fourth attempt, they found where the shouting had been coming from. The *Vindictive*'s wounded navigator, Lieutenant John Alleyne, and two seamen were clinging to an upturned boat under one of the shore batteries. *ML276* braved the pummelling of the pom-pom and machine-gun fire, hauled the survivors on board, then made off at full speed, chased by tracer.

Despite being hit again by a shell that knocked out the compressed air tank and exploded in the engine room, they made it out of the harbour. Inspecting the damage, Bourke said: 'My port acid tank had again been pierced and as my hose had been shot away I could not sluice the acid overboard so that about twelve hours after leaving Ostend it had eaten its way through the deck into the after cabin and, on contact with water in bilges, started to smoke. Lieutenant Alleyne was on a bed in the after cabin, badly wounded, so I went below to get him up before he was gassed. At this minute a monitor was reported, so I decided to go alongside and put my wounded and gassed men aboard her. I went alongside her blister and her men waded over, carrying the surgeon, who superintended the removal of the wounded slung in stretchers. We then had to be towed on account of having no air to start engines again.'

Out at sea *ML254* was so heavily laden waves were breaking over her bows and she was making slow progress.

'The forecastle was full up to the top rung of the ladder,' said Drummond. 'The wardroom was burning merrily aft, a pom-pom having landed in one of the bunks, and although we only had about 150 gallons of petrol instead of 2,000, it was right aft, only separated by a bit of galvanised iron from the fire.'

Crutchley organised parties to bail out the fo'c's'le and put out a fire that threatened to ignite the rest of the fuel. He also took a minute to put a tourniquet on Drummond's injured leg.

'I must have bled the best part of a gallon and a half,' Drummond said. There was a puddle, he claimed, on the deck, six foot across.

Using his electric torch, Drummond flashed out an SOS in Morse code. Eventually, it was answered by the *Warwick*. Coming alongside, they found Drummond still at the wheel and Crutchley waist-deep in water, still bailing.

Once the survivors were aboard the *Warwick*, she hit a mine and they had to be transferred to the *Velox*, which tied up alongside.

Arriving at Dunkirk, Bourke inspected his boat again. He found more than fifty-five holes in her. Sixteen were through the wheelhouse, but somehow he was unscathed. Despite being told that he might be in line for a decoration, Bourke headed off for five weeks' leave in Canada.

On 28 August 1918, Drummond, Bourke and Crutchley's VCs were gazetted. Drummond's citation read:

Lieut. Geoffrey H. Drummond, R.N.V.R. Volunteered for rescue work in command of ML254. Following 'Vindictive' to Ostend, when off the piers a shell burst on board, killing Lieutenant Gordon Ross and Deckhand J. Thomas, wounding the coxswain, and also severely wounding Lieutenant Drummond in three places. Notwithstanding his wounds he remained on the bridge, navigated his vessel, which was already seriously damaged by shell fire, into Ostend harbour, placed her alongside 'Vindictive', and took off two officers and thirty-eight men –some of whom were killed and many wounded while embarking. When informed that there was no one alive left on board he backed his vessel out clear of the piers before sinking exhausted from his wounds. When HMS *Warwick* fell in with ML254 off Ostend half an hour later, the latter was in a sinking condition. It was due to the indomitable courage of this very gallant officer that the majority of the crew of the 'Vindictive' were rescued.

Despite suffering severe wounds, Drummond returned to the Navy in World War II but died on 21 April 1941 from a fall. His VC is on display at the Imperial War Museum.

Bourke's citation read:

Lieut. Roland Bourke, D.S.O., R.N.V.R. (Canada). Volunteered for rescue work in command of ML276, and followed Vindictive into Ostend, engaging the enemy's machine guns on both piers with Lewis guns. After ML254 had backed out Lieutenant Bourke laid his vessel alongside Vindictive to make further search. Finding no one he withdrew, but hearing cries in the water he again entered the harbour, and after a prolonged search eventually found Lieutenant Sir John Alleyne and two ratings, all badly wounded, in the water, clinging to an upended skiff, and rescued them. During all this time the motor launch was under a very heavy fire at close range, being hit in fifty-five places, once by a 6 in. shell – two of her small crew being killed and others wounded. The vessel was seriously damaged and speed greatly reduced. Lieutenant Bourke, however, managed to bring her out and carry on until he fell in with a Monitor, which took him in tow. This episode displayed daring and skill of a very high order, and Lieutenant Bourke's bravery and perseverance undoubtedly saved the lives of Lieutenant Alleyne and two of the Vindictive's crew.

World War II found Bourke in the reserve. Initally, he served as a recruiting officer, but in 1941 he returned to sea with the Royal Canadian Navy Volunteer Reserve. He served as Commander of HMCS *Givenchy*, HMCS *Esquimalt*, and HMCS *Burrard*. In 1950 he ended his naval career in the rank of commander serving with the Royal Canadian Navy.

Crutchley's citation read:

Lieut. Victor A.C. Crutchley, D.S.C., R.N. This officer was in Brilliant in the unsuccessful attempt to block Ostend on the night of 22nd/23rd April, and at once volunteered for a further effort. He acted as 1st Lieut, of Vindictive, and worked with untiring energy fitting out that ship for further service. On the night of 9th/10th May, after his commanding officer had been killed and the second in command severely wounded, Lieut. Crutchley took command of Vindictive and did his utmost by manoeuvring the engines to place that ship in an effective position. He displayed great bravery both in the Vindictive and in ML254, which rescued the crew after the charges had been blown and the former vessel sunk between the piers of Ostend harbour, and did not himself leave the Vindictive until he had made a thorough search with an electric torch for survivors under a very heavy fire. Lieut. Crutchley took command of ML254 when the commanding officer sank exhausted from his wounds, the second in command having been killed. The vessel was full of wounded and very seriously damaged by shell fire, the fore part being flooded. With indomitable energy and by dint of baling with buckets and shifting weight aft, Lieut. Crutchley and the unwounded kept her afloat, but the leaks could not be kept under, and she was in a sinking condition, with her forecastle nearly awash when picked up by HMS Warwick. The bearing of this very gallant officer and fine seaman throughout these operations off the Belgian coast was altogether admirable and an inspiring example to all thrown in contact with him.

At the age of twenty-two, Crutchley had served on board the battleship HMS *Centurion* at the Battle of Jutland and in the final months of the war he served on HMS *Sikh* in the Dover Patrol. He remained in the Royal Navy, taking command of HMS *Warspite* in 1937.

At the outbreak of World War II, *Warspite* was assigned to the Home Fleet and fought at the Battle of Narvik. When Japan entered the war, he was promoted to rear admiral and transferred to the Royal Australian Navy, seeing action alongside the Americans at Guadalcanal and received the American Legion of Merit in the degree of Chief Commander.

SERGEANT JOHN MEIKLE, 19

SEAFORTH HIGHLANDERS

Marfaux, France, 20 July 1918

John Meikle was born in Kirkintilloch, Dunbartonshire, on 11 September 1898. He was the eldest-surviving son of eleven children, eight of whom lived into adulthood. The family moved to Nitshill, Renfrewshire. Educated at Levern Public School, he was a football fan and ran errands for Nitshill Victoria Football Club.

On leaving school, he went to work as a clerk at Nitshill railway station, then the property of the Glasgow, Barrhead and Kilmarnock Railway Company. His wages were seven shillings and six pence (37½p) a week. After the war broke out, he made several attempts to join the Army, but was rejected on the grounds that he was too young. He even took to asking his mother to make him extra porridge in the hope that his chest would expand. Finally, in February 1915, at the age of sixteen, he successfully enlisted in the Seaforth Highlanders.

After reporting to Maryhill Barracks in Glasgow, he was drafted into the 4th Battalion of the Seaforth Highlanders (Ross-shire Buffs)

Territorial Force. This later became part of the 154 Brigade of the 51st (Highland) Division. He was trained on the Lewis gun and remained in Scotland until July 1916 when, aged eighteen, he could join his battalion in France. Soon after arriving, he was promoted to corporal and he fought in the First Battle of the Somme.

Meikle had been in action for less than a month when he was bayoneted and taken out of the front lines. He was well enough to return to his unit in time to fight in the Battle of Arras in April 1917, where the 4th Seaforths captured several German trenches and took a large number of enemy prisoners. At Passchendaele he won the Military Medal, then fought on down the Menin Road.

Returning home on leave, he was presented with a gold watch at the Hurlet and Nitshill Public Hall. Already he had made his mark by carrying a heavy walking stick on the battlefield. But when he headed back to the front, he left his trademark stick behind. Fortunately his sister spotted the item, ran after him and gave it to him at the station. Back in France, Meikle was promoted to sergeant.

At the beginning of 1918, his battalion helped save the 51st Division by their stand east of the village of Beaumetz. But during the Spring Offensive the Germans advanced to the River Marne.

By the beginning of July, German prospects of victory in the West had never looked brighter. They had driven a great wedge into the Allied line at Château-Thierry. The British, they imagined, had not yet recovered from their hammering in front of Amiens and Hazebrouck.

The German Army took a brief respite. To complete their victory, they planned towards the end of the month to deliver a mighty blow at the bulge of the Lys Salient. This would finally smash the British armies in the north and open the route to Calais.

Field Marshal Douglas Haig was already considering heading for the Channel ports and evacuating the British Army, while the French commander General Philippe Pétain was planning the defence of Paris. For the Germans, victory lay in splitting the two armies.

To thwart the Germans, British Prime Minister David Lloyd George and the French Premier Georges Clemenceau decided to put their joint forces in the hands of Marshal Ferdinand Foch. They thought he was the only man who could take on the German General Erich Ludendorff, who had the military initiative and superior numbers.

They were right. Suddenly, on 18 July, Marshal Foch struck. An attack was launched against both shoulders of the Château-Thierry salient. A fortnight later, with the capture of Fismes, the whole salient had been flattened and the German dreams of victory had evaporated as ever-increasing numbers of Americans were on their way.

British soldiers had a large share in the honours of this battle, especially the divisions around Marfaux. Among them were the Scottish Highlanders of the 51st Division, men like Sergeant Meikle, who had already been tried and tested on many fields. These men had helped to break the Hindenburg Line in the Battle of Cambrai. At the end of March, they fought against tremendous odds from Boursies to Bapaume. At the beginning of April they helped to stem the tide that flowed down the Aubers Ridge. Now, in July, they took their place once more in the line near Marfaux, south-west of Rheims. Against them were massed the pick of German divisions, brought there for an intended drive towards Épernay.

On 19 July, Sergeant Meikle was with No. 2 Company in the valley of the River Ardre. The enemy were expected to cross the river there, take Rheims in a pincer movement, then move on to Paris.

257

That evening, they left the village of Champillon after receiving orders to enter the line at 08.00 hours the next morning. But in the dark they mistook Marfaux for Chaumuzy and found themselves too far over to the right. Other units also found themselves out of place.

As the front stabilised the following day, the Highlanders found themselves held up by machine guns. The 4th Seaforths held a ridge in the middle formation, but had to withdraw. At 16.30, the Germans counter-attacked and were repelled. There was a fierce bombardment around Rectangle Wood, but the brigade failed to take its objective and suffered heavy casualties.

Near Marfaux, No. 2 Company faced a machine-gun emplacement 150 yards to the front. Sergeant Meikle, armed only with a revolver and his heavy stick, rose from his place in the line, and ran forward alone across the bare stretch of bullet-swept ground towards the emplacement. By some miracle he reached it alive and leapt down over the parapet into the midst of the enemy.

He killed many of them with his revolver. When that was empty, he laid about them with his stick. As the Germans came down upon him with their bayonets, Meikle felled them one after the other.

When they were all dead, Sergeant Meikle jumped to the top of the emplacement, waving his stick and shouting to his platoon to advance.

A little while later, the progress of the company was again checked by machine-gun fire. Once again Sergeant Meikle staked his own life to save the lives of his men. Snatching up the rifle and bayonet of a dead comrade, he dashed out across the open in full view of the Germans.

This time he was not so lucky. The gun's crew shot him dead on the very threshold of the emplacement, but two of his men, who were following closely behind him, killed the Germans and destroyed their gun.

Two days later, the Seaforths participated in the liberation of the Marne district and the rout of the Germans was completed.

In a special Order of the Day General Charles Mangin, who commanded the French at the Second Battle of the Marne, paid high tribute to the valour of these soldiers.

'All the English and Scottish troops,' he wrote, 'have shown the magnificent qualities of your race – namely indomitable courage and tenacity. You have won the admiration of your brothers-in-arms. Your country will be proud of you, for to you and to your comrades is due in larger measure the victory which we have just gained against the barbarous enemies of all free people.'

Sergeant Meikle was awarded the VC posthumously for his gallantry at Marfaux, during the 4th Seaforths' advance along the River Ardre. The citation read:

For most conspicuous bravery and initiative when his Company, having been held up by machine gun fire, he rushed single handed a machine gun nest. He emptied his revolver into the crews of the two guns and put the remainder out of action with a heavy stick. Then, standing up, he waved his comrades on. Very shortly afterwards another hostile machine gun checked progress, and threatened also the success of the company on the right. Most of his platoon having become casualties, Sgt Meikle seized the rifle and bayonet of a fallen comrade, and again rushed forward against the gun crew, but was killed almost on the gun position. His bravery allowed two other men who followed him to put this gun out of action. This gallant non-commissioned officer's valour, devotion to duty, and utter disregard of personal safety was an inspiring example to all.

Sergeant Meikle's father received his son's VC from General Sir F.W.N. McCracken KCB, DSO, General Officer Commanding Scottish Command, at Maryhill Barracks, Glasgow, on 28 October 1918. His son was buried at Marfaux British Cemetery. A bronze memorial plaque was erected in Nitshill public hall, subsequently moved to Levern Primary School, and is now in Dingwall Museum. A granite memorial was erected at Nitshill Station in 1920, moved to Station Square, Dingwall in 1971.

LANCE-SERGEANT
EDWARD SMITH, 19
LANCASHIRE FUSILIERS
Serre, France, 21–23 August 1918

After the German Spring Offensive petered out in July 1918, the Allies began what became known as the Hundred Days Offensive, which brought the war to its conclusion. It began on 8 August with the five-day Battle of Amiens. This was the beginning of a new type of warfare. For the first time aircraft, tanks, artillery and infantry were all co-ordinated in a concerted effort to give the Allies one of the biggest breakthroughs of the war.

Amiens was an important rail hub, which distributed supplies to the front lines. The Germans had tried to take it in March. They began their assault on the 21st with a five-hour barrage, with 65,000 guns and 3,500 trench mortars firing along a 46-mile front.

'Such Hell makes weak things of the strongest. No body was ever built to stand such torture,' said Lance-Corporal William Sharpes of the 8th Lancashire Fusiliers.

While the British were still reeling from the effects of shelling and gas, the Germans sent in their elite storm troopers, who had maps of the British positions sewn into the sleeves of their uniforms. After two hours, the British had lost one third of their troops. Over the next two weeks, the Germans advanced twenty-eight miles. Just eleven miles short of Amiens, they ran out of steam. The rapid advance had stretched the lines and the front-line troops were starved of supplies.

The Germans dug in at Belleau Wood. On 6 June, the US Marine Corps went in. It took six attacks to clear the wood at the cost of ten thousand men. General Sir Henry Rawlinson, commanding the 4th Army, then ordered the largest concentration of tanks in World War I to gather at Amiens.

The artillery were told not to make preliminary range-finding shots that warned the enemy of a forthcoming infantry attack. They were to use maps and mathematics to make sure that their first shots in anger were on target.

At 04.20 on 8 August 1918, the attack began. Troops from Canada, Australia and Britain advanced through the early-morning fog under a creeping barrage from seven hundred artillery guns that advanced a hundred metres every three minutes. As the Allies advanced, six hundred aircraft from the RAF attacked German positions, dropping phosphorous bombs.

Heavy tanks were used to attack well-defended German positions, while smaller tanks – known as 'Whippets' – were used to probe the German defences. Rawlinson had set a target of an eight-mile advance on the first day of the attack. This seemed wildly over-optimistic and would have been the largest Allied advance, had his plan been successful. Rawlinson was helped by the weather. Early-morning fog helped to disguise Allied preparations.

The Allies advanced seven miles on the first day. They were one mile short of their goal, but this still represented the greatest Allied advance of the war. It marked the end of trench warfare. Fighting had suddenly become mobile again.

General Erich Ludendorff said it was 'the black day of the German Army'. When the battle was over on 12 August, he told the Kaiser that the war was lost.

'The Germans were surrendering everywhere,' said Major S. Evers of the Australian Corps. 'We knew it was going to be the end of the war.'

There was still a way to go, though.

Marshal Foch wanted the British to continue the push at Amiens, but Haig refused. Instead, on 21 August, he attacked twenty miles to the east at Albert, which had been fought over twice before.

The day before the battle, the 1/5th Lancashire Fusiliers assembled to the west of Beaumont Hamel-Puiseux. On the first day they would have three objectives. The first was Hill 140, a nest of machine guns south of Puiseaux. The second was the high ground to the east and the third was Beauregard Dovecot, which overlooked Ancre and Miraumont.

There was a thick mist at 04.45 hours, when they advanced on Hill 140, under a heavy artillery barrage. They managed to put the machine guns out of action with only light casualties. The second objective fell by 07.00, but the casualties there were heavier. It was at the Dovecot that nineteen-year-old Lance-Sergeant Edward Smith distinguished himself, rushing a machine-gun post and killing at least six of the enemy. He went on to help another platoon take its objective and took a leading role in staunching a counter-attack the following day.

Gazetted on 18 October 1918, the citation to his VC read:

No. 51396 Cpl. (L./Sjt.) Edward Smith, D.C.M., Lan. Fus. (Maryport). For most conspicuous bravery, leadership and personal example during an attack and in subsequent operations. Sjt. Smith while in command of a platoon personally took a machine-gun post, rushing the garrison with his rifle and bayonet. The enemy on seeing him advance scattered to throw hand grenades at him. Regardless of all danger, and almost without halting in his rush on the post, this N.C.O. shot and killed at least six of the enemy. Later, seeing another platoon requiring assistance, he led his men to them, took command of the situation and captured the objective. During the enemy counter-attack on the following day he led a section forward and restored a portion of the line. His personal bravery, skill and initiative were outstanding, and his conduct throughout exemplified magnificent courage and skill, and was an inspiring example to all.

Edward Benn 'Ned' Smith was born on 10 November 1898 at Maryport in Cumberland. His father was a seaman in the Royal Navy Reserves and served in the Dardanelles. After attending the National School in Maryland, Edward worked at Oughterside Colliery. Joining up on 11 December 1915, he was sent to the Reserves because he was only seventeen. In July 1917, he enlisted with the Lancashire Fusiliers and was sent to France to join the 1/5th Battalion. They had already fought at Gallipoli and Passchendaele.

This battalion resisted the German Spring Offensive at the Bapaume, Arras and Ancre. In the lull before the Hundred Days Offensive started, Corporal Smith took leave. On 19 June 1918, he was at home at 3 India Street, Summerseat, near Manchester, when he wrote to Captain A.B. Sackett, with whom he had served in the

⅕th Lancashire Fusiliers. Captain Sackett had won the MC, but had lost a leg.

Dear Sir,

I received your most welcome letter, with pay slips, but they have been forwarded to me at home, as I am on leave before reporting to Ripon to attend cadet school. Well, sir, we got Jukes and Needham and the other ploughmen back because they said the season was finished. Well, now a few words about the company. I arrived back from leave on the Monday, the day after the battalion went into action, so they had a composite battalion of us and we went to support the 127 Brigade. But I got fed up with it and I asked Lieutenant Parkinson if there was any chance of me getting with my own battalion, so he asked the brigade major, who said if I wished to go I could go, so I joined the company and found them in a terrible state. We made a counter attack through the village of B——y where Lieutenant Jessop was wounded so Lieutenant Blake took half of the company and myself the other half. Our new colonel was giving me a few details and then only got a few yards before he got killed, so I can tell you we was a bit unlucky with our officers. But I can tell you I thanked the Lord when Lieutenant Waugh took charge of your company, and I suppose you know he has the MC. Captain Tickler, a bar to his, and Captain Page has got the MC. As for the old boys, we lost a few of them. We have heard nothing else of CSM Banks or Captain Feerick, but Private Tweedale is a prisoner and wounded. When I left the company Sergeants Lea, Andrews, Bardsley and Greenhalgh were with them. Sergeants Needham and Howell went into hospital. CSM Hemmings is on leave at the present time, so I will hand pay slips to him to take back. Well, sir, I have no more news at present. Hoping you are getting quite well again and will always look back with pleasure on the time I served under you.

I remain

Yours very sincerely
CSM Smith

Corporal Smith was back in France on 10 August 1918. He was leading a daylight patrol near Hébuterne in the Somme region to reconnoitre the German lines. As the patrol was about to retire, Corporal Smith saw a party of Germans about to take up outpost duty. Despite being heavily outnumbered by the enemy soldiers, Corporal Smith and his party ambushed them. As a result, he was promoted to Lance-Sergeant and awarded the Distinguished Conduct Medal. The citation read:

On 10 August, south-east of Hébuterne, this N.C.O. led a daylight patrol. By skilful handling and use of cover he examined two points of the enemy line about which information was required. This information he obtained. When on the point of returning, Sgt Smith noticed a party of forty of the enemy coming forward from their main line of resistance, obviously to take up night outpost dispositions. Sgt Smith decided to wait for the enemy, and engage them, though outnumbered. He inflicted heavy casualties on the enemy, who at once scattered. His initiative and determination to inflict casualties on the enemy was a fine example.

It was just eleven days later that he won his VC and was subsequently promoted to sergeant. He was decorated at an investiture in Buckingham Palace on 9 November 1918. Two days later the war was over.

According to *The Whitehaven News*, a local West Cumbrian newspaper, when he returned to his home town of Maryport after the Great War in 1919, he was greeted by a cheering crowd of six thousand people – the town's entire population at the time. At a civic reception in the market place, Sergeant Smith and his parents were given presents, which included £200 in War Bonds, a gold watch, a grandfather clock and a silver tea service.

The local paper said: 'Sergeant Smith is not only a VC but looks it. He is a British soldier every inch of him. He is an A1 man from the crown of his head to the soles of his feet. He has not only won the VC but he has a chest on which to display it.'

In 1921, he attended a Garden Party held at Buckingham Palace by King George V of England for Victoria Cross holders, as the youngest recipient present. Having rejoined the Army in May 1919, he served in Ireland, Malaya and China, before retiring with the rank of Regimental Sergeant Major in 1935.

When war loomed again in the summer of 1939, he re-enlisted with the Lancashire Fusiliers and was among the first contingent of the British Expeditionary Force to sail for France. As a Lieutenant (Quartermaster), he was killed in action in France, on 12 January 1940, possibly due to friendly fire, and was buried at the Beuvry Communal Cemetery Extension in the Nord-Pas-de-Calais.

PRIVATE THOMAS RICKETTS, 17

ROYAL NEWFOUNDLAND REGIMENT

Ledegem, Belgium, 14 October 1918

Tommy Ricketts, from the small settlement of Middle Arm at White Bay on the Baie Verte peninsula of Newfoundland, was eager to go to war. His older brother George had enlisted on 14 July 1915. On 2 September 1916, Tommy travelled to St John's and enlisted in the Royal Newfoundland Regiment, giving his age as eighteen years, three months. Born on 15 April 1901, he was, in fact, only fifteen years, four months old.

In January 1917, he sailed on the SS *Florizel* for Scotland for training at Ayr. He left from Southampton for France in June, joining the 1st Battalion at Rouen on 2 July. The following month, he saw his first action along the Steenbeek in the Battle of Langemark, the second Allied general attack during the Third Battle of Ypres, where, in heavy rain, the Allies were pushed back.

He was injured in the left leg at Marcoing on 20 November, the first day of the Battle of Cambrai. Invalided out to England, he spent eighteen days in the 1st London General Hospital. He was then furloughed to the 24 Company Depot, before returning to France on 4 April 1918, after learning that his brother George had gone missing, presumed killed, on 3 December. His brother's body was never found. Thomas rejoined his battalion in the field on 30 April.

The Allies were well on their way to victory when the 1st Battalion of the Royal Newfoundland Regiment advanced from Ledegem, nine miles to the east of Ypres in Belgium, on 14 October 1918. The morning was misty, giving them some cover as the men climbed over a ridge and through some barbed-wire entanglements. From there, they had to cross a beet field and make for a shallow ditch three hundred yards further on.

By then, the mist had begun to lift and a German field battery began pounding them from the safety of two derelict farm buildings at the De Beurt farm, near a Belgian village called Drie Masten. The ditch provided scant protection and B Company were taking heavy casualties until Private Ricketts grabbed a Lewis gun and worked his way forward with his section commander, Lance-Corporal Matthew Brazil, in an effort to outflank the enemy.

Making their way around to the right, they were still three hundred yards from the farmhouses when they ran out of ammunition. Ricketts ran back to get some. When he returned to the Lewis gun, Lance-Corporal Brazil was nowhere to be seen. Having lost any element of surprise, Ricketts rushed forward, firing from the hip at the enemy, who had taken cover inside. Reaching the farm buildings, he planted the gun in the doorway and the entire gun crew surrendered.

Six of B Company died that day, along with another seventeen of the 1st Battalion. Captain Sydney Frost, commanding officer of B Company, recommended Private Ricketts for the VC. He also recommended that Lance-Corporal Brazil should be decorated for gallantry, along with Second-Lieutenant Albert Newman, Sergeant John Bishop and Privates Richard Power and Samuel Greenslade.

At a parade on 14 December Major Bernard announced the award of the VC, congratulated Ricketts and read out the citation. It said:

For most conspicuous bravery and devotion to duty on the 14th October 1918, during the advance from Ledegem, when the attack was temporarily held up by heavy hostile fire and the platoon to which he belonged suffered severe casualties from the fire of an enemy battery at point-blank range. Private Ricketts at once volunteered to go forward with his section commander and a Lewis gun to attempt to outflank the battery. Advancing by short rushes under heavy fire from enemy machine-guns, their ammunition was exhausted when still 300 yards from the battery. The enemy, seeing an opportunity to get their field guns away, began to bring up their gun teams. Private Ricketts at once realizing the situation, doubled back 100 yards under the heaviest machine-gun fire, procured further ammunition, dashed back again to the Lewis gun, and by very accurate fire drove the enemy and the gun teams into a farm. His platoon then advanced without casualties and captured the four field guns, four machine-guns and eight prisoners. A fifth field gun was subsequently intercepted by fire and captured. By his presence of mind in anticipating the enemy intention and his utter disregard of personal safety, Private Ricketts secured the further supply of ammunition which directly resulted in these important captures and undoubtedly saved many lives.

This was gazetted on 6 January 1919. However, Prince John, the youngest son of George V, died on 18 January and the court went into mourning. Ricketts wanted to receive his medal from the King, but he was also eager to get back to Canada.

That day, he received a message that said: 'You are commanded by His Majesty the King to proceed to Sandringham on Sunday, 19/1/19, for the purpose of being invested with the Victoria Cross. You will leave Liverpool Street Station at 9.40 a.m. 19/1/19 for Wolferton, Norfolk. You will change trains at Ely, where you will meet a King's Messenger, and you will proceed from Ely to Wolferton by a Special Coach with the King's Messenger, who will conduct you to His Majesty. You will be accompanied by Sergt. Dunphy, of this Office, to Ely.'

Arriving at York Cottage, Sandringham, Ricketts was treated to a sumptuous lunch in a room on his own. That afternoon, he was taken to meet the King, who was not in uniform, along with Prince George and Princess Mary. They chatted for about ten minutes. After pinning the VC to Ricketts's tunic, George V said: 'This is the youngest VC in my army.'

At seventeen, he was the youngest Canadian with a VC.

Also at the investiture ceremony was one of the oldest-living VC holders at the time, eighty-five-year-old General Sir Dighton MacNaughton Probyn, who had won his VC at the age of twenty-four as a captain in the 2nd Punjab Cavalry of the Bengal Army during the Indian Mutiny. His citation read:

Has been distinguished for gallantry and daring throughout this campaign. At the battle of Agra, when his squadron charged the rebel infantry, he was some time separated from his men, and surrounded by five or six sepoys. He defended himself from the various cuts made at him, and before his own men had joined him had cut down two of his assailants. At another time, in single combat with a sepoy, he was wounded in the wrist, by the bayonet, and his horse also was slightly wounded; but, though the sepoy fought desperately, he cut him down. The same day he singled out a standard bearer, and, in the presence of a number of the enemy, killed him and captured the standard. These are only a few of the gallant deeds of this brave young officer.

Ricketts was also promoted to sergeant that day.

In the *Daily Mirror* of 21 January 1919, Sergeant Ricketts explained the rush:

'I am returning home immediately,' explained the fresh-faced, fair-haired young soldier modestly, 'so it was arranged that the King should give me the Cross privately, so that I should not have to wait for a full investiture. Everything was done so nicely and considerately for me that, though I felt naturally very nervous, it was one of the most pleasant experiences of my life. There was a car waiting for me at Wolverton Station, with an equerry to explain the etiquette and everything to me. At York Cottage I was given a splendid lunch, which I enjoyed as well as my nervous state would let me. I had this in a room by myself, which was better than meeting a lot of strangers. After lunch I was taken into a kind of ante-room, where the Investiture was to take place. Princess Mary and Prince George were there, as well as the King. I was interested to see that the King was not in khaki. He wore 'civvies'. His kind manner soon put me at ease, and he talked to me for about ten

273

minutes, and I hope I made sensible replies to his questions. When he had given me the cross he turned to Princess Mary and the rest and said: "This is the youngest V.C. in the Army."'

There was a dramatic incident when Private Ricketts was being escorted from the royal presence. The youngest V.C. came face to face with the oldest (save one) – the fine old veteran, Sir Dighton Probyn, who is eighty-five. Sir Dighton gained his cross sixty years ago in the dark and bloody days of the Indian Mutiny.

Private Ricketts intends to go to college when he reaches home, to resume the education which was broken off when he joined the army.

Ricketts arrived back at St John's aboard the SS *Corsican* the first week in February and received a hero's welcome, drawn through the streets on a sleigh by the young men of the town. On 19 June 1919, he was gazetted with a Croix de Guerre avec Etoile d'Or, which was published without citation. On 1 July, he was demobilised. Then on 27 September, he was presented with his Croix de Guerre at Holickshen by Lieutenant General Sir Claud Jacob, Commander of the Second Army Corps.

A fund was set up to pay for his education, which reached over $10,000. He studied pharmacy and set up in business on Water Street in St John's.

In November 1929 he attended the House of Lords dinner for VC winners. On 17 July 1962 he attended a Garden Party at Buckingham Palace given by HM The Queen for members of the VC/GC Association.

Otherwise Ricketts was a modest man. According to the *St John's Telegraph*:

Ricketts shunned the spotlight, going so far as to decline invitations to meet with Queen Elizabeth, would never speak of his war experiences, and declined many of the privileges that came with being a VC recipient – including, for many years, his VC pension from the British government.

This may have been the result of battle fatigue, the guilt of surviving while many of his comrades died, or just the way he was engineered. While such behaviour wasn't unusual for war veterans of that era, Ricketts was in a different class. He was a VC winner.

Pat Leonard experienced it. He worked as a pharmacist at Ricketts' Water Street drugstore for nearly two years in the late 1950s.

He remembers a reporter from a national magazine coming to the drugstore one day, looking to interview Ricketts.

'He wouldn't even talk to him. He said, "You're not getting anything off me." He was very abrupt. He was not interested in any publicity,' Leonard, 72, recalls.

When Tommy Ricketts died in 1967, he was given a state funeral. When he was buried in the Anglican Cemetery in St John's, the Royal Newfoundland Regiment fired a three-volley salute and veterans dropped poppies into the open grave. His widow donated his medals to the Canadian War Museum in Ottawa.

'He did not want this VC,' she said. 'He just felt that others, everyone who went across, was just as equal to one as he was.'

ACTING CORPORAL
ROLAND ELCOCK, 19
ROYAL SCOTS (LOTHIAN REGIMENT)

Capelle St Catherine, France,
15 October 1918

T he day Tommy Ricketts won his VC, Roland Elcock was nearby
with the 9th (Scottish) Division advancing towards the
Courtrai-Roulers railway. From there, they advanced towards the
River Lys to capture the river crossings. The advance was swift and,
by noon, they had reached a small ridge named Steenen Stampkot.
There, the enemy's resistance stiffened.

Second-Lieutenant James Currie of the 6th Battalion of the Royal
Scots was mentioned in despatches for the action there. The citation
in the *Edinburgh Gazette* said:

Near Steenen Stampkot, on the 15th October, 1918, when
his platoon was held up by machine-gun fire he got his Lewis
gun immediately into action, and silenced the enemy; 100
yards further on he again came under heavy fire from two
more machine-guns, but with only half his platoon left gained
the objective, personally killing two of the enemy who were

controlling the fire. His fine courage and leadership enabled the rest of the company to advance on the right.

Lance-Corporal Roland Elcock was with the 11th Battalion. So was Second-Lieutenant James Harvey, who was also mentioned in despatches, who said of him: 'After his company commander had become a casualty, near Steenen Stampkot, on the 15th October, 1918, he took command, reorganized the company, who had become scattered, and gained the crest of the ridge, personally leading a party up to it himself, and then returning and leading forward the remainder of the company who had been held up. He then established his position, and got in touch with the company on the left. His gallantry and able leadership were most marked.'

The infantry took what cover they could in Laagacapelle Wood, where they were pinned down by German artillery firing from Hill 40, about five hundred yards to the east.

The next day, 11th Royal Scots led the 27th Brigade forward under a smokescreen towards the enemy gun positions. By then Acting Corporal Elcock was in charge of a Lewis-gun team. However, as soon as they left the wood they were immediately pinned down by two machine guns. It was at this point that Acting Corporal Elcock dashed forward amid a hail of bullets and killed the two men who were firing one of the machine guns. Then he turned the gun on to the other machine-gun crew, killing both men.

Immediately, the advance resumed and the battalion moved rapidly down the slope, while the 12th Battalion, who were behind the 11th Battalion in the wood, swung southwards and drove the enemy from Steenbeek and the southern part of Hill 40.

Three days later, Elcock was further up the line at Harelbeke, to the north-east of Courtrai, where the 11th Royal Scots had reached the River Lys. Again Elcock captured an enemy machine-gun position.

Acting Corporal Elcock knew he had done well. He wrote home to his mother: 'You ask me what I have been doing to get recommended again. Well, if I tell, you will fairly guess what I am going to get for it. So I will leave it till the decoration comes out. I am expecting the DCM, but, as rumours go in the battalion, I am in for the VC. So I hope I get it.'

His wish came true and he was awarded the VC for these two actions. It was gazetted on 26 December 1918 and the citation read:

> For most conspicuous bravery and initiative south-east of Capelle Ste Catherine on the 15th Oct. 1918, when in charge of a Lewis-gun team. Entirely on his own initiative, Corpl. Elcock rushed his gun up to within ten yards of enemy guns, which were causing heavy casualties and holding up the advance. He put both guns out of action, captured five prisoners, and undoubtedly saved the whole attack from being held up. Later, near the River Lys, this non-commissioned officer again attacked an enemy machine-gun and captured the crew. His behaviour throughout the day was absolutely fearless.

When a journalist from the *Wolverhampton Express and Star* went to tell Mrs Elcock that her son had just become the first and only Wolverhampton man to be awarded the Victoria Cross in World War I, she said she was 'overjoyed at the good news'. Elcock was presented with his VC by George V in the ballroom of Buckingham Palace on 13 February 1919.

Roland Edward Elcock was born on 5 June 1899 at 52 Alma

Street, Wolverhampton. He attended Causeway Lake Infant and Junior School from 1902 to 1913. Then he became a clerk at the Labour Assembly Rooms, Queen Square.

Eager to be a soldier, he enlisted at the age of fifteen years and four months, joining the South Staffordshire Regiment, and saw service in Egypt. He left after two years, because it was discovered that he was under-age and he was discharged. He worked briefly at the Corporation Electricity Works in Commercial Road. But he reached the age of eighteen in June 1917, when he joined the Army again, this time enlisting in the Royal Scots, serving with them in France and Belgium, where he also won a Military Medal.

On his return to Wolverhampton, he was greeted at the High Level Station by thousands of citizens, including the Mayor and other civic dignitaries. Described by the *Wolverhampton Chronicle* on 5 February 1919 as 'modesty personified', he 'did not wish to talk about one of the most remarkable exploits of the war. He was content to let the official record speak for itself'.

The streets were lined with people cheering and waving, and shaking Elcock by the hand. At the civic reception, he said: 'I thank you very much for the way you have welcomed me home. Wolverhampton is my home, and I appreciate it very much. But in winning this great distinction, I have only done my duty to my King and country.'

After being demobbed, he went back to work in his old job at the Electricity Works and in 1920 he attended the Royal Garden Party for VC winners at Buckingham Palace.

In 1923, he went to India, where he worked as an engineer for the Telegraph Service. On home leave, he attended the House of Lords VC dinner in 1929. On the outbreak of World War II, he joined the Indian Army as a major and died at Dehradun, India, in October 1944, aged forty-five. His medals are in the Royal Scots Museum in Edinburgh Castle.

PRIVATE NORMAN HARVEY, 19

ROYAL INNISKILLING FUSILIERS

Ingoyghem, Belgium, 25 October 1918

Norman Harvey was born on 6 April 1899 in Newton-le Willows, Lancashire. He was educated at St Peter's Church of England School and joined the South Lancashire Regiment in November 1914, at the age of fifteen. At that time, he was employed by Messrs Caulfield's Newton, after having worked briefly at Messrs Randall in the High Street.

Harvey was sent to France and was slightly wounded at the age of sixteen. He was still under-age when he was wounded for a second time, this time more seriously. When it was discovered that he was too young for overseas service, he was sent on a course in bayonet and physical training. He finished with excellent qualifications and was sent to Portsmouth. But there was a shortage of men and he was sent overseas again and transferred to the 1st Battalion of the Royal Inniskilling Fusiliers.

By October 1918, the Germans were in full retreat. The Hindenburg Line had been broken. Trench warfare was over. The

British were pursuing the enemy across open ground. The Germans had sent a note to US President Woodrow Wilson on the night of 3–4 October and peace negotiations were going on through diplomatic channels. General Ludendorff was still optimistic that the situation could be turned around, but when he saw the American proposals and protested that they amounted to unconditional surrender, he was forced to resign on 26 October.

The following day, the 1st Royal Inniskilling Fusiliers were advancing at Ingoyghem, east of Courtrai, when they came under attack. Harvey's platoon sergeant, who witnessed the action, said: 'Suddenly very heavy machine-gun fire opened on us from a farm about forty yards to my left front. It held my platoon up, and we all got down to fire. Five of my men were wounded, and I saw Private Harvey rush forward under heavy machine-gun fire and go round the left of the farm. Later, I heard a few rifle shots, and the machine stopped firing, and then I saw Private Harvey bring about a dozen Bosches from the farm. I went forward to the farm and found two dead Bosches and one badly wounded, with the bayonet. There were two machine-guns there.'

Harvey was recommended for a VC. It was gazetted on 6 January 1919. The citation read:

No. 42954 Pte. Norman Harvey, 1st Bn., R. Innis. Fus. (Newton-le-Willows). For most conspicuous bravery and devotion to duty near Ingoyghen on the 25th October, 1918, when his battalion was held up and suffered heavy casualties from enemy machine guns. On his own initiative he rushed forward and engaged the enemy single-handed, disposing of twenty enemy and capturing two guns. Later, when his company was checked by another enemy strong point, he again rushed forward alone and put the enemy to flight. Subsequently, after dark, he voluntarily carried out, single-handed, an important reconnaissance and gained valuable information. Pte. Harvey throughout the day displayed the greatest valour, and his several actions enabled the line to advance, saved many casualties, and inspired all.

Private Harvey was presented with his medal at Buckingham Palace on 15 May 1919 and promoted to lance-corporal. Back home in Newton-le-Willows, two thousand people turned out to welcome him home. He was presented with £100 in War Bonds and an illuminated address. Already demobbed, he went to work on the railways and married Norah Osmond, who had served with the Queen Mary Auxiliary Corps and had also seen action. He attended the House of Lords dinner for VC holders in 1929.

At the outbreak of World War II, Harvey, then forty, joined up again, this time with the 199th Railway Workshop Company, Royal Engineers, and with the rank of Company Quartermaster Sergeant. He was killed in action, near Haifa, Palestine, on 16 February 1942 and was buried in Khayat Beach War Cemetery, now in Israel.

Harvey's VC and other medals are in The Inniskillings Museum (which tells the story of The Royal Inniskilling Fusiliers and the 5th Royal Inniskilling Dragoon Guards). His name is listed on a plaque in St Anne's Cathedral, Belfast, and on a memorial stone in the grounds of the Ulster Memorial Tower in Thiepval, Picardy, France.

Peace

Now, God be thanked Who has matched us with His hour,
And caught our youth, and wakened us from sleeping,
With hand made sure, clear eye, and sharpened power,
To turn, as swimmers into cleanness leaping,
Glad from a world grown old and cold and weary,
Leave the sick hearts that honour could not move,
And half-men, and their dirty songs and dreary,
And all the little emptiness of love!
Oh! we, who have known shame, we have found release there,
Where there's no ill, no grief, but sleep has mending,
Naught broken save this body, lost but breath;
Nothing to shake the laughing heart's long peace there
But only agony, and that has ending;
And the worst friend and enemy is but Death.

Rupert Brooke, 1914